THE

EVERYTHING

INTERNET
BOOK

THE
EVERYTHING
INTERNET
BOOK

Talk to your friends, shop for bargains,
find the information you need,
and get free, cool stuff online

Sharon McDonnell

Adams Media Corporation
Holbrook, Massachusetts

An Everything Series Book. The Everything Series
is a trademark of Adams Media Corporation.

Published by Adams Media Corporation
260 Center Street, Holbrook, MA 02343
www.adamsmedia.com

ISBN: 1-58062-073-6

Printed in the United States of America.

J I H G F E D

Library of Congress Cataloging-in-Publication Data
The everything internet book / by Sharon McDonnell.—1st ed/
p.   cm.—(The everything series)
ISBN 1-58062-073-6
1. Internet (Computer network) I. Series
TK5105.875.I57M3816   1998
004.67'8—dc21   98-27124
CIP

Illustrations by Barry Littmann

This book is available at quantity discounts for bulk purchases.
For information, call 1-800-872-5627 (in Massachusetts, call 781-767-8100).

Visit our exciting small business web site at: www.businesstown.com

Contents

CONTENTS

CONTENTS

A Day In the Life Of An Internet User

7:00 A.M.   Alarm clock goes off. Sally stumbles out of bed into the bathroom for a quick shower and tooth-brushing.

7:30 A.M.   Sally starts making coffee with beans purchased from a coffee retailer, Oren's Daily Roast, whom she found on Over the Coffee, a Web site for coffee lovers she visits now and then.

7:45 A.M.   Sally eats cereal and drinks fruit juice for breakfast, part of her monthly grocery delivery from NetGrocer, a Web site supermarket, which comes by Federal Express and arrived yesterday. She puts away paper towels, toilet paper, canned goods, and some health and beauty aids from the delivery.

8:15 A.M.   Sally dresses for work. Since she runs a small public relations and marketing business from her home, every day is a casual Friday. She picks a shirt and slacks purchased at 75 percent off from Lands' End, the cataloger whose Web site has a deeply discounted overstock section.

8:30 A.M.   Sally applies her makeup, thanks to a few free samples ordered from Revlon's Web site, and uses some helpful makeup tips from its Virtual Face section.

8:45 A.M.   Sally reads and listens to the news. But she doesn't buy a newspaper or turn on her television or radio. Why bother? Instead, she turns on her computer and starts reading a free copy of *The New York Times on the Web*. She scans the headlines, reads a few full stories, then decides she will save the crossword puzzle for this evening. She quickly looks at CNN Interactive and hears a sound clip for the top news of the day.

9:15 A.M.   Sally thinks about glancing at the Dilbert comic strip on the Web. It's great to start off the day with a good laugh, especially one that jabs at the corporate world she fled two years ago. But regretfully, she dismisses the thought. There is too much work to do today. With a small sigh, she starts reading her e-mail.

9:45 A.M. Answering her e-mail, Sally wonders for a moment why so many people seem to have given up all other forms of communication. But glancing at the times the messages were sent, she realizes that since a message can be sent at any time—the person receiving it doesn't need to be awake or even in town—and it gets to the point without interruption, it's a real advantage. She sends a group e-mail to several people at a new client—of course, their e-mail addresses are kept in her online address book—answering questions they had about a project she turned in last week.

10:00 A.M. Sally dashes off e-mail responses to two other clients. One is a client she met through an online mailing list, which sends e-mail to a group of subscribers several times a week. The person asked a few questions, was impressed by her answers, and later hired her to help launch a product in her local area.

10:15 A.M. What's this? There are three e-mail reminders in her mailbox, courtesy of E-Organizer, which e-mails customers to alert them to important dates and holidays—free, of course. It's her four-year-old niece's birthday in a few days. She decides to shop at the Vermont Teddy Bear Company's Web site, and finally buys a honey colored, fifteen inch classic bear by credit card. But some of those other furry friends look awfully cute—bears dressed in little outfits from jeans to different occupations, baby bears, holiday bears—all with color photographs. There is even a discount section for Web orders only, which includes a backpack and storybook. Luckily, because Sally is ordering before 3:00 P.M. (Eastern Standard Time), her bear will be shipped in a gift box with her personalized message for little Susie today.

10:45 A.M.   It's her mother's birthday, too, next week. Her parents are living in Arizona after they retired. Sally decides to send a bouquet of flowers, so she logs on to Virtual Florist's Web site. She wants a half-dozen red roses in a vase, her mother's favorite flower, so she heads immediately for the roses section, bypassing the special occasions section. She picks her price category and types a personalized message, which will appear in the gift card. Her mother will even get same-day delivery since Sally is ordering before 2:00 P.M., a good thing since her parents are leaving in a couple of days for a weekend trip to celebrate the birthday.

11:00 A.M.   Her friend, Beth, who recently landed a job promotion she always dreamed about, deserves a congratulations card. There is simply no time to go to a card store today—Sally is swamped—so she decides to send an electronic greeting card instead, saving money and postage, as well as time. She goes to Internet Card Central, where she usually feels slightly overwhelmed by its selection of thousands of free cards. It's a really tough choice, but Sally finally turns down the sunsets, art masterpieces, pets and wild animals, flowers, poems, and famous movie scenes. She doesn't need a musical card either. Finally, because Beth was one of many fans who mourned when "Seinfeld" went off the air and has loyally watched re-runs ever since, Sally thinks she'll get a kick out of a card with a photograph of the "Seinfeld" stars. She types a personalized message: "The gang at Kramerica Industries says congratulations! Want to meet us for dinner on Thursday?" and types her name.

11:20 A.M.   Minutes later, Beth gets an e-mail at work, which notes she has a greeting card for pick-up. She clicks and smiles fondly. She e-mails a thank-you card back, picking a kitten that looks like Sally's new calico kitten from

Hallmark Cards' Web site, with a message asking if Thursday at 7:00 P.M. or Sunday at 6:30 P.M. at a certain restaurant would be okay.

11:30 A.M.– 12:45 P.M.
Sally is embroiled in a work project. She hits some major search engines to research the topic of a brochure she's writing. She's finding a lot of helpful information and goes to a multiple search engine, MetaCrawler, to speed her research.

12:45 P.M.
Sally is eating lunch in her home office today but doesn't want to bother with fighting the crowds and standing in line. She goes online instead, logging on to Daily Soup's Web site, which delivers in the part of New York City where she lives. She breezes through the online menu of the nearest branch and chooses Chicken Coconut, although that Bahian Seafood Stew and Burmese Shrimp Curry look mighty good. After less than five minutes, her nose is back to the grindstone again.

1:15 P.M.
Doorbell rings. Great—it's the two books she bought three days ago from a bookstore on the Web at 12:15 A.M. That sure beats going to a store at that hour, and the discount was pretty good, too.

1:45 P.M.
Finishing the remains of her soup, which came with fruit, bread, and a cookie, and a soft drink from yesterday's NetGrocer delivery, Sally browses through some newsgroup discussion groups. In the past, she has sometimes uncovered tidbits of information on hot topics from experts, and hopes this helps on the brochure she is writing for a public relations client.

2:15 P.M.
Sally takes a short walk in her neighborhood. She overhears a conversation between two people where one person is bragging about a cheap last-minute airfare to Europe they found from an airline that has discounts for Web surfers only. The other woman is delightfully surprised by a date with a man she met through a classical music Web site's bulletin board. Because there is no escaping the Internet, Sally decides to return home, vowing to make some travel plans on the Internet and check out that airline.

2:45 P.M.	Suddenly, a message pops up on her computer screen. "Hi Mom!" Her daughter, away at college in the Midwest, has sent an "instant message," much quicker than e-mailing Mom and waiting for a reply or—Heaven forbid—incurring a long-distance telephone charge. Sally reads the message on Laura's latest activities and request to send some money, sends a short message back, and returns to work. Laura gets it immediately.
3:15 P.M.	Sally remembers she read some articles in out-of-town newspapers on the topic she is researching, so she scans the online archives at the *Washington Post* and *Los Angeles Times* Web sites. Bingo—she has found it. But it took a little while. Sally makes a mental note to consider one of those electronic clipping services that scurry around the Web to find articles on a certain topic and bring them back to your computer. It's free and can save me a lot of time, she decides.
3:45 P.M.	Needing some synonyms for different words, Sally visits the Research-It! Web site for its Merriam-Webster thesaurus and dictionary. While there, she tracks the package she Federal Expressed yesterday to a client by plugging in the tracking number. Yes, they received it; the receptionist signed for it. Some day she will really have to use that handy currency converter on the site when she travels to a foreign country.
4:15 P.M.	Because Sally and her husband plan to go on vacation in a few weeks, Sally decides to shop for an airfare at Priceline's Web site. Shop is a bit of an exaggeration, because all you do is place a bid for an airfare and the service then tries to match it with an airline who has empty seats and is willing to sell a ticket at that price. Sally names a really low price, just for fun, and backs it with her credit card.
4:30 P.M.	Time to catch up with some industry news by browsing through a few trade publications. Their articles are on their Web sites, so Sally doesn't need to pay to subscribe.
5:15 P.M.	Sally sends an attached file by e-mail to a client who requested a proposal last week. She opens up a few

attached files from clients who have enclosed background material they want her to read.

6:15 P.M.   Priceline was able to find that unbelievably low fare she named! Jim will be thrilled. She certainly is.

6:30 P.M.   Checking her e-mail, Sally notes a few interested queries from people who saw the Web site for her small business. One or two sound like they may become clients if she plays her cards right. She'll e-mail them tomorrow, because she is ending work for the day.

6:45 P.M.   Her husband just called, confirming he is coming home late tonight from his business trip, and they talked a bit more about vacation plans. Because they already decided to spend their two-week vacation at a bed-and-breakfast in New England in a few weeks, Sally decides to shop at the B&B Finder at Fodor's Travel Service's Web site so she and Jim won't have to buy and pore over a guidebook. She picks the state she wants—Vermont—and browses through features like romantic, lakeside, good to bring kids, and activities like tennis and boating. She settles on romantic and lakeside and fills in a price range. Sally has to call the inn to check if they have rooms and to pay, but that is all right.

7:00 P.M.   She is seeing a movie with a friend in a few days, so she visits the MovieLink Web site to check on times in the evening at local theaters. The site knows her zip code—she's been there before—so she quickly glances at a recent review in the Internet Movie Database on MovieLink, picks a convenient time, and buys tickets in advance. This way, they won't risk standing on line only to hear that the movie is sold out.

7:15 P.M.   Dinner time. Because Jim has been traveling on business for the last couple of days, Sally has been cooking for herself. A foodie at heart who fantasizes about enjoying a different meal every night of the year, she whips up a tasty ethnic dinner for two with the help of a recipe found online. She printed out a batch of recipes from the Meals For You and Food TV Web sites, and hasn't used a cookbook since she started on the Web. Of course, she could order delivery service from CyberMeals—or a local restaurant by telephone—but Sally dismisses the idea.

8:00 P.M.   A couple of interesting chats and concerts are starting online now. There is a bestselling author answering questions from the public, a psychologist discussing communication between men and women, a small business expert giving a seminar and talking—or typing—about marketing tips, and a well-known actor promoting his latest movie. There are also classical and rock cybercasts—concerts without being there—at sites such as Classical Insites and Broadcast.com. Decisions, decisions. Because Sally always wanted to ask the author if he had personal experience with a topic that frequently appears in his books or if he just has a really good imagination and has read a lot, she opts for this chat located on a bookstore site.

9:00 P.M.   Is there anything good on TV tonight? Sally wonders. Logging on to TVgen, TV Guide's Web site, which has local listings, she swiftly finds the answer: no.

9:30 P.M.   Her parents are visiting New York in two months and would love to see one of the Broadway musicals they have been reading about. No problem. Sally goes to the Playbill Web site, finds out what plays are available, then orders the tickets through Ticketmaster.

9:45 P.M.   The jazz artist she and Jim like has a new recording, so Sally decides to buy it at the CD Universe Web site, an online store. First, she listens to a sound clip—yes, it's terrific. Then she hears a few others from other jazz artists and a classical musician just for the sheer fun of hearing a free mini-concert.

10:30 P.M.   The latest book by the author in the celebrity chat Sally took part in tonight sounds fascinating, and Sally succumbs to an irresistible impulse to buy it. She goes to the Amazon.com Web site. "Hello, Sally Smith," the online store's message greets her. Sally types in the author's name, picks the book, and pays.

10:45 P.M.   Her mailbox is really full by now. An e-mail from a friend now living in Italy, several newsletters from online stores notifying her of special sales, a daily recipe, e-mail from that mailing list to which she subscribes, and an e-mail that states invitingly, "MAKE $$$ FAST." No longer an Internet beginner, Sally casually discards this e-mail without reading it. A little sleepy, she will deal with the rest of these e-mails tomorrow.

11:00 P.M.   Time for the nightly news. Sally toys between National Public Radio, CNN, the New York Times, and her local television stations to hear any late breaking news. The NPR Web site wins.

11:30 P.M.   Jim arrives home from his business trip and kisses her a fond hello. The Internet can't do everything, Sally thinks with delight. Well, almost everything, she concludes as she heats up his portion of the dinner she cooked courtesy of Meals For You.

The preceding story shows the sheer variety of things you can do on the Internet. You may not want to have a day like Sally's, but this reveals the tremendous possibilities available to save money, save time, and improve your overall quality of life.

If you are new to the Internet, don't panic. You've been hearing about the Internet for months or years and are not quite sure what it is, where it is, or how to get on it. Come to think of it, you're not clear why you would want to be on it—or what being on it means.

You've heard a lot of people talking about the Internet—either praising it as the most terrific thing since sliced bread, moaning about their problems with it, or bragging about what they're doing in cyberspace, wherever that is. Many scary sounding abbreviations are being thrown around, like ISP, FAQ, and PPP, which no one takes the trouble to explain. It seems terribly complicated. You're really not sure if taking the plunge is worth it.

Learning to use the Internet is just another skill. It seems complicated at first, with some fussy rules to master, but so does learning to drive a car, riding a bicycle, playing the piano or guitar, learning a foreign language, or raising a child. You're not born knowing these things, and probably have done some—maybe all—of them. Now they're second nature, no matter how hard they seemed at first. Sure, problems may still arise, but you have the basic skills to cope or know how to ask for help. You've made mistakes, learned from them, and perhaps figured out your own way, which may be a little different from the standard wisdom. But it works for you, and that's what counts.

This book will teach you how to get on the Internet, and how to get around once you're there. You'll learn how to find incredibly useful information for yourself and your family on health, school subjects, business, and a million other topics. You'll learn how to shop online, and do it safely. You'll learn how to send messages to people all over the world through e-mail (electronic mail) for the cost of a local telephone call. You'll learn how to sit on your couch and use your television to reach the Internet—the new way of connecting—or use your computer.

But that's not all. You'll learn to find people you've lost touch with for years, such as high school or college buddies. You'll learn how to protect your children from objectionable material, and protect your computer as well. You'll learn how to locate people with common interests and hobbies. You'll also learn how to use an online newspaper or magazine and why you would want to (they're usually free!). You'll learn the names of helpful print magazines and organizations, which will teach you more about the Internet.

When you're finished, you'll understand the basic tools and essentials to enjoy the Internet and its countless riches. You'll also read about some fascinating people and businesses involved in the Internet, past and present. (Some are actually making money.)

Women and seniors are the fastest growing groups in getting on the Internet lately—don't think the Net is only for men or young kids. The Internet is too good to be wasted on just a few groups, as you'll soon see.

I've tried to make the book as up-to-date as possible. However, the Internet is changing at an unbelievably rapid pace; it's different from a year ago, even from a few months ago. Technologies are changing and new versions of software are coming out that work a little differently, and Web sites are disappearing as new ones are added. It's unavoidable that some things will be different when you're reading this compared to the time this book was written.

The Internet also has many inconsistencies. People use different hardware, different software, and many different service providers to reach it, and each operates (surprise!) a little differently. So, what you do or what you see on your screen may be somewhat different from what is described, because the Internet is not one-size-fits-all. As a result, I've tried to give a general overview and some step-by-step advice to show how certain systems work. If what is covered does not include your system and its peculiarities, don't panic! Because the Internet consists of many thousands of computers linked together, it's not like writing a manual for one software program for one type of computer.

You'll experiment, fool around, make mistakes, and finally learn, just like driving that car or playing that instrument.

My own personal story: I used to hate computers.

Really. Years ago, in a previous life as an executive at a public relations agency, I thwarted all attempts by management to thrust me into the computer age. I preferred an electric typewriter, which was a superior typing device, in my opinion. Articles you wrote never vanished, you didn't have to remember what you named them, and you didn't have to stand in line to print them. Best of all, your system never crashed, a mysterious event which provoked weeping and wailing about hours of work lost all over the office.

The agency tried to convert me to the virtues of computers, then opted for the sneaky approach. A shiny new computer would appear on my desk when I arrived in the morning, replacing my faithful IBM Selectric. No go—I wasn't fooled. That thing went straight back to the stockroom. Finally, I succumbed, a decision prompted by my decision to leave the agency and become a full-time freelance writer, entering a world where computers were shockingly prevalent. I just bit the bullet and learned.

Later I signed up for a commercial online service. I noticed questions I posted in its writers' forums about contracts, collaborations, and other things were answered quickly and intelligently, with personal examples, by writers all over the country. It was a real thrill to get these messages, sometimes within an hour after I sent them, some from writers whose names I later recognized on bestseller lists. I started exploring, and soon landed some writing jobs from the forums. Their online libraries were crammed with useful reference materials, and I could use them any hour of the day or night.

I then decided to graduate to a full-fledged Internet account. Suddenly, tons of information from all over the world was at my disposal. It was like having the New York Public Library open up a branch office in my home. The first time I ever visited a newsgroup, about food in New York City, I read about a terrific restaurant opening a branch in the neighborhood I was moving to. The first time I ever bought something from an online store, an e-mail confirmed my purchase instantly; two days later, another e-mail said my package had left the warehouse. The next day it arrived, cheaper than if I found it in a store. One day, I was shown WebTV on a large-sized television screen and fell in love with what the Internet could do, and how much easier it was becoming.

OK, computers were worth it after all. They made all that wonderful online jazz possible. You could read and see all kinds of stuff on computers from all over the world, communicate with all kinds of people—many of whom you didn't even know—and read the news before tomorrow's newspaper. The Internet suddenly brings the world into your living room, office, or bedroom—a cliche, but utterly true. This made all the difference to me.

Friends and acquaintances have often asked me questions like "Just where is cyberspace?" or "I have Internet access, I just don't know how to get to it." Then there's the complaint, "How do I find something? I always get lost."

This book hopefully will answer these questions, with a bare minimum of technical jargon. (Some is inevitable, but it will quickly be explained.) It will serve as your map and guide on your voyage to the unknown.

Everyone has their own personal reason for wanting to go on the Internet. I've learned and profited from the Internet. You can, too.

GETTING AROUND

- Introduction:
- **Chapter One**
- Chapter Two
- Chapter Three
- Chapter Four
- Chapter Five
- Chapter Six
- Chapter Seven
- Chapter Eight
- Chapter Nine
- Chapter Ten
- Appendices

Internet History 101

What Is the Internet?

Take your pick: A store which is never closed; the world's biggest library, with newspapers, magazines, television, and radio stations worldwide, medical and legal journals, United States Supreme Court decisions, full-length books and one-liner jokes; the greatest invention in publishing since Gutenberg invented the printing press where anyone can publish their articles or poems; the greatest bonanza of free services and products in the history of the world; an endless supply of information, potential friends and business contacts to anyone, anywhere.

The Internet is all this and more. Only a few years after it was introduced to the general public, it has become a mass medium, like television or print, that is changing so rapidly it's hard to keep up with. It has also changed many people's and companies' research, buying, news consumption, and communication habits as well.

The Internet is a network of many thousands of computers connected by telephone lines all over the world. It's a network of networks, where each computer can exchange information with every other computer that is connected, no matter where it is. This system is not owned by anybody, is not run by anybody, and most of it's services are free.

A History Lesson

The Internet was started in 1969 as a project of the United States Department of Defense's Advanced Research Projects Agency. Called the ARPANET, the idea was to have a decentralized computer network that linked the agency with military contractors and universities doing related research.

Conceived as a computer network that could withstand nuclear attack—it had no main central computer—the ARPANET strayed away from its military research origins as more American universities joined the network to share resources. Eventually, it split into two networks: one for general research, one for military purposes.

The National Science Foundation also got into the act, setting up five supercomputer centers for research and connecting them with the ARPANET. The foundation later designed its own faster computer network in 1986, the NSFNET, with smaller regional networks to connect researchers. The mid-1980s was a time of tremendous growth for what began to be known as the Internet, fueled by the trend toward smaller computers for individual users instead of giant computers. Many different countries joined.

In 1990, the ARPANET closed as the Cold War began thawing rapidly and its original purpose was lost. The National Science Foundation began to manage the Internet and removed prohibitions against using the network for profit the following year, which changed the face of the Internet forever. Meanwhile, the handful of big commercial networks operated by private companies that had sprung up inside the Internet evolved into Internet service providers to serve the general public as the idea dawned that this could be really big business.

Some organizations that set technical standards for the Internet include the World Wide Web Consortium, or W3 for short, whose members include all the big software companies involved with the Internet, and the Internet Society.

What Is the World Wide Web?

Often confused with the Internet, the World Wide Web is only the visual part of the Internet; a collection of linked pages of information filled with colorful graphics, text, sound, animation, and advertisements from all over the world. These pages, which offer links to other pages with related information and allow a lot of jumping around, can belong to companies, organizations, government agencies, or individuals (anyone who figures out how to design a page, even you, if you see chapter 7 on how to create a Web page).

A page is a document with text, pictures, or sound on the World Wide Web.

A Web site is a group of pages linked together that belong to a company, individual, organization, or government agency.

HTML, or Hypertext Markup Language, is the code used to create Web pages. It consist of many different commands.

HTTP, or Hypertext Transfer Protocol, is the set of rules that moves pages written in HTML between different computers.

E-mail, which stands for electronic mail, is a message you type on your computer and send to another computer.

Each page consists of computer files, which may include text files, graphics files, sound files, and so on. Each group of pages belonging to a specific company, individual, or entity is called a Web site. Traveling between these oceans of information is often called "surfing the Web."

Those funny looking addresses beginning with www that you see on television commercials, print ads, buses, and billboards are addresses for Web sites, so you can look them up easily on the Web. (See chapter 4 for more about Internet addresses.)

In 1991, the World Wide Web was born. Its father was a British researcher, Tim Berners-Lee, who was working at CERN, the European particle physics laboratory (CERN is its French acronym) in Geneva, Switzerland. His idea was to let scientists share and locate information easily using one standard program, despite different computer platforms, across a worldwide network of connected computers. He created HTML (Hypertext Markup Language), the code Web pages are written in, and HTTP (Hypertext Transfer Protocol), which allows Web pages to be transmitted to users over the network. (See more about HTML and HTTP in chapter 4.)

When the software program Mosaic was invented in 1993 at the National Center for Supercomputing Applications at the University of Illinois at Champaign-Urbana, an easy-to-use way to find things on the World Wide Web suddenly appeared. Mosaic let users point a computer mouse at something interesting, click, and then find that information immediately. The first graphical browser, which let users find information through a simple point-and-click interface—without typing text commands—Mosaic forever changed the look of the Internet, which before this consisted of not-very-exciting-looking reams of text. (They were probably exciting to the scientists who needed them, but left something to be desired for the average person.)

The invention of Mosaic was crucial in bringing the Internet to the masses. The two big browsers we have today, Netscape Navigator—most of whose designers worked on Mosaic—from Netscape Communications and Internet Explorer from Microsoft Corporation, are its descendants. (See chapter 3 for more about browsers.) They added to many of Mosaic's original features and are much faster.

Thanks to the Web and Mosaic, which made it much easier to find and view information, two more pieces were in place for the Internet's shift from its origins as a research and military tool to a new medium for the general public. Millions of pages are now on the Web—the number is multiplying at an astonishing rate—as companies, nonprofit organizations, countries, cities, and everyone imaginable grasped the enormous potential of the Internet and raced to create their own Web sites.

What Can I Do On the Internet?

Send and Receive E-mail

You can send a letter or short message to people anywhere in the world or right around the corner for the price of a local telephone call, and it will usually arrive in seconds or minutes. E-mail has become very popular for work or home use because typed messages can be sent at any hour and require no paper or postage. E-mail can be sent to friends and family, coworkers, clients, people you've met online, and people you don't know yet but want to know. If you wish, you can send e-mail to a group of people at once, or attach an article, art, or another e-mail you have received.

You can even send by e-mail free electronic greeting cards, that can include photographs, art, personalized messages, and sound to mark special days. If you feel like spicing up your e-mail with different colors, type sizes, and designs, you can do this, too. (See chapter 5 on how to use e-mail.)

Research

You can look up information on any topic: current or old movies, news, jobs, health, sports, weather, ancient Egypt, recipes, your family tree, business, schools, pet care, famous people, and religion. Newspapers, magazines, books, databases, encyclopedias, laws—any reference source you can imagine—are here. You can research at any hour, and it will often be faster than using the library or making telephone calls.

A browser is a software program that locates Web pages and other Internet resources and displays them for users. A graphical browser lets users find and move around a Web page by pointing and clicking a mouse instead of using text commands and arrow keys.

An interface is the onscreen look of a page, which allows users to interact with their computers to move around.

Virtual means almost real. For example, a virtual mall is a set of stores online where you can shop and pay for products. You don't have to go to their real world stores; in fact, some don't even have them.

Download means to copy a file or software program from another computer onto your computer's hard drive where it is stored.

Shop

Whether it's airline tickets, concert or movie tickets, books, stocks, computer equipment, hotel reservations, clothing, gifts, or music CDs, the virtual mall is always open. (It takes credit cards, too.) On the Internet you'll see famous brands like Barnes & Noble, J. Crew, American Airlines, and Dell Computers with full descriptions and often pictures of their products. But you'll also see companies without stores in the physical world who exist solely online.

Often, you'll get lower prices by buying on the Internet than you will in real world stores. You can get on e-mail lists that notify you of current sales and bargains. You can even buy things at auction on the Internet. (See chapter 9 for some great shopping sites to visit.)

Join Newsgroups

Thousands of special interest discussion groups have formed around every imaginable topic, hobby, or professional field. You can read messages posted on online bulletin boards, and you can post your own. Many newsgroups are serious and offer good reference sources. Others are just for fun. (See chapter 6 for more about newsgroups.)

Sell Products or Services

Whether you are posting your resume, promoting your country inn or shop, offering your legal services, or selling antiques, you can set up a storefront that may attract interested queries from people all over the world, not just your local community. Instead of a brochure, people you meet can look at your Web site for prices and information. You can accept payment over the Internet and keep in touch with your customers regularly by e-mail.

Chat

Real-time chat (actually, typing messages that instantaneously appear on other people's screens) can be found at many places online on an ongoing basis or scheduled at specific times. Some chats are held with celebrities, such as actors, television talk show hosts, and authors, while others are held with experts. (See chapter 6 for more about chat.)

Download Software or Information

You can download all kinds of software to add new features to your computer, such as browsers, plug-ins (things to make browsers play sounds or show animation or videos), and filters to protect your children by blocking sexually explicit or other objectionable material. (See chapter 4 for more about plug-ins, and chapter 8 for filtering software to protect children.) Many software products are free or cheap.

Software can be downloaded from many Web sites as well as from FTP (File Transfer Protocol) sites. FTP sites are computers that hold directories of files transferred to other computers by FTP, a method which does not involve the Web. FTP can be for either private or public use. If the files are for public use, the servers are called anonymous FTP servers.

In addition to software, you may want to download information—in the form of text, images, sound, or video—including Web pages, e-mail, or newsgroup messages so you can read or play them without paying Internet access charges. (Of course, if you have unlimited Internet access, this doesn't matter.)

Play Games

Tease yourself or your children with puzzles, riddles, quizzes, or multiplayer games from action adventure scenarios to golf, poker, and backgammon. (See chapter 6 for some game sites.)

Who's on the Internet?

Anywhere from 30 to 50 million Americans were regularly using the Internet in 1997, depending on what study you read. In a study by FIND/SVP, a New York market research firm, half of this group used the Internet daily, while two out of five used it weekly. In addition, over nine million Americans tried the Internet but are not current users. Worldwide, many more were Internet users in 1997, with 100 million expected in 2001.

Plug-ins are add-on software programs that enhance the ability of your browser to play sounds, display images or virtual reality, or take part in chats.

Filtering software screens and blocks access to objectionable material on the Internet, either on the World Wide Web, e-mail, or newsgroups. It can be used by parents to protect their children, or by businesses to monitor their employees.

FTP (File Transfer Protocol) is a way of obtaining or sending files over the Internet from certain sites, which can be public or private.

Women are almost one-third of the current users—9.9 million—more than three times as many compared to late 1996, the study noted. Men and women browsed the Internet for different reasons, with men outnumbering women in sports and product information—the biggest gap—as well as news, hobbies, entertainment, and games. Women outnumbered men in health/medicine and travel content.

Many noted they were watching less television, reading fewer magazines and newspapers, and watching fewer videos in 1997. The biggest proportion of current Internet users (35 percent), said their television watching had dwindled. Sixteen percent said their magazine/newspaper reading had fallen off, while 19 percent said their video watching had slackened. Only 10 percent were listening to the radio less, perhaps because it's easy to have a radio in the background while Web surfing.

How Does the Internet Really Work?

If you're using the Internet, your computer (or television set—see chapter 2 for using your television to reach the Internet) is able to obtain access to computer files from any other computer in the world that is also connected to the Internet. This means you can view text, pictures, animations, and videos and hear sounds from computers in Germany, Russia, Malaysia, and England just as you can from your friend's or employer's computer across town or in another state. Often, locating these resources takes merely seconds. It's like calling up a file on your own computer. This is truly awe-inspiring and deserves some thought next time you're wondering why it's taking so long to reach a Web site.

Very simply, a computer uses a client (a software program to contact and talk to another computer to access files and programs) to connect to a server (a central computer or software program that offers services over a computer network). A server can perform a specific service, such as sending and receiving e-mail, carrying newsgroups, or offering access to or hosting Web pages. A server is often named after its function. For example, there are mail servers, news servers, or Web servers. A server can also run software packages to offer a variety of services to clients on the network.

When your computer dials up a computer that offers services to other computers on the network, your modem is calling a host machine. A host can be an Internet service provider, or it can be a computer whose text and graphics files you want to access.

Your computer asks for files from the Internet by giving commands to your browser either by typing in a specific Internet address or by pointing to and clicking on a link (a word, phrase, or picture) that displays the page you requested on your computer. It doesn't bring the actual page; in fact, other people may be viewing a page at the exact time you are. Your request and the text or graphics it locates may travel through several computers on its merry way across the globe, but because it's automatic, you aren't aware of it.

We've just dropped a bunch of unfamiliar technical terms, but don't worry. We'll thoroughly explain browsers, Internet addresses, and links in chapters 3 and 4. But that, in a nutshell, is how information travels across the Internet.

But Where Do I Find the Internet?

You need an account with an Internet service provider to hook up your computer (or television) to the Internet, so it can take advantage of resources from all the other computers hooked up to the Internet. Your account can be with a commercial online service, which offers its own private content and articles, discussion forums, shopping areas, reference sources, e-mail, and chat areas to its subscribers in addition to Internet access. (Well-known commercial online services are America Online, Compuserve Interactive, Microsoft Network, and Prodigy Classic.) Each uses its own special software.

Your account can also be with an Internet service provider that provides Internet access but no special content. There are now thousands of providers across the nation, including many big telephone companies such as AT&T, Ameritech, and Pacific

A client is a software program that lets a computer contact and talk to another computer, a server, to access its files and programs.

A server is a central computer or software program that provides services for other computers over a network, including sending or receiving e-mail, carrying newsgroups, or offering access to or hosting Web pages. A server can perform a specific function or several.

A host is a computer that provides services to other computers on the network. It can be a computer offering access to its files, or an Internet access provider that a computer dials up for a connection.

An Internet service provider is a company that sells dial-up access to the Internet over telephone lines.

A commercial online service sells Internet access plus extra content to subscribers, such as articles, discussion forums, shopping, chat areas, and e-mail.

Bell, some cable television companies, and WebTV Networks that let you view the Internet on your television.

The going rate for unlimited access from either a commercial online service or straight Internet service provider tends to be about $20 per month ($25 for Compuserve). The rate is considerably less for a specific number of hours per month plus extra per-hour charges. Free trial versions are generally available.

Heads or Tails: Commercial Online Service or Internet Service Provider?

Differences are blurring between commercial online services and Internet service providers, as some content that began on commercial online services has expanded to the Web to draw a bigger audience. For example, The Motley Fool, a personal finance site, started on America Online but now is on the Web. Also, some Internet service providers offer a limited amount of content and recommended links, particularly local or regional providers.

Commercial Online Services

Many people like the fact that each commercial online service is its own self-contained small world. You'll only meet fellow subscribers in discussion forums and chat areas, which fosters a reassuring feeling of safety and belonging to a community among many. Some subscribers, in fact, venture only rarely, or perhaps never, past its cozy confines to the Internet.

Of course, this is somewhat misleading, since at 10 million subscribers, America Online, the biggest online service, can hardly be considered a small town where everybody knows each other's name. But many subscribers to online services enjoy certain discussion forums centered around common interests—plus friendships and contacts formed with fellow members—that they are unwilling to give this up for an Internet-only account.

In terms of sheer number of Internet users, the United States takes the cake worldwide. Considering the origin of the Internet as an American defense project—and the fact that English is its primary language—it's not too surprising. But if you look at the number of Internet host computers per person, three Scandinavian countries are among the top five countries across the globe.

Finland, a country of five million people where about 780,000 are online, has 62 Internet host computers per 1,000 people, compared to 31 in the United States, 30 in Norway, and 24 in Australia. Iceland, which came in second, has 42 per 1,000 people, according to the early 1997 study by Matrix Information and Directory Services, an Austin, Texas, market research firm. In Finland and Iceland, which has only about 270,000 people—smaller than many United States cities—high literacy and education rates, high standards of living, and the teaching of several languages in school, because few people speak Finnish and Icelandic outside these countries, are believed to be factors accounting for such widespread Internet usage.

Finland is also home to a maker of cellular telephones, Nokia Oy, whose products let users browse the Web and send e-mail as well.

All commercial online services offer parents ways to protect their children from sexually explicit and other objectionable material (read more about filtering software in chapter 8).

Many people prefer to get their feet wet through an online service, then later move to an Internet service provider when they feel more independent and adventurous.

While you can access the Internet if you subscribe to an online service, it doesn't work the other way around. An Internet user can't reach the content and services of an online service unless he or she subscribes to the service. That is, the Internet user can send mail to people if he or she already knows their e-mail addresses, or reach the online service's home page on the Web, but not its members-only content.

Internet Service Providers

Internet service providers often offer faster access and fewer service shutdowns because none has anywhere near the number of subscribers as America Online's millions. In contrast to a privately owned commercial online service, no one owns the Internet, it has no members, and anyone can get to it with the proper software, which is offered by countless different providers. Many Internet users assert that they have found a strong sense of community on various Web sites and in newsgroups without subscribing to a commercial online service.

A Brief Overview of Top Commercial Online Services

America Online

The biggest online service, America Online (AOL) is easy to use and install, its content is well-organized and appeals to many different age groups and interests, and there are lots of colorful graphics. Its content is divided into different topics, called channels; each can be found quickly on the main channel menu, or by typing in the proper keyword.

For example, the Entertainment channel contains sections on movies, television, music, comedy, fiction, and the arts. You can read movie reviews from the *New York Times*, Gene Siskel and Joel Siegel, celebrity gossip at the Daily Fix, David Letterman's Top Ten Lists, and hear interviews with movie stars and directors and attend premieres at Entertainment Asylum. Fans can discuss genres, such as action or science fiction, and stars at many forums. Career help can be found at the WorkPlace channel, which offers resume tips, regular discussions with small business owners and professionals in various industries, and job postings.

Investment advice, financial news and analysis are offered by the Finance channel's The Motley Fool, whose experts have written several books on investing. Tax help and forms, mutual fund ratings and reports, and insurance advice are also available at the channel. In the Families channel, parents can obtain advice from experts and each other on many child-rearing topics. Its timesavers section enables busy parents to pay bills, plan vacations, and handle other tasks in one place, while a genealogy forum teaches how to research your family tree. Hobbyists meet and exchange tips in the Interests channel, which also offers a food area with recipes, a pet care forum and an auto center with expert advice and price deals.

At the Travel channel, you can book airfares, hotel rooms, and car rentals from Preview Travel, explore travel bargains, and share prize finds with others in various forums. Arts and leisure, including book and movie reviews and gossip, can be found in the Influence channel, while AOL Today offers the top news headlines and top AOL features of the day. Meanwhile, the Lifestyle channel offers a women's network, communities where you can find others with similar interests, plus a Love@AOL section, featuring personal ads.

Breaking news, the *New York Times* newspaper, and ABC News are located at the News channel. Reference help, such as encyclopedias like Grolier's, Compton, and Columbia, homework help on different topics, and for-credit college courses from the University of California can be found at the Research & Learn channel. For the more playful-minded, the Games channel lets

Overwhelmed by the vastness of the Web? Friendly guides, each an expert in a certain specialty, share the treasures they've collected—Web sites, articles, newsgroups, and mailing lists—at The Mining Company (www.miningco.com). The directory has nearly six hundred categories, including food, family, travel, health, freebies on the Web, and the arts, and can be easily searched by a keyword or alphabetically by site.

If your taste buds run to sweet potato pie, ham jambalaya, chicken-fried steak, and other gems of Southern cuisine, check out Southern Food (http://southernfood.miningco.com). There are extensive links to Web sites for chile peppers, breadmakers, recipes, and gourmet shop sites among many others, and mailing lists such as EAT-L for recipes and ideas about food, and Recipe A Day, which sends recipes daily by e-mail.

users play action games with others across the world, exchange tips, read reviews, and buy games.

Starbucks, Eddie Bauer, and 1-800-FLOWERS are some of the name-brand merchants at the Shopping Channel, but there are many more, selling computers, clothing, books, sports equipment, and gifts.

A special Kids Only channel offers homework help from online teachers, chat rooms, and a variety of puzzles, trivia, and word games. Besides these channels, which come with the 4.0 version of AOL—if you have an earlier version, you may not have all of them—the Internet button is the jumping-off point to the Internet, including the World Wide Web, newsgroups, and Personal Publisher, which gives you free tools to design and publish your own Web site. The People lets you meet people in real-time chats, which can be general or organized by topic.

America Online's Web site (www.aol.com) offers a detailed index for help on all features of AOL, whose software can be downloaded from the site.

Its membership is considered more diverse in age and more middle-of-the-road than Compuserve, which it bought in 1997. A huge surge in membership followed its decision to offer unlimited monthly access and resulted in constant busy telephone signals that prevented many members from using it for hours at a time and delayed e-mail service. Since then, however, AOL has focused more on improving its network and keeping current members than attracting new ones.

Compuserve Interactive

The oldest online service, which started to serve the public in 1979, Compuserve has a reputation for an older, more serious, more business- and professional-oriented, and more international audience than AOL. Since its purchase of Compuserve, AOL has pledged to let the smaller service keep its distinct identity. It's known for over one thousand highly specialized discussion forums devoted to over sixty categories, including work at home, journalism, music/arts, family services, travel, and many computer and Internet issues. Databases offering business information and thousands of magazines, newspapers, and trade journals at per-article or per-hour rates are a real boon to researchers.

Available in 185 countries, Compuserve has no separate children's section, but there are educational forums.

Microsoft Network

The newest online service was formed in 1995 by the Microsoft Corporation, who belatedly realized the importance of the Internet. Much of the content on MSN, which you have automatically if you have Windows 95, is available free at its Web site (www.msn.com). This includes MSNBC, a news outlet and joint venture with NBC, which has a cable channel as well; Sidewalk, a guide to local events and restaurants in certain cities; Cinemania, movie reviews and interviews.

Business and legal experts, as well as authors, are forever showing up for conferences—real-time chats whose subject matter is far removed from what often passes for chat online. *Time*, *Money*, and *Fortune* magazines and newspapers such as *USA Today* are also found on Compuserve.

MSN also offers Expedia, an extensive travel resource for making reservations and a guide for researching destinations, and the Internet Gaming Zone, which offers many games, from classic board and card games to action and combat simulation (some games charge fees). MSN also includes the Encarta encyclopedia, Microsoft Investor, which helps users track their stock investments, a shopping area, chats, and new programming which has changed often since MSN's launch.

Prodigy Classic

Formed in 1990 as one of the earliest online services, Prodigy underwent an overhaul to become more Internet-oriented. Now there are two services: Prodigy Classic, an online service with its own private content, and Prodigy Internet, an Internet Service Provider which divides popular Web sites into channels—each topic also features links to related newsgroups and chat rooms—to make Web surfing organized and easy.

Prodigy Classic's content is divided into topics such as Business & Finance, Education, Entertainment, Computing, Games,

A newbie is a beginner in the online world.

A POP (Point of Presence) is a city or location that an Internet service provider can connect to with a local telephone call.

Home & Family, Music, News, Reference Center, Travel, and Sports. There is also a special Kids Zone, while a Shopping section includes merchants like J.C. Penney and Amazon.com. The Communications section offers message boards, e-mail and chat.

What Kind of Account Do I Get With An Internet Service Provider?

You'll want a PPP (Point-to-Point Protocol) or SLIP (Serial Line Internet Protocol) account. This means your computer is really part of the Internet network and lets you use the most popular browsers, Netscape Navigator and Internet Explorer, which do all kinds of fantastic things. (Read more about browsers in chapter 3.)

UNIX shell accounts, which let you access the Web as text-only, used to be the only way to connect to the Internet before PPP and SLIP. Most Internet service providers will still give you a UNIX account for an older computer, which needs no special software since it runs all programs you need on the provider's computer, not yours.

How to Select An Internet Service Provider

1. Decide if you want a commercial online service (such as America Online, Compuserve, Microsoft Network, or Prodigy) or a straight Internet service provider (ISP). Because online services have their own private content and serve as guides to the online world in general, they can be a good choice for newbies, or people new to cyberspace. A straight Internet service provider is more like an unguided tour of the Internet. Many users start with an online service then jump to an ISP when they feel ready. Many, in fact, keep both so they can still take part in favorite forums or avoid changing their e-mail address.

2   Ask if it is a local call to reach the ISP. It is important for an ISP to have a POP (Point of Presence) connection in your local calling area. You can expect a much higher telephone bill if there isn't. If you have a regional, not national, ISP, make sure there is a local number that you won't be charged extra for using.

    Sometimes, an ISP's local access numbers might be changed to 800 numbers. Users assume these are free or local calls, then are surprised to receive $90–$100 monthly telephone bills for usage, instead of $10–$20. When they check, the 800 numbers turn out to cost $6 per hour. Check with your telephone company to make sure the telephone number your modem is dialing is, in fact, a local call.

3   Ask the basic rate. Find out how many hours per month this rate includes and the per-hour rate for extra hours. Ask the monthly rate for unlimited access. Determine which is the best deal for you based on whether you will be a heavy or occasional user. A good idea is to start with the basic rate, then see what your bill is. Those hours always pile up faster than you think. Most ISPs now charge about $20 for unlimited access, but will charge half that for only a couple of hours per month.

4   Decide if you want a national or local/regional ISP. They vary wildly. If you live in a city, you probably can choose between national and local providers. If you live in a rural area, you may only have a local ISP. National ISPs, because they are offered by very large companies such as AT&T, MCI, IBM, and Sprint, are stable. Local ISPs go out of business much more often. National ISPs have bigger technical support staffs, but local ISPs may give more attentive service and be more willing to go out of their way for you. Local ISPs often host community chats and offer resources involving their regions.

Diane Rattray, the guide to Southern Food, is a devoted cook living in Tupelo, Mississippi, who takes special pride in the over 600 crockpot recipes on her site, as well as articles on the history of certain foods. One focuses on Kentucky cuisine in honor of the Kentucky Derby race, and others on cornbread and okra. Her readers, who live nationwide, particularly enjoy the chat room on her site "because it's filled with adults who love Southern cooking," adds Rattray, whose personal Web site, Diane's Kitchen (www.ebicom.net/kitchen) is filled with many types of recipes.

Configure means adjust software settings to connect properly with an Internet service provider to reach the Internet.

If you're looking for a delightful spot for a vacation, the Elegant Resorts, Hotels, Inns (elegantresorts@miningco.com) guide offers reviews and photos from around the world including the Caribbean, France, New Mexico, and the Spanish island of Ibiza. Links include Affordable Elegance, Kid-Friendly, Ski, and Villas.

If you travel a lot and want Internet access on the road, a national ISP is your best bet. They most likely have a POP in big cities, plus 800 numbers for smaller towns that lack access through a local telephone call.

5. Make sure all the software you need to connect your computer to the Internet is supplied by the ISP. This should include a Web browser, connection software, an e-mail program, a newsreader to read newsgroups, and an FTP (File Transfer Protocol) program to move files between computers connected to the Internet.

6. Talk to sales and support departments at the ISP before signing on with them. Find out if there is twenty-four-hour technical support. You don't want to be stuck with an Internet glitch at 2 A.M. or on Sunday with no support for hours. Ask the staff a list of questions to see if they are knowledgeable and polite. If you prefer to e-mail technical support queries, ask how long a response takes.

7. Look for an easy, automated process to install and configure your software and instructions written in plain English. A simple on-line registration, where you fill in various numbers and other information your ISP gives you, is what you want.

8. Talk to other people about their ISP. Do they often have trouble connecting? Do they get frequent busy signals? Do they get disconnected often? Do they think technical support is helpful? Ask friends, colleagues, or family, or ask the ISP to supply customer references.

9. Find out the fastest modem speed the ISP can accommodate. If you have a 33.6 Kbps or 56 Kbps modem or an ISDN line, make sure your ISP can support these higher speeds.

10. Consult the ISPs own promotional materials. Read their ads in the Yellow Pages (under Internet Services) and in business and technology sections of newspapers and magazines. Check out their Web sites.

11. Read articles comparing ISPs. See what computer trade magazines and business and technology sections of newspapers and magazines have to say about their differences. Some offer blow-by-blow comparison charts.

There are lists of ISPs on the Web. A directory of over 3,000 providers, divided into categories by area code, state, and country, with links to profiles and costs, can be found at The List (http://thelist.internet.com). It is published by Mecklermedia, a publisher of Internet trade magazines.

The television network, CNET, has an excellent comparison list on the Web (www.cnet.com).

12. Ask if there is a setup charge. So many ISPs have no setup charge that it seems unfair to pay one.

13. Find out what percentage of newsgroups your ISP includes. Some include only a fraction. If you planned on discussing your favorite hobby and its newsgroups are omitted, you won't be a happy camper. Ask if any particular categories are left out.

14. Take advantage of the trial offers, which offer free service for a limited time. Try more than one to see if you like it, can get around well, and find its support staff helpful.

15. Ask about the peak hours for usage. Then, try an ISP at those times to see if you get through or if you get constant busy signals or frequent disconnections.

How to Compare Internet Service Providers

Sounds like a dizzying lot of information to digest, right? How will I ever choose a provider, you're thinking.

Remember, the right provider is what's right for you. Think of your priorities. What do you really want the Internet for? A bargain is not the same for everyone. Do you want the cheapest possible rates? Do you prefer several e-mail addresses that share one account so you can have an e-mail account for yourself, one for your spouse or partner, others for the kids; or an e-mail account for personal

National

AIS Network
www.solutionprovider.net
847-882-0493

AT&T WorldNet
www.att.com/worldnet
800-967-5363

Blue Sky Internet
www.blueskyweb.com
503-669-1497

Brigadoon.com
www.brigadoon.com
425-586-2497

Concentric Network
Corporation
www.concentric.net
800-745-2747

EarthLink Network
www.earthlink.net
800-395-8425

FlashNet
www.flash.net
800-352-7420

Global Net
www.globally.net
703-715-1829

GTE
Internetworking
www.gte.net
888-GTE-
SURF

HoloNet
www.holonet.net
510-704-0160

IBM Internet Connection
www.ibm.net
800-888-4103

InterNET Resource
NETworks
www.inr.net
603-880-8120

Kampus Networks
www.kampus.net
888-826-1985

MCI Internet
www.internetmci2000.com
800-550-0927

MindSpring Enterprises
www.mindspring.com
800-719-4332

Netcom On-Line
Communication
Services
www.netcom.com
800-638-2661

Nova Internet Services
www.novaone.net
214-904-9600

PSINet
www.psi.net
800-827-7482

Sprint Internet Passport
www.sprint.com/sip
800-747-9428

TOAST.net
www.toast.net
888-TOAST-ME

UniDial
Communications
(www.unidial.com)
502-244-6666

Voyager Online
www.vol.com
800-864-0442

WebTV Networks
www.webtv.net
800-GO-WEBTV

ZipLink
www.ziplink.net
947-888-5465

The Internet Access
Company (TIAC)
www.tiac.net
617-276-7200

Regional Internet Service Providers Serving Major U.S. Cities

Boston
Cyber Access
Communications
www.cybercom.net
617-876-5660

Galaxy Internet Services
www.gis.net
888-334-2529

The Internet Access
Company (TIAC)
www.tiac.net
617-276-7200

Chicago
I Connect
www.iconnect.net
847-662-0877

InterAccess
www.interaccess.com
312-496-4400

The Ads
www.the-ads.com
815-741-1645

Urbancom.net
www.urbancom.net
708-687-2090

Denver
Denver.net
www.denver.net
303-573-5020

Rocky Mountain Internet
www.rmi.net
307-332-3755

Houston
Compass Net
www.compassnet.com/index.html
713-776-0022

Netropolis
Communications
www.netropolis.net
713-977-9779

Internet Service Providers

Regional Internet Service Providers Serving Major U.S. Cities (continued)

Southwestern Bell
Internet Services
www.swbell.net
972-238-3600

Miami
CyberGate
www.gate.net
800-NET-GATE

Internet Providers of Florida
www.fla.net
305-273-7978

Netpoint
Communications
www.netpoint.net
305-891-1955

Los Angeles
aNet Communications
www.anet.net
800-395-0692

BNS Internet
www.bassett.net
714-227-7503

BeachNet Internet Access
www.beachnet.com
310-823-3308

Brand X Internet
www.brandx.net
310-395-5500

Direct Net
www.directnet.com
213-640-6246

InterWorld Communications
www.interworld.net/default.htm
310-726-0500

Pacific Bell
www.pacbell.net
800-708-4638

New York
ASANet Internet Service
www.asan.com
718-539-2362

BrainLINK International
www.brainlink.com
718-805-6559

bway.net
www.bway.net
212-982-9800

Erol's Internet
www.erols.net
888-GO-EROLS

GAIN-NY
www.gainny.com
212-779-8715

Interport Communications
www.interport.net
212-989-7448

i-2000, Inc.
www.i-2000.com
800-464-3820

Internet Quick Link
www.quicklink.com
212-307-1669

Link America Communications
www.link-net.com
212-334-0331

Panix
www.panix.com
212-741-4400

Spacelab Net
www.mxol.com
212-966-8844

San Francisco
BAIS (Bay Area Infoserve)
www.bais.com
408-447-8690

Pacific Bell Internet
www.pacbell.net
800-708-4638

Sirius Connections
www.sirius.com
415-865-5000

Verlo Northern California
www.wco.com
800-226-3848

Seattle
Emerald Net
www.emeraldnet.net
206-363-1818

Seanet
www.seanet.com
206-343-7828

Washington D.C.
Cornerstone Network
www.cstone.net
800-325-9848

Erol's Internet
www.erols.net
888-GO-EROLS

The Hub Internet Services
www.knight-hub.com
703-553-6790

Verio Washington D.C.
www.veriodc.net
888-VERIO-DC

use, one for business use, one for people you don't want to hear from (and never open up)? (IBM and WebTV networks offer six, America Online five.) Do you want more server space to store your Web pages (many offer several megabytes of storage space; some offer five; America Online offers two for each user, a total of ten for all five users, which one user may hog), if you're planning an elaborate Web site?

Do you prefer to surf the Web and write your e-mail on your television because you've never really warmed up to computers? Will you be on the road a lot, Web surfing as you go?

Finding the Internet in Public Places

The Internet can be found in some surprising places nowadays. Besides many of the almost 10,000 public libraries in the United States that offer free access if they have Internet-connected computers, you can surf the Web and send e-mail for a fee at airports, cyber cafes, Kinko's copy shops, auto dealerships, even the mall. Public libraries with Internet access, including many in small towns and rural areas, vary greatly in their policies. While many allow anyone to come in and use their computers, others require a library card, which can cost a fee. The time limit is usually a half-hour, although you can continue if no one else is on the waiting list in some libraries. In New York City, the New York and Brooklyn Public Library systems—which cover 100 libraries—you don't need a library card and can print out ten pages free. (They even supply the paper.) Free classes on how to use the Internet are offered at public libraries. Many organizations—such as Webgrrls, a networking group for women interested in Internet issues with chapters in many cities in the United States—continuing education programs, and community centers offer very cheap classes.

At airports serving New York (Kennedy, LaGuardia, and Newark), Chicago, Houston, Orlando, Baltimore-Washington, D.C., Oakland, and Minneapolis, among other cities, passengers and visitors can

Web surf or send e-mail at almost 200 ATM-style kiosks. The rate for the machines, located in main terminals or in TWA Ambassador's Clubs and Continental President's Clubs, is $.35 a minute, plus a $1.95 access fee, payable by swiping a credit card. The company that installed the kiosks, TouchNet Information Systems in Kansas City, upgraded them from offering fax and copying services only.

In Los Angeles, San Francisco, and Newark, there are large stand-alone Internet stations from QuickATM, a Berkeley, California company, which cost $2.50 for ten minutes. The terminals are also convenient for travelers with laptop computers who normally have to hunt for data hookups to check e-mail or snatch a quick Internet break before a flight. You can also sip and surf at many cafes nationwide that offer Internet access as well as coffee, pastries, and often sandwiches as well—making the word "wired" doubly meaningful. In New York these include Cyber Cafe in Soho, a loft-like space, alt.coffee in the East Village, a Beat-type coffeehouse with comfortable couches, chairs, and eccentric fixtures, and Internet Cafe in the East Village, a funky space with loads of Internet reference books and a large dog. Directories of Internet cafes, with addresses, phone numbers, and links to their home pages, are on the Web at Cyber Cafes of Europe (www.xs4all.nl~bertb/index.html) and Cyber Cafe Guide (www.easynet.co.uk/pages/cafe/ccafe.htm), an international guide.

Early in 1998, a major mall developer began installing Internet kiosks and giving free CD-ROMs to its shoppers to alert them of merchant discounts at its malls and permit on-line buying, Web surfing, and e-mail. The Simon DeBartolo Group, which owns or manages over 200 regional and local shopping centers nationwide—including the nation's biggest, the Mall of America, plus The Forum Shops at Caesar's Palace in Las Vegas, and Newport, in the New York area—is also rolling out cyber cafes in its malls. Some of the 3,500 square-foot cafes, which will have an average of forty computers and kiosks, will be ready in time for the 1998 Christmas season. The cyber cafes will be run by Cybersmith, a New York chain of technology stores.

Interested in creating your own personal Web site? Check out the Personal Web (http://personalweb.miningco.com) section, with many articles and links that showcase the tremendous variety out there, including many diaries.

If you want to spruce up your home garden, guides from the Gardening (http://gardening.miningco.com) and Birding (http://birding.miningco.com) sites teamed up to create "Feathers and Flowers," a feature on how to create gardens that appeal to birds, which appears on both sites.

Can I Get the Internet for Free?

Sure you can. Besides public libraries, colleges and universities give their faculty members and students free Internet access, as do many companies with their employees. More and more high schools and grade schools are getting wired as well. An increasing number of community organizations also let local residents use their Internet-connected computers for free, or cheaply.

Some cities have "freenets," where people register for free and get limited Internet access with lots of local content. Then there are companies that offer free unlimited Internet access. In the San Francisco area, @Bigger.net has offered access to area residents, in exchange for a setup fee of about $60–$70, for the past few years. Tritium Network, based in Ohio, offers access in certain cities in exchange for viewing ads running along the bottom of the screen like a news ticker and monthly surveys on users' buying preferences.

But a number of firms that promised free Internet access folded after a couple of months, some, sadly enough, with users' setup fees. So be suspicious toward any firm touting free access and look up their track record. As is so often the case, what seems too good to be true, often is.

How to Get on the Internet

A modem is an electronic device that connects to your computer and telephone line and lets your computer talk to other computers. It can be either external or internal, that is, outside or inside your computer.

TCP/IP (Transmission Control Protocol/Internet Protocol) is the set of rules computers connected on the Internet follow to communicate. Your computer needs TCP/IP software to be on the Internet.

Y ou're all set to cruise the information highway, right? Here's the hardware and software you need to connect to the Internet.

1. A computer or television set. A computer that can run Windows 95, Windows 3.1, or a Macintosh will work. Because the Web is so rich in images, which take longer to download than text, you'll need more memory and probably more hard disk space than what usually comes with an older computer.

   A growing number of people are using their television for Internet access. If you subscribe to WebTV or similar services that use a set-top box atop your television, you get the added thrill of reading a Web page or your e-mail lying on a couch or even across the room.

2. A modem. This is an electronic device that lets your computer talk to other computers and obtain information over telephone lines. Most new computers now come with pre-installed modems. If you belong to a company, university, or school network, however, Internet access may be delivered through a network card inside your computer, which then talks to the company's or school's own network, which communicates with the Internet.

3. A telephone line. Any analog line, which tends to be used in homes, is generally needed.

4. Software. You need telephone dialer software to dial the Internet, communications software called TCP/IP (Transmission Control Protocol/Internet Protocol) so your computer can communicate with the Internet, and a browser that finds Web pages to display on your screen. The software will generally be supplied by your Internet service provider when you sign up, except perhaps for the browser. If you choose Windows 95 or an online service, a browser will be included. (See chapter 3 for more on browsers.)

5. An account with an Internet service provider. This can be a national, regional, or local provider, which offers full Internet access, or one of the commercial online services, such as America Online, Compuserve, Prodigy, or Microsoft Network, which offers original content to members plus a gateway to the Internet. (See chapter 1 for more on ISPs and a list.)

A megabyte is a million bytes, or tiny pieces of computer data, and is equal to 1,000 kilobytes.

A gigabyte is 1,000 times a megabyte.

What Kind of Computer Do You Need?

To really experience the Web fully and be able to use up-to-date browsers with all sorts of nifty features, you'll need the following:

1. You need to have a minimum of a 486 PC (which is no longer sold new today but available secondhand) with at least 8–12 MB (megabytes) of RAM (random access memory, or memory for short), but preferably anywhere from 16–32 MB of RAM. The preferred Pentium processor, commonly sold today, is a 586, has more power and so is even better, but not necessary. A 386 with a handful of MB and Windows 3.1 is possible, but you'll miss a lot and won't be able to use the latest browsers. For a Macintosh, you'll need at least a System 7 with at least 8–12 MB of RAM, but ideally 16–32 MB. The more memory, the faster and more efficiently your computer will run.

2. A hard disk with at least 400–500 MB. The size of your hard disk determines the amount of permanent space on your computer for storing files and programs, and this should do. But if you plan to download a huge number of files or play lots of games (with or without your kids), you'll want more room, like 1–2 gigabytes.

3. A video card that supports 256 colors and a high-resolution VGA graphics display for clarity. You can still see the Web if your video card supports only sixteen colors, but your browser may not show pictures. To

Computer Buying Do's and Don't's

DO buy a computer from a reputable store, computer maker, or Web site. Buying a bargain used computer from an individual as a result of an ad, flyer, or word of mouth may seem tempting but offers almost no protection for the buyer compared to a brand name that repeatedly deals with customers and stands behind its products.

A bargain is no bargain when the computer doesn't work and the seller has moved or won't return your frantic calls. But if you do buy a used computer, ask for the original sales receipt and manufacturer's warranty, because some warranties only cover the owner who has proof of purchase.

see pictures the way their designers intended, you'll need a 256-color card.

4. A 16-bit (or 32-bit) sound card (SoundBlaster or compatible) and speakers (or a headset). There is lots of sound on the Web, such as music, radio and interview clips, but if you can live without this, you can skip the sound card. If you plan on listening in privacy without blaring sound in front of your family or others, get a headset. If you want to try making Internet telephone calls (see chapter 4), you'll need a microphone as well.

5. A color monitor (15" is standard, but 17" is sharper and no longer so expensive), keyboard, and mouse. These generally come with your computer.

6. A printer. An inkjet, which produces good quality, or a laser printer, which produces excellent quality but is much more expensive, is preferable. Don't get a dot matrix printer, which produces poor quality, is slow, and needs paper fed one sheet at a time. If you don't need to print out Web pages in color, buy a black-and-white printer, which is cheaper.

7. A CD-ROM drive (16X or higher; X refers to the speed). It's not necessary to reach the Web, but a great deal of software, including Internet connection software, and children's educational and game programs are available on CD-ROMs.

See the Internet in Black and White

If you don't need the full pictures-and-sound experience of the Web, don't want a fancy new browser, and have no interest in upgrading an old computer, you can get by with a 286 or 386 PC with a very slow modem (14.4 Kbps or less) and a shell account.

A shell account gives your computer access to the powerful UNIX operating system, which is how people used the Internet before the Web, Mosaic, and Windows were invented. It's called a shell because your computer will only display the results of programs that actually run on another computer. Many ISPs will still give you a shell account that comes with a browser, which shows text only, called Lynx, plus e-mail and newsgroups.

Choosing a Computer

When you buy a computer, comparison shop. Read articles in magazine and newspaper technology sections on computers and computer magazines, which always run articles on "Best PCs," "PC's Under $1000," and "Best New Product," etc., and review different brands. Talk to computer salespeople at several stores, ask questions about how the products differ, and what they recommend for your needs and price range. If you want to buy by mail order, obtain several catalogs, not just one.

Don't be swayed by the latest, most expensive models which come on the market. You can always upgrade your computer with fancy new software and other accessories—like a faster modem, bigger monitor, and better sound card. You can also buy a more advanced model later when you can afford it or want loads of extra features. Don't think you have to buy a new machine every year or so; many computers are still thriving several years after they were bought.

Leasing a computer is an option. Paying a small monthly amount over the term of a twenty-four-month or thirty-six-month lease may be more affordable in the short run. When the lease ends, you can either buy the computer at a specific percentage of the sales price or lease a newer, more sophisticated model. But read the fine print in the leasing agreement, which is subject to credit approval because it is in effect a loan, carefully to see exactly how much more the computer will cost in the long run. Leases vary widely from different computer makers, so be sure to comparison shop here, too.

When you're ready, buy—or lease—the model with the best mix of features that suits your needs and fits within your budget.

Computer Buying Do's and Don't's

DON'T pay for a computer by check or cash. If worst comes to worst, if you pay by credit card you can always challenge the charge on your bill with the credit card issuer. Most issuers will limit the dollar amount a buyer is liable for if there is a problem with a charge. Trying to get your money back if you have paid by check or cash is much harder. Payment by some credit cards even entitles you to a longer warranty period.

Where Do I Buy Computers, Software, and Other Accessories?

Stores

Circuit City
800-251-2665

CompUSA
800-266-7872

Computer City
800-843-2489

Staples
800-333-3330

Mail Order Catalogs or Online

Compaq
800-888-2339
www.compaq.com

Cyberian Outpost
www.outpost.com

Dell
800-WWW-DELL
www.dell.com

Egghead.com
800-EGG-HEAD
www.egghead.com

Gateway 2000
800-846-4208
www.gateway2000.com

IBM
800-426-7235
www.pc.ibm.com/us/index.html

Internet Shopping Network
www.isn.com

Micron
888-346-3006
www.micronpc.com

MicroWarehouse
800-367-7080
www.warehouse.com

NetBuyer
www.netbuyer.com

OnSale (on-line auction)
www.onsale.com

Modems

Traditional Modems

Modems come in different speeds, can be external or internal, and are made by many different manufacturers for desktop computers or laptops at varying costs. Some have additional features and can act as fax, voice mail, and speakerphone systems. You'll want at least a 28.8 Kbps modem (kilobits per second, or a speed of 28,800 data bits per second). The Web is filled with images, sound, and video clips, which take a lot of time to download. Don't settle for a slow 14.4 Kbps modem unless you have the patience of Job and the tolerance of the late Mother Teresa.

When you buy a modem, make sure it is Hayes-compatible, which means it is standard and should work with your computer. If you have an older 386 computer, most modems made today will not be compatible; a 486 or Pentium, however, will be able to use the fastest modems around. Also, make sure your Internet service provider will support your modem's speed. If you have a high-speed 56 Kbps modem, but your ISP is at the 33.6 Kbps speed, you'll be cruising at the slower 33.6. The two different and incompatible standards for 56 Kbps modems—x2 from 3Com/U.S. Robotics and K56flex from Lucent Technologies/Rockwell International—merged into one standard in 1998. Thankfully, this means you should easily be able to upgrade your 56 Kbps modem to the new single standard.

Modem Tips and Tricks

Decide if you want your telephone and your modem to share the same line. A second telephone line is not necessary, but callers will get a busy signal during the time you are using your modem unless you have voice mail or an answering machine. Family members may also want to use the telephone. On the other hand, a second line means higher monthly bills, an installation charge, and interruptions (from friends, family, and telemarketers) during Internet usage.

If you have only one telephone line, make sure your modem is connected to the telephone jack in your wall from its line in

Computer Buying Do's and Don't's

DO approach the right company if your computer has problems. This means calling the company whose warranty covers your computer, which may be the manufacturer or the retailer.

DO keep records of your computer's problems and the people you spoke with. This means dates, names, telephone numbers, and any error messages that appear on the screen.

Computer Buying Do's and Don't's

DO call the Federal Trade Commission's consumer hot-line at (202) 326-3128 (business hours only) if following the steps in the warranty fails to achieve any results. You will be told which agency in your state to contact. Generally, it will be the consumer protection agency or state attorney general's office.

or line jack for a clearer connection. Your telephone and answering machine should be connected to the modem's line out or phone jack.

If you have call waiting, dismantle it while using your modem. Otherwise, an incoming call is likely to break your online connection; worse, you may end up with no call and no online connection. Dismantle it by adding *70 (or *71) before your telephone number in your dial-up connection (in Windows 95 go to "Dial-Up Networking," then "Dial Properties.") If you have pulse, not tone dialing, use 1170 or 1171. Call waiting will resume when you finish Internet usage.

Internal modems are a little cheaper than external modems. They also save precious desk space. However, they are harder to install; you have to open your computer. It's best to have a computer expert do this instead of trying it alone.

If you have a laptop computer, you may want an internal modem or a credit card-sized PC card modem, which fits into the card slot. This makes it easier for travel than lugging around an external modem.

If you have a fax modem, your top fax speed will be 14.4 Kbps, despite the higher speed for your modem.

Ask if your ISP can support a faster modem connection, such as 56K or ISDN.

If you have trouble connecting with your modem, or keep getting disconnected, check all the modem settings with your ISP to make sure all information has been entered properly. If this doesn't work, call your telephone company to see if you have noise on your line. If you do, perhaps they can fix your line. Sometimes, switching your modem to a slower speed will ease things. Other times, removing another appliance, such as a fax machine, from the same telephone line will help reduce interference.

A modem works by switching digital data from a computer into analog data for transmission over telephone lines, then to digital data for the other computer and back again to analog data. A 56 Kbps modem runs so fast because the data sent over telephone lines in the first place from the ISP remains digital. Even with a 56 Kbps modem, uploading data—transferring files from your computer to another computer—remains at the 33.6 Kbps speed.

ISDN (Integrated Services Digital Network)

Much faster than a traditional modem—four to nine times as fast as many home users' modems—ISDN runs at up to 128 Kbps, more than twice the speed of a 56Kpbs, because it uses a special, completely digital telephone line. It's also more expensive, both in terms of installation and monthly charges, although this varies widely depending where you live. Buying a special ISDN terminal adapter is also required.

Ask your telephone company if it supplies ISDN, which is now available in most urban and suburban areas. One advantage, besides the speed, is that you can use your regular telephone line while using ISDN at the same time.

Cable

Hundreds of times faster than a traditional modem, cable can far surpass the super speedy T1 lines businesses often use which run at 1.5 Mbps (one-and-a-half megabytes). Because a cable connection means you are permanently connected to the Internet over the coaxial cable used for your television, you don't need to dial up your ISP every time you want your computer to go on-line.

Unfortunately, only a couple of hundred thousand people in a few test areas of the United States have cable Internet access at this time, and special cable modems sold at some stores tend to work only with the ISP in that area. However, this is expected to change rapidly because the biggest computer companies and cable operators in the country—Microsoft, Intel Corporation, and cable giants Tele-Communications, Inc. and Time-Warner—pledged as a group in 1998 to work together on a common standard to bring cable Internet access to a broader audience. Interestingly, a cable company that operates mainly in the South and Midwest, Charter Communications, plans to offer cheap Internet access on television sets through special cable set-top boxes in St. Louis by the end of 1998. Access will be at a slower 192 Kbps—still much faster than a 56 Kbps modem—because analog boxes will be used in contrast to the speedier digital boxes some cable operators are planning.

Computer Buying Do's and Don'ts

DO make sure you get a money-back guarantee. Thirty days or more is a good amount of time in case the computer doesn't work.

DO read all the fine print about the features included, especially if the price seems low. If it seems too good to be true, maybe it isn't. Make sure the monitor is included, which costs several hundred dollars if bought separately.

Computer Buying Do's and Don't's

DO make sure you understand the manufacturer's warranty. Know if it is full or limited, where repairs will take place, the length of time (often one year) covered, under what conditions repairs will occur, and steps to follow for repairs. In some cases, you may have to pay to ship the computer back to the seller, who will arrange for repairs. In other cases, you may be able to call the service bureau. Limited warranties, which are more common, often note that repairs are for defects of workmanship or materials only—not to fix problems caused by accidents, moving, well-intentioned efforts by people other than authorized service people, or mistreatment, such as spilling food or drinks over the machine. Be certain the warranty notes replacement parts will be similar or better so you won't get stuck with parts that are outdated or inferior.

Television is getting more like the Internet, and the Internet is getting more like television. The bottom line is to ask your local cable company if it offers Internet access.

Satellite

A satellite dish can also offer very high speed, about 200–400Kbps for downloads, but a standard dial-up connection to upload. The dish itself costs several hundred dollars.

T1

You probably don't want a T1 line, since its 1.5 Mbps speed for a dedicated line comes with a hefty price tag—at least $1,000 per month. Many corporations, as well as some Internet cafes and even apartment buildings, sport T1 lines, though.

ADSL

Asymmetric Digital Subscriber Line (ADSL), also called DSL or XDSL, is a new technology that uses ordinary telephone lines but can achieve tremendous speeds of up to 6 or 7 Mbps. Found only in a few trial areas of the United States, DSL uses the nonvoice part of the telephone line, which means you can talk on the telephone while Web surfing.

Prime-Time Internet: Watching the Internet on Your TV

For those who don't want or can't afford a computer and all kinds of software, or have a computer but enjoy the thrill of surfing the Web and using e-mail while lying on their living room couch, WebTV (www.webtv.net) is an ideal choice.

It's cheap, fast, much easier than a computer, and even lets you print pages in color. At only $99 for WebTV Classic, the original version (plus a wireless keyboard for about $50-$80), and $250 for WebTV Plus, the advanced version and its keyboard, it's a bargain whose quality has won many rave reviews in computer publications. Since six e-mail accounts come with each unit, it's easy for a family to share. Of course, the Web pages, e-mail, and newsgroups displayed are the size of your television screen—pretty impressive if you own a 31" screen.

Sold in electronics stores, WebTV looks like a black cable box, which you plug into your telephone line and the back of your television. Turn it on and off with its lightweight wireless keyboard or its remote control if you prefer. There's no mouse, so you zip around with up, down, and side arrow keys, which automatically jump to links if you're on a Web page, and with scroll up and down keys. To find a Web page, press a "go to" key and a window pops on the screen so you can type its address.

WebTV comes with a fat list of interesting Web sites to visit, so you'll have a map and won't get lost on your Internet safari, in a directory on its home page and a monthly online newsletter. Its online directory, "explore," features links to national and foreign newspapers from *USA Today*, *New York Times*, *Chicago Tribune*, *Washington Post* to the *International Herald Tribune* and *Jerusalem Post* in its News channel. Entertainment offers links to book information and bookstores such as Barnes & Noble and Amazon.com, arts event finders, famous museums such as the Smithsonian and the Louvre, and movie articles from E! Online, the cable channel. Money links to job hunting and career resource sites, while home life links to home improvement, decoration, garden, and parenting sites, and games ranges from mysteries to children's games and puzzles.

WebTV has a built-in search engine to find Websites. You can personalize its home page with news, sports, stock quotes, and local event listings, just as you can with search engines (read more about search engines in chapter 3). You can also choose background music while you use WebTV, from classical pieces such as Beethoven's *Fifth Symphony* or *Moonlight Sonata*, to jazz, popular or world music. Its Plus version even lets you watch television and Web surf at the same time, in case you want to look up facts on a movie, sports game or product. This sounds a little distracting to me, but to each his or her own. You can also build your own Web site with its free online help.

By the way, Bill Gates, of Microsoft—no slouch when it comes to brilliant ideas—bought WebTV Networks for $400 million in 1997. If that doesn't show faith in this product, what does?

You can't see everything on the Internet with WebTV that you can with a sophisticated computer, but then you haven't spent $1,000 or more. But you can see many animations and

Upload means to transfer files from your computer to another computer.

hear some sound clips; pages also seem bigger than they do on a similarly sized computer screen because space at the top and bottom is not taken up by rows of icons. In addition, you don't have to worry about updates—they're automatic—and viruses. A red light can go on at a preset time each day to alert you that you have e-mail, without the machine being on.

WebTV Plus comes with a 56K modem, a 167 MHz 1.1 GB hard disk, and 8 MB of RAM. All of this means it both connects to the Internet fast and sends pages rapidly, and its picture and word quality is superior to WebTV Classic, which has no hard disk and the speed of a 28.8 modem. The versions sold by Sony, Philips Magnavox, and Mitsubishi look slightly different but operate the same way. These companies licensed the revolutionary technology invented by WebTV Networks, a Palo Alto, California, start-up formed by three Apple Computer veterans. The first WebTV's were introduced in late 1996 and sold for about $250 plus the keyboard.

The monthly rate for unlimited Internet access is $19.95 for WebTV Classic, which is more or less the going rate for all-you-can-eat plans from many Internet service providers and commercial online services such as America Online and Compuserve. (It drops to $9.95 monthly if you use your own ISP.) It's $24.95 for unlimited monthly access for WebTV Plus, or $19.95 if you use your own ISP. Certain color printers from Hewlett-Packard and Canon can be plugged into the back of the WebTV box.

Where Do I Get Software to Connect to the Internet?

1. Your Internet service provider will probably provide what you need on a floppy disk or CD-ROM. (Of course, if it comes on a CD-ROM, you'll need a CD-ROM drive to run it.) Sometimes, you'll find a free sample in your mailbox, in a magazine, or given out at events on the street because some providers find this a good way to win more customers.

2. Stores sell it.

APT. With Riv Vw, 4 BR, WBFP, and T1 Line For Sale or Rent

As more people crave speedy Internet access, some apartment complexes are being built or refitted so they are wired for special T1 lines, connections that carry computer data fifty times faster than a 28.8 Kbps modem, at up to 1.5 million bits per second. Usually too expensive for homes or small businesses and used generally by big companies, residential T1 lines are being installed in New York City and the San Francisco area, densely populated areas with a high concentration of Internet users. Signing up for the lines, which let users download a video clip in less than a minute as opposed to a sluggish forty-five minutes, is optional for residents.

It may never be as popular as a wood burning fireplace or water view, but some apartment dwellers with home-based businesses, or lovers of Web sites filled with graphics or video, find sharing a built-in T1 line a delightfully novel feature. In New York, the Grand Millennium, a 31-story, 200-unit luxury condominium near Central Park and Lincoln Center, installed T1 lines in 1997. Service starts at $71.95 per month at the condominium, where each apartment can have up to a dozen telephone lines.

Other New York buildings that offer T1 access at a cheaper $50 per month are One Columbus Place, a 51-story, 700-unit rental on the West Side; the New Gotham, a rental with over 500 units at 43rd Street and Tenth Avenue; and City Lights, a Queens middle-income co-operative apartment building with over 500 units. At West End Towers, a rental complex with over 1,000 units on the West Side, speedy Internet access is provided through ADSL, which uses the nonvoice part of standard copper telephone lines, also at $50 per month. All these buildings, which have full-time "cybercierges" who handle Internet troubleshooting for residents, were wired by Dualstar Technologies Corp., a New York company. The first building to install T1 lines in New York was a small East Village twenty-eight-unit rental, back in 1996.

In California's Silicon Valley, the home of many technology companies, a new apartment building where each unit can have up to four telephone lines and T1 service from Pacific Bell, the regional telephone company, was built by Bay Apartments Communities. The company, which owns about four dozen rental buildings in California, plans to add the lines to more buildings in the next two years.

Computer Buying Do's and Don't's

DON'T buy a computer with a warranty that notes service is "at the company's discretion." The deck is stacked in favor of the maker in this case, and getting repairs will be tough unless it meets the narrow conditions specified by the owner.

DO notice if the warranty says you have to ship the computer back in the same box and packing materials it came with. Many do. Shipping is generally at your expense.

[3] It can be downloaded from the Internet. Maybe a friend or relative can download the proper programs for your system onto their hard drive and give you a copy on a floppy disk.

Connecting to Your Internet Service Provider or Online Service

Follow all the printed instructions from your ISP or on-line service on how to install its software and configure it properly. Pay particular attention to the information you are supposed to enter to log on for the first time. This includes:

- :-) IP address
- :-) domain name
- :-) mail server
- :-) news server
- :-) type of IP address (static or dynamic)
- :-) dial-up telephone number
- :-) e-mail address
- :-) host name

Some, particularly the commercial on-line services, offer highly automated software that is simple to install and basically runs itself, asking you to choose a local access number and password and little else. Others require more work. Call the technical support line of your provider if you have any problems connecting.

Of course, if your modem and your telephone share the same line, you will not be able to execute their instructions during the phone call, and will have to hang up. Two telephone lines make this much easier.

Connecting with Windows 98

Released in mid-1998, Windows 98 offers a faster, easier way to connect to the Internet for the first time and sign up for an ISP (or use the ISP you already have) due to its Internet Connection Wizard.

1. Click "start," then "programs," "online services," and follow the instructions of the ISP you pick. The Connection Wizard will automatically configure your computer and install any special software your ISP requires.

2. If you already have an ISP which is unlisted but no sign-up software, click "start," "programs," browser icon, then Connection Wizard. Follow its instructions, and it will automatically set up your account.

3. Either way, to connect to the Internet from now on, click "start," "programs," "Dialup Networking," and your ISP icon. Type your user name and password (unless saved on your computer), then click "connect."

Connecting to an ISP with Windows 95

The good news is your system already has everything it needs to connect to the Internet. If you have the Internet Setup Wizard software, the connection process is a lot easier. The Internet Setup Wizard may be in your computer, or that part of a product that enhances Windows 95 called Microsoft Plus!.

If you don't know if your computer has Microsoft Plus!, do this:

1. Click "start" on the vertical row of icons on the left side of your screen. Click the "programs" menu, then "Windows Explorer." If you find a "Plus!" folder on your C:\ drive, make sure the "Microsoft Internet" folder includes "Internet Tools."

2. Click "start," then "programs," then "accessories." Click "Internet Tools." You should see Internet Setup Wizard

Protect Against Electrical Surges

Buy a surge protector and plug your computer into it. This will protect your computer system against electrical surges, which can be caused by a heavy-duty appliance—such as an air conditioner or dishwasher—on the same power line, lightning storms, and fallen power or telephone lines. Look for a certification mark on the packaging and the product itself—"UL-approved," the best-known, should be on a holograph label—and the make and model number on the unit. The Consumer Product Safety Commission has recalled many low-cost surge protectors recently, so it's wise to look for this mark.

(Hooray!). If you didn't find that "Plus" folder on your C:\ drive—or other drives if you have them—you don't have Microsoft Plus!. You should buy and install it in the correct drive. (By the way, you can also use the Internet Jumpstart Kit, available from your ISP or your retailer, to connect to the Internet) Then, follow these tips.

If you have Microsoft Plus!, do this to configure your system:

1. Click "start," then "programs," "accessories," "Internet Tools," and "Internet Setup Wizard." Then, click "next." (Unless your modem is not set up yet—in that case, set it up ASAP.)
2. Choose the option which states you have an account with a different service provider, then "next."
3. Type the name of your ISP, then click "next."
4. Type the local access telephone number of your ISP, including area code. Choose "bring up terminal window after dialing," then click "next."
5. Type your user name (login name), which is the first part of your e-mail address—for example, "msmith," leaving out the "@mindspring.com" part—and password. Then, click "next."
6. Choose the way you obtain your Internet Protocol (IP) address. (Your ISP will tell you either it is a fixed address or that they automatically assign it each time you log on to the Internet.) Click "next."
7. Type the Internet Protocol address of your Domain Name Service (DNS) server. (This is a series of 12 numbers, which your ISP will give you.) Also, type the address of an Alternate DNS server, if your ISP gave this to you. Click "next."
8. Choose "Use Internet Mail," then type your full e-mail address and name of your mail server. (Your ISP will give you this.) Click "next."
9. Type "Internet Mail Settings" in the box in the big Exchange Profile box. Click "next."
10. Click "finish." You're done. Congratulations!

Now, to connect to the Internet for the first time, do this:

1.   Double click the "Internet" icon on your screen.
2.   Click "connect" in the big Connect To box.
3.   After it says "status: dialing" and then connects, type your user name, password, and other information given to you by your ISP in the big Post-Dial Terminal Screen box. Click "continue."
4.   It will say "connected" at a certain modem speed, if you're lucky and all the required information was typed properly. You can now minimize, but don't close, the Connect To box—closing it means your connection is lost and you will have to start from 1.

If you don't have Microsoft Plus! (or the Internet Jumpstart Kit), you may have to do more work to configure your system. OK, a lot more work, perhaps doing something like this:

1.   Insert the software from your ISP into the appropriate drive of your computer.
2.   Establish Dial-Up Networking. Click "start" button, then choose "settings," and then the control panel. Click on the "add/remove programs" icon. Choose the Windows setup tab, then click on "communications." Click the "dial-up networking" box, which allows you to connect to other computers over telephone lines, then click "OK."
3.   Install TCP/IP.

   This sets up the proper language (or protocols) to allow communication among computers on the Internet. Click "start," then "settings," then "control"—just like you did in step 2. Click on "network" to see a box that lists network components. Click "add" for a list of network component types, then click "protocol," then "add." Select "Microsoft," then TCP/IP, and finally click "OK." To make sure you have done this correctly, at the control panel—click "start," then "settings" to reach it—click "network" to see TCP/IP listed under "configuration."
4.   Configure Your Connection to Your ISP.

At the control panel, double-click on "network." Click "TCP/IP" and then select "properties" to see a box with six different categories. On the "IP address" option, click on "obtain an IP address automatically" if your ISP has told you to do so. (If not, type in the address, a series of numbers.) On the "DNS configuration" option, disable DNS if your ISP has told you so. (If it hasn't, type your ISP's name in "domain," your user name in "host" box, and the IP address of your ISP name server in "DNS server search order". You can usually ignore the rest of the options, which are at a default setting.

5. Establish Your Dial-Up Connection to Your ISP. Click "my computer," click "dial-up networking" and also the "make new connection" icon. Fill in the boxes, typing in a name for your ISP (its real name or a nickname will do), seeing if your modem type appears, then click "next." Type the access telephone number of your ISP; no area code is needed if it is a local call. When you see message stating you have made a new dial-up connection; click "finish."

6. You're almost done (whew!). Click "my computer," click "dial-up networking" and choose the new connection icon you just created. Make sure all the information you typed earlier is there, then click "properties." Click "general" to verify your ISP's local access number and your modem type. Click your new connection icon, and type in your user name and password (plus your ISP's local access number, in case it's missing.).

7. Click "connect"—you'll hear your modem dialing, which will be music to your ears at this point—and stare exultantly as "connected" at a certain modem speed comes up.

Congratulations! You've connected successfully to the Internet. Reward yourself somehow, you deserve it. Don't worry, you don't have to do this again—unless you get a new ISP.

Again, because there is so much variation, pay attention to how your specific ISP tells you to connect.

Connecting with Windows 3.1

If you have an older computer, not Windows 95, you have to connect to the Internet by adding Winsock (Windows Socket) software because your system lacks the software for Internet access. The most popular is Trumpet Winsock, although there are many Winsock software products around. This inexpensive product can be supplied by your ISP or downloaded from the Trumpet Software site (www.trumpet.com).

Once you have a Trumpet Winsock program and dialer, follow your ISP's instructions on how to install them. Some versions are more automated than others. Basically, you'll do something like the following. (If you have another product, not Trumpet, the process is similar.)

1. At the DOS prompt (C:\), type "MKDIR\TRUMPET." Or, in the Windows File Manager, create a directory called "\TRUMPET."

2. Copy every file by typing "COPY *.*" at the DOS prompt, or using the Windows File Manager.

3. Add the "\TRUMPET" directory in the file called "AUTOEXEC.BAT" after the "PATH" phrase.

4. Restart your computer. Go to the "\TRUMPET" directory and click "TCPMAN.EXE."

5. Pick "Internal SLIP" or "Internal PPP"—whichever connection you have with your ISP. Then, type the Internet Protocol address, name server, domain suffix, netmask and default gateway (your ISP will give you this).

6. Enter your modem speed and the communications port to which your modem is connected—for example, 28,800 and COM1.

7. Click "OK."

8. The information you have typed will appear. Click the "dialer" menu, then select "edit." Follow the instructions for editing in the "readme" file in the new "\TRUMPET" directory.

Winsock (Windows Socket) is software you add to a Windows 3.1 computer because it has no built-in Internet connection software, unlike Windows 95.

You now have a Trumpet icon on your computer. Click it and follow all the instructions from your ISP to connect to the Internet. Congratulations! You are connected. Your ISP should also give you a Web browser and an e-mail program.

Connecting with a Macintosh

You belong to a small but solid minority. The special software you need to connect to the Internet is:

1. MacTCP or TCP/IP control panel (System 7.5 and higher comes with MacTCP. But if you have an older version, it's best to upgrade to 7.5. If you have system 7.5.3, TCP/IP is pre-installed.)
2. MacPPP or FreePPP (system 7.5.3 needs FreePPP instead)

If you want to buy connection software, Apple's Internet Connection Kit is a good bet. Pre-installed in the newer Macintoshes that use System 8.0 or 8.1, Apple's Internet Connection Kit is an all-in-one, automated package which includes a browser, e-mail and newsreader program, dialer and manual. It can be used by systems 7.5 and higher, and makes connection and configuration much easier. The iMac is the turquoise-colored, translucent unusually-shaped Macintosh introduced by Apple this year.

Your ISP may also supply it. Follow the instructions on how to install and configure carefully. You also can download from the Web, America Online, or Compuserve (for example, FreePPP can be downloaded from www.rockstar.com/ppp.shtm).

Connecting to America Online

America Online offers a highly automated connection software. Do this to install:

1. Insert your diskette or CD-ROM into the appropriate drive of your computer.
2. Go to the Start menu, then choose "run."
3. Type "a:\setup" to start the installation.

4   Click "install." After this concludes, click "OK." Then, double click the "AOL" triangle icon. Reboot your computer if this icon doesn't come up.

5   If all the information on the next screen is accurate, click "yes." If not, click "no."

6   Click "OK." Your modem will now dial into AOL's toll-free number so you can select a local access number.

7   Carry out the online instructions. Type your area code and choose a local access number from those which appear. AOL will disconnect at this point.

8   Dial in with your new local access number. Type your registration number and password (see the diskette's packaging) and the remainder of the online registration form. Congratulations! You're an America Online member now. Sign on with your password whenever you return.

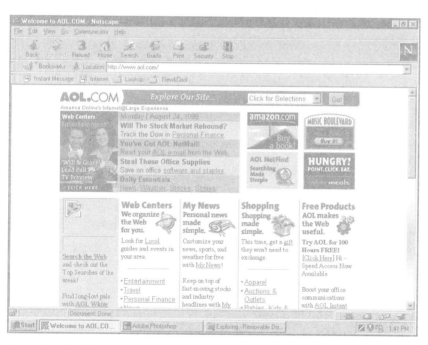

America Online www.aol.com

Connecting to WebTV

The easiest of all is saved for last (and just goes to show you how lack of a computer simplifies everything). Connect your set-top box, which looks like a black cable box, to your telephone line and television with the cords that come with it. Then, fill out the on-line registration form and you're ready to Web surf. No software, no installation, no configuration. Congratulations!

A wireless keyboard, which uses arrow and scrolling commands to navigate instead of a mouse, is a good bet to buy instead of using the on-line pop-up keyboard. If you have an older television, you'll have to buy an accessory called an RFU adapter.

Print Magazines About the Internet

Equip (www.complife.com) features easy to read how-to stories and trends, involving computers, the Internet and digital products.

Family PC (www.familypc.com) includes easy to read features on best Web sites and CD-ROMs for children and parents, Internet-on-TV products such as WebTV, and filtering software to protect objectionable material. Published jointly by Disney and Ziff-Davis.

Home Office Computing (www.smalloffice.com) is geared to people who run businesses from their homes, and includes helpful features on creating your own Web site, saving time, and being more productive and successful through the Internet and other technology.

Internet Computing (www.zdimag.com) is geared to Web professionals, with stories on Web site design and makeovers, increasing site traffic, and doing business over the Internet.

Internet World (www.internet.com) is a weekly, technically written business publication about Internet trends and news.

Online (www.onlineinc.com) features easy to read, practical stories about using commercial online services, as well as the Internet.

PC Computing (www.pccomputing.com) features in-depth, round-up stories and reviews of computers, software, and related products.

PC Magazine (www.pcmag.com) includes in-depth, round-up stories, such as "best products of the year" and "best Web sites," and reviews of computers, software, and related products.

PC Novice (www.smartcomputing.com) has easy to read single-themed issues about computers for beginners, including some about going online.

PC World (www.pcworld.com) features in-depth articles such as "top 5 home PCs" and "top 20 budget desktops," with features on Internet issues such as freebies, fraud and regulation, how-to, and product reviews.

Wired (www.wired.com/wired) is full of hip commentary, profiles, and trends on how technology has influenced culture. It uses flashy colors and fairly hard-to-read type.

Yahoo! Internet Life (www.yil.com) features easy to read stories about Internet issues, celebrity interviews, Web site reviews by topic with ratings, how-to tips, and a handy tear-out guide to Internet addresses of sites in each issue.

Three Online Newspapers: Chicago Tribune, New York Times, Wall Street Journal

Chicago Tribune Internet Edition
www.chicago.tribune.com

The *Chicago Tribune* is known for its many story packages. Certain stories are enhanced by a batch of sound clips, interactive graphics, and, sometimes, video clips, which almost turns them into mini CD-ROMs. For example, a Leisure feature on the discovery of the most complete dinosaur skeleton ever found relives the excavation through sound clips of the scientists, plus icons to click for sights of the dig itself, and lots of fossil facts. To fully experience the discovery of Sue, a 67-million-year-old Tyrannosaurus Rex exhibited by Chicago's Field Museum, you need three software plug-ins: Macromedia Flash to view graphics, RealPlayer to hear audio, and IPIX to see 360-degree photographs. (Read more about plug-ins in chapter 4.)

Portrait of An Online Retailer: Amazon.com

The first big bookstore to really sell books in a large-scale way on the Internet wasn't Barnes & Noble, Borders, B. Dalton, or another familiar name. It wasn't even a real world bookstore at all, but one that existed only in cyberspace. To add to the surprises, Amazon.com—named after the earth's biggest river—wasn't even founded by a bookstore owner, book publisher, or author.

When Jeff Bezos launched Amazon.com on the Web in the summer of 1995, he was a former Wall Street hedge fund principal at D.E. Shaw & Co. who became captivated with the possibilities of on-line retailing. Despite his lack of experience in publishing, Bezos sensed the Internet was growing at a truly exponential rate that dwarfed other industries. He was also struck by the fact that books are a category with an enormous number of individual units. So in 1994, he moved his family to Seattle from New York, writing a business plan for his brainstorm on his laptop and hiring a staff along the way. He set up shop in his garage, and later in a converted warehouse in Seattle.

Today, Amazon.com, which claims to sell about 2.5 million titles—much larger than any superstore—at discounts from 10–40 percent, is regarded as one of the major shopping sites on the Web. Many books are shipped out to buyers within twenty-four hours, and most within two or three days. Customers can search for books by name, author, or topic, and pay by credit card on-line. Amazon.com resembles a bookstore whose friendly owner remembers your tastes and can recommend similar titles after you buy a book, send e-mail reminders that new books by the same author or on the same topic have come on board, or try to match your mood. Outstanding new books are described, interviews with authors are included, and readers can play book reviewer by posting their own comments for the world to see.

One of Bezos' favorite books is the biography of Sir Richard Francis Burton, the British explorer who discovered the origins of the Nile. Bezos is an explorer in the uncharted territory of cyberspace whom many think changed the online shopping experience forever.

If you don't want or can't use plug-ins, you can still get the gist by reading the text—broken up into short, bite-sized portions—and seeing the photographs.

A story package on Israel's fiftieth anniversary, in May 1998, aired a cybercast—a discussion between an American who fought in Israel's war for independence and a Palestinian-American, which could be heard over the Web in real time. Readers were invited to e-mail questions and comments before the cybercast was held. Diary entries (and photographs) of a young Israeli soldier that told of his hopes and fears for the future were also part of the package.

The top stories of the day flash alternately every few seconds on the Tribune's rather sparse front page, with links to sections of the paper.

New York Times on the Web
www.nytimes.com

Aiming to be as thorough and up-to-date as the newspaper itself, The New York Times on the Web offers vast resources for book lovers and technology fans in particular. Its Book Review section contains over 50,000 reviews, dating from 1980, which can be searched by author, title, and topic. Sound clips of book readings, first chapters, and discussion forums are also available. An online section, CyberTimes, covers online trends and culture with five weekly columns that cover the arts, education, law, travel, international issues, and other stories.

Breaking news is reported every ten minutes from the Associated Press' wire service, while news sound clips are heard every half-hour.

Early birds can scan a huge array of job and real estate listings from the Sunday papers hours before home delivery customers receive them. They're posted online Friday at midnight.

The Front Page, which resembles the print paper's front page, offers links to top

Is your hometown newspaper on the Internet? If it is, why would you want to read it online?

Well, for one thing, it's free. For another, it may report breaking news you won't see in print until tomorrow's paper. Special features, like sound clips of interviews and book readings, or fancy graphics, may turn your dose of current events into a multimedia event. You may even get a jump on classified help wanted or real estate ads before they hit the print edition. If you feel strongly about a story you've read, you can discuss it with others in forums set up for this reason, or shoot off an e-mail to an editor.

Of course, you can read out-of-town and even foreign papers without paying expensive prices or waiting days or weeks for them to arrive by mail. This comes in very handy if you want to catch up with news and people from your original hometown—or country—or want to brush up on your knowledge of a new city.

Over 2,000 newspapers in the United States are online. Most are dailies, but there are over 700 weeklies now on-line according to AJR NewsLink (www.newslink.org), the online version of the *American Journalism Review* magazine. In fact, all fifty states have at least one daily, which is updated at least once that day, notes AJR NewsLink, whose fascinating site has links to the over 3,600 newspapers online worldwide. These are organized by country and, in the United States, state and type—such as dailies, nondailies, business, alternative, and special (ethnic or religious)—making for easy browsing.

Illinois, interestingly enough, is the state with the most newspapers online, at 173. California is the runner-up.

Newspapers have scrambled on-line— only 855 were online worldwide in 1995—and most of the recent growth has come from smaller American and overseas papers, says AJR NewsLink. There are strikingly different online editions to reach distinct audiences, and some even charge for subscriptions.

stories in a variety of sections, plus links to the sections themselves. Stories are full-text from the paper, a bargain given that the Sunday paper edition is $2.50. Dozens of forums discuss a wide range of issues, both local and international.

Although free in the United States, the New York Times on the Web requires password registration, meaning you fill out an online form with some personal details and receive future e-mail of additions to the online paper.

Wall Street Journal Interactive Edition
www.wsj.com

Daringly charging $49 for an annual online subscription—which includes *Barron*'s and *Smart Money*'s on-line editions as well—the Wall Street Journal offers several features found only online. You can chart a specific stock, tracking it against other stocks and market indexes, and find extensive background data, such as financial results for the past five years and corporate history. Small business owners will find the Small Business Suite section, which is part of Tech Center, filled with informative articles.

Searches of over 3,600 publications in the Dow Jones News/Retrieval Library are free, although reading the articles is not—each costs $2.95. (But once you have the headlines and dates, read them on-line at their own Web sites or at a library.)

A sizable career management/job hunting section (http://careers.wsj.com) offers articles from the print edition's career columnists, as well as outside experts, on topics from getting a promotion to negotiating a salary. There is a career Q&A with the editor of the *National Business Employment Weekly*, also owned by Dow Jones Company (owner of the Wall Street Journal). Over 11,000 job listings worldwide are included from the papers' domestic and foreign editions.

Top Ten Web Sites for Home Surfing

In 1997, the most popular Web sites for users at home, according to Media Metrix, a PC Meter company in New York that is part of the NPD Group, were (in order):

Yahoo!
Netscape
America Online
Microsoft
Excite
Infoseek
GeoCities
Lycos
ZDNet
Digital Equipment Corp. (Alta Vista)

Five out of ten were search engines (Yahoo!, Excite, Infoseek, Lycos, and Alta Vista, whose Internet address is digital.com because its maker is Digital Equipment Corporation). Two were makers of popular Web browsers (Netscape and Microsoft). America Online is the most popular online service, while GeoCities is a popular community site offering free home pages, and ZDNet is Ziff-Davis Publishing, a publisher of Internet magazines.

Attention, All Shoppers: Who Shops on the Internet, Why, and How Much?

The number of people visiting shopping sites on the Internet rose by 54.8 percent during 1997, according to a survey by Media Metrix.

On-line consumers spent about $2.4 billion in 1997, estimated Forrester Research, Inc. in Cambridge, Mass. According to its report, "Retail Revs Up," this is expected to soar to over $17 billion in 2001, with nearly half coming from travel bookings from airlines, hotels, and trips, and most of the rest from computer hardware and software, entertainment, books and music. Convenience and "surgical shopping"—focused buying, not leisurely browsing—will drive the online buying boom, says Forrester.

Meanwhile, a survey of online shoppers found 19 percent said they are shopping less at real world stores, while 14 percent noted a similar drop off in catalog shopping, said Cyber Dialogue, a market

Moore's Law: Computers Add Power, Reduce Price

Back in 1965, Gordon Moore, the co-founder of Intel and its chief executive officer from 1974-87, noted the power of computer chips doubles every year, while the cost declines at a similar rate. He predicted this trend would continue. Although the rate slowed somewhat—Moore later revised his prediction to every 18 months—this theory, called "Moore's Law," has held true for 35 years. In 1998, most computer experts, including Moore, now a billionaire, saw no reason why this trend would not continue for at least 20 more years.

Moore studied the number of transistors, which are microscopic devices made from semi-conductor material, per square inch in integrated circuits in microprocessor chips, which give computers their computing power.

It's a good idea to remember Moore's Law when buying a computer. Don't buy a new computer when it first comes out. Wait a while, and the price will drop steeply over time. In a few months, you will be able to buy a more powerful computer at the same price. After more months pass, you can buy a much more powerful computer for the price you originally considered, or the first computer you wanted at a much lower price. You can always upgrade.

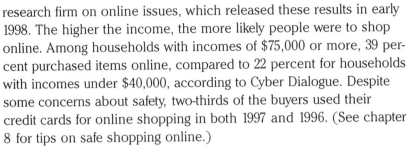

research firm on online issues, which released these results in early 1998. The higher the income, the more likely people were to shop online. Among households with incomes of $75,000 or more, 39 percent purchased items online, compared to 22 percent for households with incomes under $40,000, according to Cyber Dialogue. Despite some concerns about safety, two-thirds of the buyers used their credit cards for online shopping in both 1997 and 1996. (See chapter 8 for tips on safe shopping online.)

The top five shopping sites for 1997 were:

Amazon.com (books)
CNET Download.com (software)
ColumbiaHouse.com (CDs)
    Hotfiles.com (software)
    Surplusdirect.com (computers)

Source: Nedia Metrix survey

Web Sites with Technology News

CNET Online (www.cnet.com)

This terrific site from CNET, the Computer Network, is rich in resources from its daily technology news, reviews of hardware, software, and Internet service providers, a search engine for the Web, information on browsers and building Web sites, software downloads, and content from its television shows "The Web" and "The New Edge."

HotWired (www.hotwired.com)

Articles on Internet news and culture plus vivid graphics are featured on this online offshoot of *Wired* magazine.

Internet.com (www.internet.com)

Excellent features on this site from Mecklermedia, a publisher of Internet magazines, include The List, a directory of over 3,000 Internet service providers, Search Engine Watch, Browser Watch, Product Watch, and an electronic commerce guide with hundreds of links.

MSNBC (www.msnbc.com)

This joint effort between NBC and Microsoft, which also has a cable television channel, offers technology articles with interactive features, plus news, business, and lifestyle sections.

TechWeb (www.techweb.com)

This site includes daily technology news, product reviews, software downloads, an online store, plus The Net Insider—people profiles and articles on the Internet, with sound clips—and a Net guide from CMP Media, a publisher of a dozen computer magazines.

ZDNet (www.zdnet.com)

This site features daily technology news from Ziff-Davis, links to its computer magazines (*Yahoo! Internet Life*, *PC Magazine*, and *PC Computing*) an Internet section, product reviews, software downloads, and an online store.

Pick Passwords Wisely

You will need a handful of passwords in your journeys around the Internet. The most important password is the one you pick when you connect to your ISP for the first time, which can be saved on your computer if you don't want to type it every time you go on the Internet or get your e-mail. But many Web sites will ask you to pick passwords as well, so you can use their bulletin boards and read their special content, and they can track your visits to their sites. To prevent you from forgetting your password, some sites will ask you to think of a question and its correct answer, to verify that it is really you.

The best type of password is one you can easily remember, but hard for others to guess, over five letters and/or numbers long. Computer security experts recommend these tips in choosing passwords so other people will not be able to access your account and read your e-mail: (This includes co-workers, nosy relatives or strangers.)

:-) Don't use your full name, first or last name, initials, or any combination of these in any order

:-) Don't use your user name

:-) Don't use your telephone number, birthdate, address, or social security number

:-) Don't use the name of your child, spouse, girlfriend, or boyfriend, pet, favorite sports team, or any other obvious personal information someone who knows you may guess

:-) Don't use a word in the English dictionary

:-) Don't use the same password for every system; if you don't want a different password for every system, at least use several

:-) Don't tell anyone your password; if you do, change it immediately

:-) Don't carelessly display your password (for example, taped to your computer monitor or atop or under your desk)

:-) Do use a combination of letters and numbers

:-) Do use a word which has deep personal meaning for you but which almost no one knows (for example, a word your child has invented; a name from your distant past, such as your first pet, the street you lived on as a child, a character in a favorite book)

:-) Do write it down and keep it in a safe place (for example, your wallet, unless you tend to misplace it often, or under lock and key)

GETTING AROUND

What to Do Now that You Are on the Internet

A search engine is a software program that searches for topics, words, or phrases on the Web or in newsgroups and displays them as links for you, usually with descriptions. They can be directories or indexes.

Point and Click

When all is said and done, all the thousands of words written about how to get around on the Internet—all the technicalities and high-sounding gobbledygook—can be boiled down to three little words: point and click.

This means that when you see something that looks interesting—words, a picture or a button—move your mouse so its cursor rests on it, then click. If you don't have a mouse because you have WebTV or Lynx, a text-only browser that doesn't show pictures, use arrow keys to move around. If the interesting word or picture is a link, you'll suddenly be transported to another place, either on the same Web site or a different site. You're here, next thing you're there.

You know it's a link because if it's a word or phrase, it's underlined. Links are generally blue, in contrast to the generally black text (if the colors are different, it's still fairly easy to tell the link apart from the rest). Your cursor will suddenly change to a pointing hand, and the Internet address of the new location will appear at the very bottom of your screen. Buttons that say "contact us," "products," "search," or "company news" are generally links. Pictures that are links have borders; often, they tell you to "click to see a larger image," "click on the area of the country where you are located," or something similar.

Before you know it, you're suddenly navigating the interface, computer talk for moving around and interacting with the screen you're viewing. Some interfaces are easier to travel than others, depending on how clearly they were designed.

When you want to see more of a Web page than what is shown on your screen—some are quite long—press your scroll down key (or scroll up to reread what you've already seen). If you want to move more slowly, click the down arrow on the bottom right of your screen to read more (or click the up arrow to reread). To scroll faster with your mouse, click the vertical box above the down arrow for more, or click the vertical box below the up arrow to reread. Many Web pages also have links called "next" or "continued," or arrows, which you can click to take you to the next page.

Let's first discuss Web browsers, indispensable tools that you need to move around, and various commands. Then, we'll discuss different search engines, which are helpful directories and indexes that search for topics, words, or phrases when you don't know the specific Internet address. Once you know how to use browsers and search engines—both of which are elaborate software programs—you'll be zipping around in no time.

The Browser: Your Essential Tool

Browsers are software programs that scan the Internet to locate Web pages and show them on your screen. They also respond to commands to perform many other tasks. The most popular browsers, Netscape Navigator and Internet Explorer, are locked in a dog-eat-dog battle to outdo each other by offering more and easier features to win the hearts of users everywhere. As a result, their recent 4.0 versions are workaholics: they handle e-mail, read newsgroups, create Web pages, find people and businesses, connect you to search engines, send customized news and information, and let users work together easily by sharing documents.

The higher the number of the version, the more recent a browser is and the more features it has. For example, 3.0 is more advanced than 2.0; 4.0 versions, which came out in late 1997 for both Netscape and Microsoft, surpass 3.0, and 4.5 surpasses 4.0. You don't have to have the absolute latest version of a browser, but you will be able to do more with it. Many Web pages note they can be seen best with a certain browser or version: "Netscape and Internet Explorer 3.0 or better."

Some sites note, thoughtfully, that users of other browsers, such as AOL, which has its own browser (a version of Internet Explorer), or text-only browsers, can click to view their pages properly. Web sites look different, depending on the browser you use, which creates a challenge for Web designers and adds to the infinite variety of the Web. Both Netscape Navigator, from Netscape Communications Corporation, and Internet Explorer, from Microsoft Corporation, work on many operating systems, such as Windows 95, Windows 3.1, Macintosh, and UNIX. Specific system requirements, including the amount of memory and disk space your computer needs to use the browsers, plus detailed descriptions and technical support to answer likely

questions are located on the Web sites for Netscape
(www.netscape.com) and Internet Explorer (www.microsoft.com/ie).

Netscape Navigator comes either as a stand-alone product, or as
part of a package called Netscape Communicator, which lets you
create Web pages, share documents to work with others, even make
telephone calls without paying long-distance charges (see more
about what's called Internet telephony in chapter 6.) in addition to e-
mail and newsgroups.

Major Features of Netscape Navigator and Internet Explorer Browser Versions

Because browsers come in many different versions, it is sometimes hard to keep track of which version offers what features in
addition to browsing the Web. Here is a short list:

Netscape Communicator 4.0
> E-mail and newsreader programs, Web page design, cus-
> tomized channels for news and information, instant mes-
> saging, sharing documents to work together. Standard Edition
> is free; Professional Edition for companies is not, after a 90-
> day free period.

Netscape Navigator 4.0 Stand-Alone Edition
> Customized channels for news and information. Free.

Netscape Navigator 3.0 Gold
> E-mail and newsreader programs, Web page design.

Netscape Navigator 3.0
> E-mail and newsreader programs.

Netscape Navigator 2.0
> E-mail and newsreader programs.

Internet Explorer 4.0
> E-mail and newsreader programs, Web page design, cus-
> tomized channels for news and information, instant mes-
> saging, sharing documents to work together.

Internet Explorer 3.0
> E-mail and newsreader programs.

Internet Explorer 2.0
> E-mail and newsreader programs.

How Do I Get A Browser?

Browsers are either free or fairly cheap. It may be already installed
in your operating system. If you have Windows 95 or 98, both
Microsoft products, you probably have Microsoft's Internet Explorer
browser. You do not have to use the browser that comes with your
computer, however, and may choose another you like better, as
many do.

A browser may already be included in the connection software
from your Internet service provider when you sign up for an
account. The ISP may give you Netscape or Internet Explorer, or its
own more limited version of one of these very common browsers,
as America Online does. If you have WebTV, its own browser is
built in.

You can also download some browsers for free from its maker's
Web site. Set aside some free time: the download takes a couple of
hours (six hours estimated for Explorer, two hours estimated for
Netscape) and may be a pain in the neck if installing software is not
one of your natural gifts.

How to Download A Browser

Go to its maker's Web site, for example Netscape Navigator
(www.netscape.com/download) or Internet Explorer
(www.microsoft.com/ie). Both Internet Explorer and Netscape
Communicator (or Netscape Navigator, the stand-alone browser) are
entirely free.

Say you want Internet Explorer. Choose the version you want
(3.0, 4.0, etc.) from the pulldown menu. After you are sent to the
download area, choose the server located closest to where you are,
from which the file will be sent. When you are asked where the file
will be stored on your hard disk, choose an easy-to-remember
folder name, such as downloads. This way, all your software
downloads are grouped in one place, so you won't
have to hunt for them.

Then, occupy yourself while you wait for it to
download—which will be no time soon. (Pick
something that will take a couple of hours.)
You can watch the progress in the
window on your screen (and cheer it

BASIC STEPS

In April 1994, an unlikely pair cofounded a new company: Dr. James Clark a former Stanford University associate professor and the founder of Silicon Graphics, a Fortune 500 computer systems firm, and twenty-two-year-old Marc Andreessen, who helped created Mosaic, an early Web browser, as a University of Illinois college student at its National Center for Supercomputing Applications (NCSA). Later that year, the company, Netscape Communications Corporation, made the first copies of its new browser, Netscape Navigator, available for free downloading from its Web site. A graphical browser that built upon the revolutionary features of Mosaic, Netscape Navigator (often called Netscape) rapidly became the world's most popular Web browser.

In mid-1995, its first retail product was released, Netscape Navigator Personal Edition. In August, Netscape Communications went public, selling shares in what was considered the hottest initial public offering ever by a new company. Although at the time the Mountain View, California, company had no sales to speak of—not to mention profits—many investors were eager to cash in on the potential of the Internet. The shares' price zoomed in a buying frenzy.

Earlier that year, the company gained an experienced CEO and president in James Barksdale. The former president of McCaw Cellular Communications, a cellular telephone company that later merged with AT&T, and former chief operating officer of Federal Express, Barksdale oversaw Netscape's launch of a full line of software products for sale to corporations. The software products enabled companies to set up server computers to publish and share information with other computers, host Web sites, and set up their own internal computer networks, called intranets. Money from ads and software sold from its Web site grew enormously. The year 1995 was one of huge growth, as Netscape opened a subsidiary in Japan and offices in Paris, London, and Munich.

In 1997, revenues for Netscape grew to over $500 million, of which $95 million came from its heavily trafficked Web site—compared to 1995, when only $1.8 million came from its Web site. But the company simply broke even for the first two quarters of 1998. In January, it announced the first layoffs in its history, and decided to give away Netscape Communicator—its package of browser, e-mail, and newsreader programs, and Web site building tools.

A major reason for these changes was that Navigator's great popularity aroused the jealousy of Microsoft Corporation. Microsoft released its own browser, Internet Explorer 2.0, in late 1995—just a few months after Windows 95 was launched amid worldwide fanfare—and began to include it free in newer versions of Windows 95. Displaying the can't-miss-it Explorer icon on Windows 95's opening screen and releasing newer, souped-up versions to challenge Netscape meant an all-out battle of the browsers. Microsoft released Explorer 4.0 in September 1997, and many more users began to abandon Netscape for Explorer.

Fast-forward to today: In December 1997, a Federal court ordered Microsoft to stop requiring computer makers who sell Windows 95, or later versions, to include Internet Explorer. Appealing the order, Microsoft agreed to modify Windows 95, but its new product, Windows 98, was just a few months away from being shipped. In May 1998, the Federal government under Attorney General Janet Reno, plus twenty other states,

sued Microsoft for antitrust violations. Accusing the world's biggest software maker of using its monopoly in personal computer operating systems to force its own browser down the throats of a captive audience, the suit demanded that Microsoft remove Explorer from Windows 98, or offer users a choice between Navigator or Explorer.

The Federal government also required Microsoft to let computer makers choose the browser they want, or include more than one with Windows 98, and hide Explorer on the opening screen. However, the government suit did not prevent Microsoft from shipping Windows 98 to computer makers, which took place in May 1998, for sale to consumers in early summer.

Meanwhile, Netscape beefed up its Web site, Netcenter, in 1998, turning it into something that looks more like many search engines with different channels of content—from kids and family to business and entertainment—plus free e-mail. The company partnered with the search engine Excite, which is now the major search engine powering the Netcenter site, and helped develop some of the channels of content in exchange for paying Netscape over $70 million over the next two years.

A pull-down menu is a list of a variety of choices. Click on the choice you see to view the selections, then click on your selection and hit your enter key or the button next to the menu.

Shareware is software that is free for a trial period, then requires a small fee paid to its developer if you continue to use it.

along). When it's done, log off and get ready to install your browser.

To install, find it in your cleverly named downloads folder. Click on the file name and it will install automatically. Follow the instructions on the screen. If you're asked if you want optional components, select "yes" if you want Microsoft's e-mail program and newsreader program (to read newsgroups), unless you want to use other programs from other companies, such as Eudora or Pegasus, which some people prefer. (See chapters 5 and 6 for more about e-mail and newsgroup programs.)

When done, you may need to start up your computer again. Then, connect to your ISP or commercial online service and click the browser icon on your screen (labeled The Internet for Internet Explorer; Netscape's is called, not surprisingly, Netscape) to make sure all is well.

You can also buy a browser. Stores and mail order retailers sell CD-ROM versions. Netscape's and Explorer's Web sites can also ship a CD-ROM for just a few dollars in shipping charges.)

Other Browsers Besides Netscape and Explorer

Yes, there are other browsers, but you would almost never know it from all the press the big two get. Some work just fine for older computers because they require a lot less memory (RAM) and speed. Some show graphics. Others, however, only show text—meaning you miss all the color, images, sounds, and excitement of the full Web experience. (Since you also miss all the delays when these images and sounds load, you can hop around pretty fast with a text-only browser.)

Here are a few of the lesser-known browsers, which have their loyal fans:

Opera (www.operasoftware.com)

Showing almost all graphics at a good speed, Opera runs fine on an older 486 PC with 8 MB of RAM on Windows 3.1. It works on a 386 and even a 286 with a lowly 4 MB of RAM, and takes up a little more than one tenth the disk space of Netscape and Explorer. You can also keep two or more Web pages open

Download Tips

No matter what kind of software you are downloading—a browser, a plug-in to add abilities to your browser, an e-mail or newsreader program—it helps to remember some tips.

1. Most software programs today have an automatic installation feature to make the process easier. If not, they will probably include step-by-step instructions. Read the "read.me" or "readme.txt" help files. The software maker's Web site almost always has detailed instructions as well; look under "technical support" for the specific product.

2. Be sure you know where your downloads are located. This is why it is a good idea to name the folder "downloads" when the program asks you where to store the software.

3. Copying the file from the download folder to an installation folder on your hard drive before you install it is also a good idea. This way, if there is any problem, you have a copy of the download left. Give the installation folder an easy-to-remember name, such as "install."

4. If the program asks you to name a drive and folder, use the already-supplied default names to avoid confusion.

5. The bigger the size of the file in megabytes, the longer it will take to install.

6. If the program asks if you want a "full," "common," "optimal" or "minimum" installation, choose "common" or "optimal." These provide the essentials without grabbing too much hard drive space. "Full" includes files you rarely need, while "minimum" lacks help files.

7. Clean up after you install a download. Delete the installation file, and any other unneeded files, on your hard drive, so they don't hog space which can be used for other things. Remember that you have two download files to delete if you made a copy before installation.

The toolbar is a horizontal row of icons and verbal commands on your screen. Each is a button for a different command.

Status indicator is the browser icon that changes to show the browser is active.

at the same time in different windows, reducing the size of the type to make them easier to read.

No e-mail program is included, however, so you'll need to get one. Opera also won't show sites with heavy animation and interactive elements the way Netscape or Explorer do.

Lynx (www.fdisk.com/doslynx/lynxport.htm)

A text-only browser that requires no mouse, just arrow keys to jump to links and view a link plus other single-key commands, Lynx dates back to the good old days before the Web was born, when people used the UNIX operating system on the Internet. Lynx can be used on Windows 95 if your standard browser is not working well. It cruises around much faster than the latest browsers because of its lack of graphics, only needing a 386 PC with a slow (under 14 Kbps) modem, which is truly impressive.

It requires so little power because the program runs not on your computer, but on a UNIX server. Your computer merely shows the results. If you are using Lynx on a UNIX operating system, you will need a telnet software.

In place of a picture, the word "image" or brackets will appear, letting you imagine what might have been. If you have a UNIX shell account from your Internet service provider, Lynx and its e-mail program, Pine, will come free.

Two excellent Web sites with news and product information on browsers are CNET's Browser.com (www.browser.com) and Mecklermedia's BrowserWatch (www.browserwatch.com).

How Do I Get It to Browse?

After you have installed the browser—by downloading it or following instructions on the installation package that comes with the CD-ROM—and connected to your Internet service provider or commercial online service, just double click the browser icon on your screen to launch it. Look for a capital "N" for Netscape, or a small "e" for Explorer.

Try a command, which can be found in the toolbars—the horizontal rows of icons and verbal commands—at the top of your screen. Many commands are duplicated in both icons and verbal menus, which may either delight or confuse you, but it's your preference. Your browser shows it's busy working for you when you see an hourglass or a clock replace the cursor on your screen. You will also see changes in the browser icon at the top right corner of your screen, called a status indicator. For example, on Netscape, you can admire a status indicator which looks like a comet cruising through the sky.

The following commands refer to the 4.0 versions of both Netscape Communicator and Internet Explorer, unless just one is specified. Older versions or different browsers will have similar functions and more-or-less similar commands, except for a text-only browser like Lynx, where you will use single-key commands because there are no icons.

Icons Toolbar

This is the row of icons (pictures) near the top of your computer screen, below the Menu toolbar. Each is a command you can click on.

Back

This returns you to the Web pages you've seen before the current page. Click "back" once to reach the immediately previous Web page, keep clicking for the page visited five pages ago, ten pages ago, etc. Copies of pages you've viewed are stored in order in your hard drive's cache, which is why clicking on "back" is much faster than reaching a Web site in the first place.

Forward

This takes you to the next Web page you have already seen, once you have started viewing past pages stored on your cache. It is not used to view a new page you have not yet seen.

An icon is a picture—such as an envelope, pen and paper, mailbox, etc.—that you can click on to perform a command.

The cache is the part of your computer's hard drive where recently viewed Web pages are stored for quick access.

Cool Places to Find Free Stuff

"The best things in life are free," the saying goes, and it certainly applies to the Internet. There are countless sites offering free information, services, or products of one kind or another. We agree wholeheartedly with this philosophy, and have chosen a few to showcase the gigantic variety.

Movie Reviews
Cinemachine (www.cinemachine.com)
Why limit yourself to your local newspaper when you can read dozens of movie reviews from newspapers, magazines, and online publications nationwide? Just click the link to the specific review you want.

Internet Movie Database (www.imdb.com)
This vast resource has facts on over 100,000 movies, new or old, from cast, crew, running time, plot summary, and reviews, to awards searchable by title, keyword, actor, or director.

Mr. Cranky's Guide to This Week at the Movies (http://internet-plaza.net/ zone/mrcranky/thisweek.html)
Mr. Cranky has never seen a movie he's liked, but don't let that stop you from browsing reviews at this often wildly amusing site. Bulletin boards for each movie reviewed let readers debate his latest howlers, which use a unique rating system from "almost tolerable" to "as good as a poke in the eye with a sharp stick" and the feared "so godawful that it ruptured the very fabric of space and time."

Products and Samples
Club FreeShop (www.freeshop.com)
This site features hundreds of product samples, trial offers and memberships, catalogs from magazines, software, and consumer products.

Birth Announcements
Babies Online (www.babiesonline.com)
It's never too early to be on the Web. Birth announcements, which feature photographs of your newborn, size, and other vital statistics—searchable by the baby's name or birthdate—are free to parents who supply scanned photos. Free t-shirts, toys, and many links to sites with resources for parents and babies.

Web Pages
GeoCities (www.geocities.com)
Build your own Web site with GeoCities' page building tools, then locate it in a "neighborhood" in a community site based on your interest or hobby. (See chapter 7 for more on how to create your own Web site.)

Tripod (www.tripod.com)
Tripod allows you to build your own Web site with its page building tools, then house it in a "pod" in a community site. Mainly for people in their twenties or thirties.

Maps

MapQuest (www.mapquest.com)

Type in an address or the junction of two streets anywhere in the United States and see an instant map that you can zoom in on for a closer look. Driving directions from where you are located are included.

Classes

America Online Courses (keyword: courses)

Choose classes from a wide array of teachers in the arts, business, the humanities and math.

Foreign Language Lessons (www.travlang.com)

Learn some vocabulary in over sixty foreign languages, including sounds you can mimic. Translation dictionaries and currency converters are also included.

Genealogy Lessons (www.ancestry.com/home/academy.htm)

Research your family tree with these detailed lessons, which explain how to use public records like birth and death certificates, the Web, and databases.

The Nine Planets (www.seds.org/billa/tnp)

This site has astronomy, history, and mythology about our solar system, with great photographs, sounds, and movies.

A Short Course on Shakespeare's Hamlet (www.hypermart.net/hamlet)

This site has the entire text of *Hamlet*, plus questions and answers.

Quick Reference

E-Organizer (www.eorganizer.com)

Forget important dates like anniversaries, birthdays and upcoming meetings? Not any more, plug in the dates, as well as your to-do lists and notes, and you'll get reminders by e-mail.

Research-It! (www.itools.com/research-it)

Dictionaries—including translation and biographical—a thesaurus, *Bartlett's Familiar Quotations*, the Bible, maps, people and business finders, and much more are included at this handy site.

Travel

Expedia (http://expedia.msn.com)

Book flights, make hotel reservations, and read detailed, practical information about destinations worldwide. Receive notification of the lowest airfares to your destination by e-mail as well.

The Trip (www.thetrip.com)

Book flights, make hotel and car reservations, and travel to the airport (airport map included) at this helpful site.

Stop

This immediately stops browser action, so a new page won't continue to download, or an image or sound clip on a page will be prevented from downloading. Use this when you've made a mistake or are just plain tired of waiting for those pages or sound clips to kick in.

Reload (or Refresh)

This gives you the most current version of a page, handy if the site's content changes often. It's also handy if you are viewing an older version stored in your cache.

Home

This returns you to the Web page at the very start of your journey. It's generally either the home page of the Netscape or Explorer browser or a page you have selected as your home page.

Search

This will bring up several search engines at once, such as Yahoo! and Lycos. This way you don't have to type in their Internet addresses or bookmark them. (See more on different search engines later in this chapter.)

Bookmarks (or Favorites)

You're tired of typing in all that www. stuff—some of those Internet addresses are as long as your arm. Leave out one little letter, slash, or period and you can't reach the Web site. There should be a shortcut.

There is. Once you find a site you like—and know you will want to return—you need only type in its Internet address, or do a search, once. Then, click on "bookmark" to save it. When you want to return, just click "bookmark," then click the site's name, which is a link to that favorite site. Some users even bookmark pages which look mildly interesting with abandon on the theory that it's much easier to delete a bookmark than to find that scrap of paper with the address or wait for a search engine to respond.

You can save tons of sites this way, and even organize your book-marks into topic folders for easy reference. For example, you may want folders for work, personal finance, and entertainment categories.

When you look at a saved site, you'll often see just icons, no images. Just click on the icon to see the image.

Print

This will print the current Web page, e-mail message, or news-group posting you are seeing. (But only if you have a printer hooked up!)

History (in Explorer only)

This shows a batch of recent Web pages you have visited with links to those pages. Just click on the name of the desired page. (In Netscape, you reach your history by clicking on "Communicator" in the Menu toolbar, then clicking on "history." Or, click "Go" in the Menu toolbar, and see a shorter list of recent Web sites visited since you launched your browser. Either way, click on the page you want.)

Channels (in Explorer; Netcaster in Netscape Communicator)

This offers a batch of Web sites—news, business, and entertainment—whose current content can be sent to you on a regular basis so you don't have to search for it. This is the Microsoft and Netscape version of push technology (see Chapter 4 for more on push), and lets you decide how you want to receive the content. For example, you may want it full screen, as a screen saver while your computer is idle, or in a small window. You can also decide how often you prefer updates.

Mail (in Explorer; Mailbox for Netscape Communicator)

This is for sending and receiving e-mail, reading newsgroups, and composing Web pages. In Explorer, these features are bundled into a package called Outlook Express. (In Netscape Communicator, "discussions" is the newsgroup icon, "composer" is the Web page composer icon.)

Fullscreen (in Explorer only)

This means the Web page you are viewing will now be much larger than just the size of the window. It also means a few more icons will appear on your toolbar, such as "print" and "edit." Since all icons will now have no text commands attached, rest your mouse on one for its description to appear.

Guide (in Netscape only)

This brings up five easy ways to find information on the Web, including categories from the search engine Yahoo!; a people finder to look up telephone numbers, street addresses or e-mail addresses; a business finder to look up telephone numbers and addresses; "What's New" and "What's Cool," new sites that just came on the Web and interesting sites such as Cool Site of the Day, Category of the Day, cool sites grouped by category, even This Day in History. It's an easy way to keep track of new or noteworthy sites on the Web (or just amuse yourself).

Security (in Netscape only)

This indicates whether the Web page you are viewing is secure, meaning you can safely purchase on it, by showing a closed lock. An open lock means the site is not secure. (Read more about safe buying in chapter 8.)

Component Toolbar

This is the row of icons at the bottom of your screen. If you have Netscape Communicator, each icon will refer to a different part. The ship steering wheel icon is for the Navigator browser. The mailbox icon is for sending and receiving e-mail. The balloons with messages inside are for reading newsgroups. The paper and pen icon is for composing Web pages. Rest your mouse over each icon to see the description.

In Explorer, "Mail" is for sending and receiving e-mail and reading newsgroups, "Channels" is push technology. Rest your mouse on each icon and its description will appear.

Menu Toolbar

This row of commands at the top of your screen lets you move around the Web and your files and perform many tasks. Each has a pull-down menu with a variety of choices. You'll notice some do the same thing as the row of icons (pictures) below. It's a matter of choice which to use. For example, in Netscape Communicator here are commands you can click on:

File

The "open page" command lets you type an Internet address and takes you to that Web site. "Send" means you can e-mail the Web page you are viewing to a friend or colleague. "Print" lets you print the Web page. "Edit" means you can edit—change or move around words or sections—in the page you are viewing. "Quit" allows you to end your browsing.

Edit

The "search Internet" command lets you find a topic or keyword on the Web, if you don't know the Internet address, by giving you a variety of search engines to choose from. "Search directory" lets you locate people's telephone numbers or e-mail addresses in a variety of directories. "Find in page" means you can zero in on a specific word in a Web page you are viewing. Commands such as "copy," "cut," and "paste" let you duplicate or move around words or sections after you highlight them.

"Preferences" allows you to change the first page you see when you start Web surfing. So if you've tired of admiring the beauty of your browser's home page, you can type the Internet address of the Web page you'd prefer to start with—or start automatically with the last page you visited earlier—by clicking your browser icon and following the instructions.

You can also change the number of days your browser will track the Web sites you have visited—it will even conveniently finish an

Stop the Internet: I Want to Get Off!

When you are finished for the time being, you get off by clicking the "file" menu, then "exit," or "quit." You can also press the "control" key, then "Q" on your keyboard. Then disconnect from your ISP.

If you have WebTV, press the power button and your television will go on at the last channel watched.

Internet address you have begun typing, like a friendly elf—by typing the preferred number or by clicking your browser icon in the "preferences" menu. The look of Web pages, such as colors, font size, and the toolbars themselves can be altered by clicking on the "appearance" option.

View

This lets you change the look of Web pages, including "reloading" with the most current version of a page, stopping the display of images, enlarging or reducing font size, and displaying only the toolbars of your choice.

Go

This will take you to the last Web pages you have viewed (click "back"), the next already viewed Web page (click "forward"), or your home page ("home"). By the way, "back" even numbers your recently viewed sites in order.

Communicator

This reaches the various components, such as the Navigator browser, Messenger for e-mail, Collabra for newsgroups, Netcaster for push technology, Conference for sharing documents for working cooperatively, and enables you to make telephone calls over the Internet. (The caller and recipient will need sound cards and microphones for Internet telephony.)

Help

This offers a variety of assistance including how to get technical support for problems, information on updates, and increased computer security.

Location (or Address or Netsite) Box

This long white box under the Icons toolbar is where you type in the Internet address of a page you want to see. Start with "www" because the "http://" which begins a Web site address is implied. In Explorer, you can also type a keyword or topic, preceded by "?," "go" or "find" (for example, "go Paris" or "?U2" for the rock band). First, click inside the box so that little up-and-down line appears on the side. Then, type the address. Last, hit "enter" on your keyboard.

If you make a mistake typing the address, click at the start of the mistake, drag it across the screen, then hit your "delete" key, which will erase the mistake, now highlighted.

How to Find Information on the Web

If you know the Internet address of a site, type it in the Location or Netsite (in Netscape) or Address (in Explorer) box—precisely the way it is. This means no misspellings, omitted letters, spaces between letters, or wrong punctuation. If you don't know the Internet address and don't have it on file anywhere, you can use a search engine.

There are several different ways to find a search engine.

1. You can click the "search" icon near the top of your screen, or the "search Internet" command in the "Edit" menu to bring up a handful of popular search engines like Yahoo!, Lycos, or Alta Vista.
2. You can type the Internet address of a search engine.
3. You can click on a bookmarked search engine you have visited before.

How to Use Search Engines

To start the engine, click your browser icon to launch your browser and type the Internet address of the search engine you want, or pick one from the list in the "search" icon your browser probably has.

Then type words or phrases that describe what you're looking for in the Search box, then click Search (or hit the Enter key). A page will soon appear, which lists links to the pages that match your words or phrases and short descriptions. If a list of subject areas appears, click on whichever subject seems appropriate and pages that list sub-category areas will appear. Again, click on whichever link seems closest to narrow the search down to what you're looking for. Results the search engine thinks are closest to your request appear first.

Here are some tricks to improve your searching. Narrow your search by using terms like "AND," "OR," and "NOT" so you won't be swamped by a huge list of results. Using "AND" means both words should be included in the search. "OR" means either word can be included, so you'll get a bigger list. "NOT" before a word means the next word should be excluded from search results.

For example, if you're looking for Venice, California, type in "Venice AND California," which means both words are required to appear in the search results. If it's Venice, Italy, you want, type "Venice AND Italy." Use "OR"—"Venice OR California"—only if you want a massive list of all the Web pages that include either city plus the state of California. If you want the city in Italy as well as the California beach town, just type "Venice."

Putting phrases—words which must go together in order—in quotes also works. For example, "walking tour of Venice" should turn up only pages listing this phrase; the phrase without quotes will turn up many more pages with the words walking, Venice and tour, such as trips to Italy that include walking. Plus and minus signs before words—no space in between—also work the way "AND" and "NOT" do in some search engines. For example, "Venice+California" or "Venice-Italy" will both turn up the California town.

Type your words or phrases in lowercase, unless they are proper names starting with capital letters. A search for Rock Hudson should serve up dish on the actor; lowercase, it will turn up results on the Hudson River, rock music, and rock climbing.

Using a wildcard—placing an asterisk or another symbol after a word—means you welcome results with different word endings. Typing "gold+" means golden, goldfinger, and goldfinch are all acceptable. You'll get everything from James Bond movies, birds, the precious metal, and companies and people whose names begin with "gold" or "golden."

Comparing Different Search Engines

The many different search engines—Yahoo!, Alta Vista, Web Crawler, Infoseek, Excite, Lycos, HotBot, and Northern Light—all have their fans. Each has its own distinctive features, and some are better for certain searches than others.

There are two main types of search engines. The first, called the index type, scours the Internet for the same words or phrases you're seeking by using an automated computer program, and tends to return an enormous list of matches. The second, the directory type

Will the Real Kurt Vonnegut Please Stand Up?

Don't believe everything you read on the Internet. In August 1997, a quirky but inspiring speech supposedly given by writer Kurt Vonnegut to the graduating class at the Massachusetts Institute of Technology appeared in many people's e-mail, around the world.

"Ladies and gentlemen of the class of '97: Wear sunscreen. If I could offer you only one tip for the future, sunscreen would be it," it began. "Do one thing every day that scares you," it went on. "Remember compliments you receive. Forget the insults. If you succeed in doing this, tell me how."

About goals: "Don't feel guilty if you don't know what you want to do with your life. The most interesting people I know didn't know at 22 what they wanted to do with their lives. Some of the most interesting 40-year-olds I know still don't." About where to live: "Live in New York City once, but leave before it makes you hard. Live in Northern California once, but leave before it makes you soft." About not being envious: "Don't waste your time on jealousy. Sometimes you're ahead, sometimes you're behind. The race is long and, in the end, it's only with yourself."

Vonnegut's wife, photographer Jill Krementz, liked it so much she passed it on to many people, including his children.

But Vonnegut didn't write the speech or give it. In fact, the MIT commencement speaker in June 1997 was the Secretary General of the United Nations. The author of the speech was Mary Schmich, a columnist for the *Chicago Tribune*, which ran in her column on June 1. But she was as surprised as Vonnegut himself that someone, whose identity was never revealed, started circulating Vonnegut's alleged speech as an e-mail chain letter.

She tried to track down the origin of the chain, with no success, but did track down Vonnegut, who by then had heard about his speech from many people, even a women's magazine who wanted to reprint it. An Internet skeptic, his comment was that cyberspace was "spooky." Schmich then sent her own e-mail message around explaining things and admitting authorship of the column.

Repeat: Don't believe everything you read on the Internet. A fake press release was even circulated a few years ago that noted Microsoft was acquiring the Roman Catholic Church. The company was forced to issue a denial, as many people who received it by e-mail believed it.

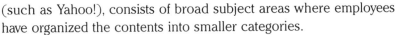

(such as Yahoo!), consists of broad subject areas where employees have organized the contents into smaller categories.

Search engines vary in terms of how they display results, how many pages they cover, how they index, and extra features they offer, such as searching newsgroups as well. Each offers detailed advice on how to best use its specific service—click the "help," "tips," "options," "advanced search," or similarly named button near the search box.

That's the most important tip on getting good results from search engines: Read the search engine's own help and tips sections for clear advice on how it works. Because search engines are owned by different companies, they don't work exactly the same way.

An excellent site that compares search engines and offers reviews and news of updates is Search Engine Watch (www.searchengine.watch), from Mecklermedia, the Internet trade magazine publisher.

Many Web sites, from companies, news, community to personal home pages, have their own internal search functions, so you can easily look through the databases on their sites. Often, their rules and tips are posted as well.

Some Popular Search Engines

Yahoo! (www.yahoo.com)

In 1994, Yahoo! began humbly enough as Jerry and David's Guide to the World Wide Web, a directory of favorite Web sites compiled by two Stanford University graduate students in computer science and engineering with time on their hands.

Fast forward to today. Yahoo! Inc. went public in 1996 (it's listed on NASDAQ), was getting over 50 million page views per day (that's one billion per month) in 1997, and over 25 million users per month in the United States according to Mediamark Research. It's a partner in a popular magazine, *Yahoo! Internet Life*, with the magazine publisher Ziff-Davis. Its Web site has become a hot spot for advertisers, from computer makers to booksellers.

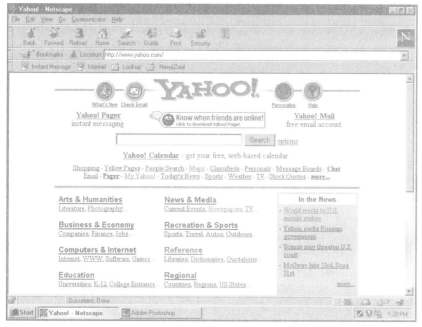

Yahoo! www.yahoo.com

The first guide to navigate the Web, Yahoo! also became the first search engine to broaden its services well beyond searching. Other search engines have followed in its path in efforts to convince users to stay a while on their sites, which makes it better to win advertisers. Yahoo! now offers a spate of services, from free e-mail for anyone, chats (see chapter 6 for more about chat), Internet guides for other countries such as Scandinavia, Japan, Korea, Italy, the United Kingdom/Ireland, a Chinese-language guide, an instant messaging paging system to reach other Internet users without using e-mail, and My Yahoo!, a customized home page of news and sports scores based on users' interests.

In 1998, it even launched its own commercial on-line service, powered by MCI Internet, offering lower rates than other commercial online services and ISPs.

There's also a Yahoo! Visa credit card, launched in 1998, with rewards good for online as well as store purchases.

Jerry Yang, who emigrated from Taiwan to San Jose, California as a child with his mother, brother and grandmother, and David Filo, who grew up in Louisiana, didn't start the directory as a business. It

Alta Vista can search for Web pages in two dozen languages besides English, including: Chinese, Czech, Danish, Dutch, Estonian, Finnish, French, German, Greek, Hebrew, Hungarian, Icelandic, Italian, Japanese, Korean, Latvian, Lithuanian, Norwegian, Polish, Portuguese, Romanian, Russian, Spanish, and Swedish.

was a pet project, a free service with a whimsical flair for the two graduate students in their twenties, with categories like Cool Links and Hard to Believe. In the summer of 1994, they changed the name to Yahoo!, an acronym standing for "yet another hierarchical officious oracle"—breezily ignoring the word's definition as a rude, obnoxious person. The name was inspired by their favorite acronym at the time, "yacc," a computer program that stands for "yet another C compiler."

Living on the Palo Alto campus while pursuing their Ph.Ds., the students began to get many views worldwide for their site, as many as 170,000 hits daily in late 1994. Press attention started and has never stopped. A strategic partnership with Netscape, which offered Yahoo! as the search engine for its browser users, was another stroke of luck. When the demands of cataloging the exponentially growing Web and user traffic began to get out of hand, the duo offered Stanford the chance to take over their project. Stanford declined. Through a contact, they met and obtained their first outside investment, $1 million from the venture capital firm Sequoia Venture Partners, allowing them to move into an office building in 1995.

In that momentous year, they also found a chief executive officer and hired a staff—including Srinija Srinivasan, a former Stanford student with a background in artificial intelligence, who built its current category system—to look at and catalog each Web site submitted by applicants to Yahoo! The company also began to accept ads to make money.

Revenues totaled over $67 million in the 1997 fiscal year at the company, which is one of the major cyber-millionaire success stories.

A directory search engine, Yahoo! offers a choice of typing in keywords or phrases or picking a broad category, such as Business and Economy, Arts and Humanities, or Entertainment. Easy to use and clear, it's one of my favorite search engines—there's something reassuring about all those humans toiling behind the scenes, classifying sites, and often offering ratings. Some topics appear under more than one heading so they are easier to find.

You'll note each category is divided into many subcategories, as well as news of the day, chats, other Internet events of the day,

A Sample Search on Yahoo!

Here's what a search for the word "health" turned up in Yahoo!. Remember, each is a link to click on to reach that site. These are only the first twenty categories found. A link to "next 20 matches" at the bottom of the page will bring more of the over 14,000 sites found.

Yahoo! Category Matches (1–20 of 3,411)

1. Business and Economy: Companies: Health
2. Business and Economy: Companies: Health: Mental Health
3. Business and Economy: Companies: Health: Software: Health Care
4. Management
5. Health: Public Health and Safety
6. Health: Reproductive Health
7. Business and Economy: Companies: Books: Health
8. Business and Economy: Business Opportunities: Multi-Level
9. Marketing: Health
10. Business and Economy: Companies: Financial Services: Insurance:
11. Health
12. Net Events: Science: Health
13. Regional: Countries: United Kingdom: Health
14. Health: Health Care
15. Health: Children's Health
16. Government: U.S. Government: Executive Branch: Departments and Agencies: Department of Health and Human Services
17. Health: Women's Health
18. Regional: Countries: Canada: Health
19. Business and Economy: Companies: Health: Home Health Care
20. Regional Countries: Australia: Health

and indices. For example, Entertainment is divided into movies, music, humor, and what the staff optimistically calls "cool links," for starters. Movies is further divided into actors and actresses, reviews, titles (in alphabetical order or by genre), filmmaking, and many others, even into separate sites the staff feel merit special attention, such as Internet Movie Database (a listing of thousands of movies, crews, and years) and Hollywood Online.

Results turn up as names of sites and descriptions. If Yahoo! can't find something, it offers results from Alta Vista due to a friendly arrangement.

The buttons for What's New and What's Cool on the Yahoo! home page reveal new sites added in the past few days and staff recommendations. A people finder search, free e-mail service, today's news headlines (in categories from business to sports), and stock quotes are also available.

A dandy Web guide for children—Yahooligans!—offers categories like School Bell (homework help and clubs) and Science & Oddities. Regional indexes for cities like Atlanta, New York, and Washington, D.C. make searching for a local topic simple. You can also order a personalized version, My Yahoo!, which will bring news headlines, stock quotes, industry news, and Web resources customized to your interests on a regular basis.

Alta Vista (www.altavista.digital.com)

Alta Vista began as a research project of the Digital Equipment Corporation, a major computer maker, and performed so well the company spun it off as a separate product. The biggest search engine in terms of the number of pages it indexes, over 100 million in early 1998, Alta Vista can search newsgroups as well as the Web and searches in twenty different languages. Without the variety of categories and extra features on Yahoo!, Alta Vista's home page is rather naked and unadorned. Alta Vista is a tool for the serious searcher and is famous for scaring off novices by turning up millions of results for keywords or phrases.

Alta Vista is known for its "refine" feature. This presents results arranged in different categories; you choose which to require or exclude to get a closer match. If you're ready to see more results, click "search"; if not, keep refining to narrow your search further. Plus and minus signs, "AND," and "NOT" are important in your original request since Alta Vista is so literal minded.

Results—which appear with name, Internet address and description—can also be limited by date or in the form of a question in its Advanced Search section.

Excite (www.excite.com)

Much like Yahoo!, Excite allows you to search by typing keywords or phrases or choosing a topic category. Excite also offers another helpful feature. Click "Search for more documents like this one" after a match you particularly like after a keyword search, and similar results will obligingly appear, with name, Internet address, and description. Excite claims its search system understands synonyms and related concepts thanks to intelligent concept extraction technology. For instance, it knows pet grooming sites should be included in a search for dog care without your typing those exact words.

Categories of topics, or channels, include links to newsgroups and articles as well as Web sites. Channels range from autos, home/real estate, money/investing, relationships to travel. Today's news headlines, a people-finder, a product finder (prices and reviews for products from computer equipment, games and toys, home and garden supplies), chats, and an instant messaging paging system are also found on its home page. In addition, Excite also offers free Web-based e-mail accounts to anyone, plus its own commercial online service for Internet access with special content, powered by MCI Internet. But Excite boasts a really nifty feature, NewsTracker, which acts as a free automatic clipping service. Pick a topic and NewsTracker will scan hundreds of top newspapers and magazines on the Web, fetching articles for you like a digital dog. But like any dog, it requires training. Click the "learn what I like" button after clicking several "liked it" buttons when it has behaved well, and it will retrieve more on-target articles for you. Look for it under "my News Tracker topics."

Free e-mail, a people finder search, today's news headlines and stock quotes are also offered by Excite.

A Sample Search on Excite

Here's what a search for the word "health" turned up in Excite. These are the top 10 matches of over 1,650,000 sites found, some repeat. Excite suggests a list of words that you can add to limit your search, like "mental," "disease," "medicine," or "nutritional."

1. Latest News About Health Visit the Excite Health & Fitness Channel
2. Shop for Food and Drink Online
3. 64% Medicine more like this
4. 64% The Global Health Network more like this
5. 64% ATSDR's Home Page (Agency for Toxic Substances and Diseases Registry
6. 62% Healthwise @ Columbia University
7. 61% National Health Security Plan Table of Contents
8. 61% United States Public Health Services
9. 61% California Health Insurance
10. 61% Planet Health: The Best of Health

A Sample Search on Infoseek

Here's what a search for the word "health" turned up in Infoseek. These are the first matches of over 5 million pages found. Infoseek suggests some best bet categories, each of which is a link to click.

1. Best bets: health/school of public health/environmental health/ health insurance/women's health etc.
2. World Health Networks
3. National Institutes of Health
4. The WIRE—Associated Press
5. Philadelphia Online/ Health Philadelphia
6. The Vimy Park Health Magazine
7. U.S. Department of Health & Human Services
8. World Health Organization
9. Mental Health Net
10. Health on the Net Foundation
11. Pregnancy Health: A Comprehensive Index on Diet, Exercise, Complications

Infoseek (www.infoseek.com)

Accompanying its categories—from Good Life (food and drink, home and garden, classical music, theater) to Kids & Family—Infoseek features a healthy selection of recommended sites for each, like Zagat Survey and Epicurious for Good Life, and Parent Soup for family advice, plus appropriate tips and chats.

Besides searching newsgroups, newswires, and the Web, Infoseek also uses intelligent agents, which it claims understand phrases and full questions in plain English. Plus and minus signs can also be used here.

A helpful reference section includes a dictionary, thesaurus and stock ticker symbols.

HotBot (www.hotbot.com)

Indexing over 80 million pages in early 1998, HotBot, owned by the company that owns *Wired* magazine, is the second biggest search engine in terms of number of pages covered. Nifty features allow you to specify a search on front pages of Web sites, or front and index pages of directories on sites to limit the results. Or you can specify page title, time frame, which words may or must appear in the results, country, and even type of media (image, sound, or video files).

Besides these vast choices, you may opt to use the category directory. Top news sites, newsgroups, people finders, and classified ads are also available.

Lycos (www.lycos.com)

The only search engine that can look for sound and image files, Lycos also offers handy Web Guide categories, its list of the top 5 percent quality Web sites, and free personal Web pages as well. (Lycos bought Tripod, a community site with free home page building tools, in 1998.) You can also choose if all your keywords must appear in the search results, if the exact phrase must appear, or if a close match is desired.

A helpful City Guide lists local events, restaurants, news, people finders, and company finders in your area.

Web Crawler (www.webcrawler.com)

Also organized into categories—such as Arts & Books, Business & Investing, Careers & Education—Web Crawler rates the relevancy of its results on a scale from zero to 100. Another nice touch is its list of recommended sites, as well as chats and message boards, for each category. For example, the Louvre, Pulitzer Prize, and Dance Online sites appear on the Arts & Books page. The Entertainment page recommends National Enquirer Online, The Official X-Files Site, and The Smoking Gun (a site which exposes confidential documents from court and public records).

A small search engine compared to the big guns, Web Crawler is easy to use and searches newsgroups as well as the Web. It lets you choose if you want an exact match, partial match, or a match to any word or phrase in your search request, and claims its search system is based on natural language searching—ordinary English. The awkward search syntax of using "AND," "NOT," etc. is not needed. But if you miss using these terms, just click Advanced Search and they're yours, since Web Crawler seems to be in a let's-keep-everybody-happy frame of mind.

A people finder search, today's news headlines, and stock quotes are also offered.

Northern Light (www.nlsearch.com)

A newer search engine, Northern Light searches a special collection of over 3,400 magazines, journals, books and reviews not covered by other search engines, in addition to the Web. Summaries of results found in its special collection are free, but reading each document requires a small fee. A low-cost monthly subscription is also available.

Northern Light automatically organizes its results into folders for easy reference, by subject, type (such as product reviews or press releases), source (such as magazine, commercial or personal Web page) and language, besides listing the results themselves. Click on the folder to read the documents, listed by title, type, and Internet address.

Keyword searches can use "or," "not," plus and minus symbols, and quotes for phrases.

A Sample Search on Northern Light

Here's what a search for the word "health" turned up in Northern Light. These are some of the top matches of over four million results found:

Its folders are divided into special collection, public health, health insurance, government sites, commercial sites, Centers for Disease Control & Prevention, non-profit, exercise & fitness and psychiatry, among others. (Click on "special collection" for documents in publications such as Population Reports, Health Management Technology and Journal of School Health.) Results included Health Sciences graduate programs in eastern U.S., ABC Radio's health report summaries, a government health care commission report, Mathematica Policy Research's health publications, and Environmental Health newsletter.

An *agent* is a software program that scouts around for information and brings it back to your computer. Intelligent means it is designed to understand context, instead of being literal-minded.

Deja News, Reference.com, Cyber Fiber, Liszt (www.dejanews.com, www.reference.com, www.cyberfiber.com, www.liszt.com/news)

Newsgroups are searched by these search engines. So if you want to monitor what's being said about your favorite hot topic in the thousands of discussion groups on the Internet, you can easily search by subject, newsgroup name, date, or writer of the posted messages.

A word to the wise: any gossip or bad-mouthing about a person or topic may be read by the person or persons involved. You may want to restrict personal comments to private e-mail messages, not public newsgroups.

How to Personalize a Search Engine

Some search engines, such as Yahoo! and Excite, let you customize their home pages. This means whenever you visit them, you can read news headlines, stock quotes and sports scores tailored to your interests, in a layout you prefer.

To sign up for this free service at Excite, for example, click "personalize my page" on its home page. Type your name, e-mail address, password, and zip code on its online registration form. Then, click "change content." Choose the type of information you want, from news categories, columnists, services (airfares, books, flowers, etc.), television listings, stock quotes, sports, cartoons to lottery listings. If you want to read only business news, follow a certain stock, cartoon and sport, and scan television listings for your town, you can.

To change the background color of your page, click "change color," and choose a color. To list your content in a certain order, so that news and weather will appear at the top, with sports and stocks underneath, click "change layout" and number your preferences. You can even specify the number of news headlines you want to see, and add new topics after you have personalized your Excite page.

If you personalize the newsgroup search engine Deja News, it will subscribe you to discussion groups which match your interests. Choices are offered, from fashion, food/drink/cooking to kids, but you can pick whatever you like. This means whenever you visit your "My Deja News" page on its Website, links to these newsgroups will appear. You can easily read and post messages, without hunting for the newsgroups or using a special newsreader program. (Read more about newsgroups in chapter 6.) Register by filling out your name, sex, birthdate, country, zip code, user ID, password and job on its online form.

Multiple Search Engines

It is possible to search using a bunch of search engines at once. Some of the multiple search engines you can use include the following.

Savvy Search (http:guaraldi.cs.colostate.edu:2000)

This uses two dozen search engines—like Yahoo!, Excite, and Infoseek—other giant databases—like the Internet Movie Database—and people finder directories. It works several search engines at a time, with results compiled by search engine, unless you specify otherwise.

Meta Crawler (www.metacrawler.com)

This queries only the major search engines—Yahoo!, Excite, AltaVista, Infoseek, Lycos, and WebCrawler—and combines the results in one list, noting which engine found the result. MetaCrawler can scour newsgroups as well as the Web. Searches can be limited to certain domains, a certain number of results from each search engine, or a certain continent.

Dogpile (www.dogpile.com)

Two dozen search engines are used by Dogpile, three at once. Newsgroups and newswires—news media which supply breaking news throughout the day, such as Associated Press (AP) and Reuters—as well as the Web can be searched. If it finds less than ten results, it will keep going until it reaches that number.

Why Do I Get 11,980,764 Results When I Search for Something?

Tens of millions of pages exist on the Internet, and many more are being added every day. To prevent a gigantic list of results and get a smaller, manageable list to sift through, follow these tips.

You should narrow your search request as much as possible at the outset, being as specific as possible. For example, search not on classical music, but on Beethoven symphonies; not cake recipes, but chocolate cake recipes; not Vermont, but bed-and-breakfasts in Manchester, Vermont.

Index search engines, such as Alta Vista, tend to return more matches than directory search engines for the simple reason that their automated software grabs words and phrases from Web page titles, page contents, and Internet addresses that resemble the search request instead of following subject classifications compiled by humans. This means indexes more often return results that are off the mark—sometimes wildly—unless you carefully read their online instructions about words and symbols to limit your request.

Directory search engines are often more efficient in returning exactly what you're looking for—sometimes just two or three matches—but their scope is less broad and they lag days or weeks behind indexes in adding new sites.

Spending ten minutes or so reading a search engine's search tips and advanced help is worth its weight in gold in saving your time, reducing your frustration level, and making your search more efficient. Some search engines can even restrict their search to words appearing on a site's home page, or return results ranked by category so you can hone in on a closer match.

Always expect the unexpected. Imagine the surprise of a friend of mine, browsing for photos of kittens, when a scantily clad photo of a stripper came up. (Her first name, it turns out, was Kitten.) He was probably as surprised as I was when searching for a friend's name and *Buckets of Blood* turned up. (It turns out this is a horror movie starring an actress with her name.)

You'll probably develop a favorite search engine over time as you grow familiar with its quirks and it consistently produces the kinds of results you want—or at least doesn't disappoint too often! Bookmark this search engine so you can find it immediately without having to type its Internet address.

A search engine that lets users pose questions in natural language—without the keywords, "and," "or," and plus and minus symbols—and is actually polite and easy to use is a blessing. Ask Jeeves! (www.askjeeves.com) allows you to ask a full question—this works better than a phrase—and returns results for variations of your question. It even returns a few top results from several search engines, such as Alta Vista, Infoseek, and Lycos.

"Hello, Jeeves here," the home page greets users. "I know the answers to the following questions," the results page notes. The search engine thoughtfully supplies sample questions to show the great variety it covers, such as:

What is my car worth?
How much do I need for retirement?
Why is the sky blue?
Where can I find a job in advertising?
Who won the Nobel Prize for
physics in 1937?
Am I in love?

For example, the question "How do companies sell stock on the Internet?" returns "Where can I trade on-line?," "Where can I find the publicly traded companies?," and "Where can I find information on the American Stock Exchange?"

There is even a special Ask Jeeves! for children, which uses filtering software to block objectionable material from other search engines.

Using Ask Jeeves!—which is often uncannily accurate—can feel a little spooky. But employees at the Berkeley, California-based Ask Jeeves, Inc., formed by software developer David Warthen and venture capitalist Garrett Gruener in 1996, have devised a huge number of likely questions, found the answers from standard search engines, and packaged them in a database that greatly simplifies the search process.

Internet Hijacking?

The Yahoo! rags-to-riches saga has had its bizarre episodes. In December 1997, someone tried to hijack Yahoo! briefly by posting a message on its home page threatening to unleash a computer virus on Christmas day upon all the search engine's users for the past month. The only way to stop the virus, the note said, was if the Federal government released Kevin Mitnick, an imprisoned computer hacker who was caught in 1995.

Mitnick, who had broken into government, corporate, and university computer systems, had developed quite a following on the Web, and admirers have created a Web site and legal defense fund in his honor. He is the subject of the book, *Takedown*, by *New York Times* reporter John Markoff.

The hijack message was visible only to users of the text-only browser Lynx for a few minutes because Yahoo! security experts removed it after its detection. No virus was found, experts said.

Compare the Easy Way

It's easy to do price and other comparisons when you're shopping on the Web. But it's not even necessary to visit one site after another, scribbling down information to hunt for the best deal. Some helpful sites do the legwork for you, offering price quotes from various competitors or recommending products based on specific criteria you plugged in.

For example, Price Scan (www.pricescan.com) offers price quotes for computer hardware, software, and related equipment from many vendors and manufacturers, with links for online buying. ZDNet's Net Buyer makes it simple to pick a computer with the right amount of memory, hard drive size, and CD-ROM drive speed based on your specific needs, whether it's simple word processing, games, or graphics.

Kaplan Educational Centers (www.kaplan.com), a publisher of test preparation and college guides, streamlines college selection by letting you pick a school based on factors such as region, type, cost, and student life. The educational publisher, Peterson's (www.petersons.com), lets you choose a graduate school or college by type of degree, program type or major, or location.

If you would like a dog, you can even choose a pet by size, temperament, or activity. But perhaps you're thinking of buying a car, bicycle, or truck, investing in mutual funds, or relocating to a city based on cost-of-living or low crime rate first.

Guides to all these choices can be found at PersonaLogic's (www.personalogic) product showcase. The company makes decision-making software for companies, and its investors include Home Shopping Network head and former studio chief Barry Diller and Paul Allen, cofounder of Microsoft. Some of its guides are found at Excite's topic channels.

Internet Basics for Everyday Use

There are some basic terms you need to grasp that will explain a bit more how things work on the Internet. We've touched on some in passing, but others will be brand new. Without understanding these terms, you will truly be lost. Understanding them, you will learn how to add to and improve your overall experience.

Hypertext

Hypertext is the name for the system of linked pages that make up the Web. Web pages are written in HTML (Hypertext Markup Language), a programming language your browser reads, and use links to easily connect to related information either on the same Web site or a different site. These links to other Web pages or to sound, image, or video files—also called hot links or hyperlinks—can be either words or phrases, pictures, or icons on a Web page.

Links are generally underlined and blue in color (although this can be changed). In fact, your cursor turns into a pointing hand when it is on a link, while the Internet address of that new page appears in the lower left corner of the page. Links you've already seen will change color afterward, a handy reminder that you've been there, done that.

When you reach a Web page, your browser translates the information and commands in the HTML file it receives—plus files for pictures, sound or video that may be on the page—into readable words and viewable graphics.

What Is an Internet Address?

The long addresses for Web sites follow a format, starting with "http://" and followed by "www" (without the quotes). For example, "http://www.xyz.com" is the Internet address, or URL (uniform Resource Locator, pronounced you-are-el) for the fictional XYZ Company. Let's break it down. Think of the prefix "http," which stands for Hypertext Transfer Protocol, as a command to your browser to connect with the Web and find the site whose name follows.

URLs are often lengthy because they can specify the name of a directory and the name of a file or document in the directory. These appear separated by front slashes in the URL. For example, typing the URL "http://www.xyz.com/products/widget" will show the page for the document named "widget" in the directory called "products" on the Web site of the XYZ Company. Because every page within a site has its own URL, you can type the URL for a specific page, if you know it, to find that page without going to the site's home page first. This saves a lot of time, because you don't have to explore the whole Web site to reach that page.

You must type a URL EXACTLY the way it appears in the Location, Address or Netfinder box—no matter how weird it looks—including every bit of punctuation, the whole string of letters, or sometimes numbers and capital letters in the middle. Otherwise, you won't find that site. This is probably the single main reason for not finding a Web site and the major cause of people throwing up their hands in despair and complaining they can't find anything on the Internet.

Remember, if you bookmark a Web site, you never need to type its long, complex address again! You can find it in one click. By the way, most URLs are entirely lowercase. But if one includes some capital letters—this means the host computer is case-sensitive—use them.

While "http" is how an address signals to your browser the location is part of the Web, other prefixes signify other parts of the Internet. For example, an address that starts with "news:" means it is a newsgroup. For example, "news:rec.arts.movies.current-film" tells your browser to find the discussion group on current films called "rec.arts.movies.current-film." (See chapter 6 for more about newsgroups.)

The Home Page

A home page is the front page of a Web site that appears when you type its Internet address. Often, people use the term home page to refer to the entire Web site. Sometimes, it looks like a table of contents, with links to different areas of the site. Companies, government agencies, individuals, countries, nonprofits, and even some family pets have home pages.

Many Web sites have dozens, even hundreds or thousands of pages. You can reach an interior page without accessing the home

The Internet offers a new way to look for a job. You can browse through thousands of jobs listed by employers across the United States on some huge job hunting Web sites. You can also post your resume on some of these sites, hoping an employer will find you. Articles by experts on many aspects of the job search and career management—from interviewing, networking, and resume tips, to getting a promotion—are also available.

For example, at Career Mosaic (www.careermosaic.com) thousands of job listings can be searched by occupation, region, or zip code. You can even browse postings in newsgroups, post your resume, and read employer profiles and information on certain industries, such as accounting or health care. You also can take part in online job fairs for certain cities.

Its career resource center lists salary information, both general and for specific fields, trade associations, and tips from career experts. Career Mosaic also has a special section on entry-level jobs for recent college graduates.

Monster Board (www.monster.com) will even send job listings by e-mail to you that match a profile of your desired job. But you can also sift through its job listings database, post your resume, and read articles on hot jobs, opportunities for women and minorities, and many other topics.

America's Job Bank (www.ajb.dni.us) only lists jobs obtained from state public employment services, but this covers a very broad range from shipbuilders to public relations executives.

Many company Web sites also list their own openings. Look for a jobs button to click.

page first if you know the URL for that page, or you can follow the directions on the home page to jump around. After reading this book, you may want a home page too. (See chapter 7 for how to create a Web site.)

Twelve Tricks to Speedier Surfing

1. Use a faster modem. Get a 56 Kbps modem, or at the very least a 28.8 Kbps modem. You'll connect to the Internet faster and pages will load faster. If cable is an affordable option where you live, go for it.

2. Stop a search or a page from loading if it's too slow. Click the "stop" button; you're not honor-bound to continue a search or wait for a page if it's just taking too long.

3. Turn off the images off. You don't need to see all kinds of pretty pictures if you are surfing just to read information. Change the feature that automatically shows images. Depending on the browser version you have, in Netscape click the "edit" menu, then "preferences," then "advanced," and delete the checkmark from "automatically load images," or click the "options" menu and remove the checkmark from "auto load images." In Explorer, click the "view" menu, then "options," then "appearance."

3. Bookmark with abandon. If you think you may return to a Web site again, bookmark it. You can always delete the bookmark later. Bookmark search engines in particular, although your browser may include links to some search engines. The goal is to avoid typing in long URL's all the time.

5. Organize your bookmarks into categories. It will take time to find a bookmark if they are in no particular order. Place them in easy-to-find topics like fun, work, finance, and family, or whatever suits you best.

6. Think before you search. Using two or more keywords, terms such as "and," "or," "not," or plus and minus symbols is always better than just one keyword to narrow your search results and increase the chance of finding what you're looking for.

Hey, It's too Small

Reading tiny type on Web pages is hard sometimes. But you can increase the font of your typeface with your browser. For example, in Netscape Navigator 4.0, click "view," then "increase font." In Netscape Navigator 3.0, click "options," then "general preferences," then font. In Internet Explorer 3.0 and 4.0, click "view," then "fonts," and pick a size.

7. Specialize in a search engine. Why use several search engines half-heartedly for mediocre results? Learn one search engine in and out by following its instructions carefully and seeing how it works, so you can depend on it.

8. Use the Internet at nonpeak times. Late at night, weekends, and very early in the morning seem to produce faster results.

9. Use the "history" button often. This way, you can quickly return to a site you've viewed before in one click instead of retyping its URL. You can also click the "back" button repeatedly if you wish.

10. Use a personalized service. Tailor a service such as Point Cast or My Yahoo! to your interests and it will send news, sports, stock quotes, weather, and other features to your computer automatically on a regular basis so you need not search for them. Automatic news clipping services such as Excite's NewsTracker will scout for articles on specific topics from many publications for you.

11. Use the "find" button often. Zoom in on the specific name or word you're looking for to avoid constantly scrolling down a page.

12. Open another browser window. Surf while you wait for a search to end or a page to load on another part of your screen. Click the "file" menu in Netscape or Explorer, then choose "new Web browser" or "new window."

Domain Names

The domain name is the name registered for an Internet address. The very end of an Internet address, or top-level domain name, shows the domain, or type of organization supporting it. The top-level domain names are com, which means it is a business; gov for government; edu for an educational institution; net for a computer network; mil for military; and org for a nonprofit organization.

The first part of the domain name is called the second-level domain names, which precedes the top-level domain and shows the specific organization or person to whom the site belongs. For example, in "nytimes.com," the domain name for the New York Times, "nytimes" is the second-level domain. In "census.gov," the domain name for the U.S. Census Bureau, "census" is the second-level domain.

Each domain name is unique in the world. Each is coupled with an Internet Protocol (IP) address, a series of numbers that refers to a specific host computer in the routing system of the Internet. Typing in these numbers will bring up the same Web site as typing its Internet address, but generally only a computer, not the average person, knows the numbered IP address.

Different countries have country codes, two-letter endings to their domain names, such as "fr" for France, "uk" for United Kingdom, and "it" for Italy. When there is no country code, a location in the United States is implied. Some American domain names do have "us" as an ending, however, preceded generally by a state and city or county.

The Domain Name Chronicles: Playing Games With Names

As more people realized a domain name that was easy to remember and quick to find was a valuable property—a great way to promote a business—the cyberspace version of gold rush fever swept the land. Because each domain name has to be unique—even though many companies in the world may share the same name—the situation produced many bizarre twists.

Companies began suing other companies for real or imagined trademark infringement. Cyber squatters began grabbing domain names similar to names of big companies, itching to sell them at a profit. Obscure South Pacific islands began cashing in on the frenzy of the nameless, due to a quirk that some countries do not require that only their citizens be able to register a name under their country code. Companies began suing Network Solutions, which has operated the only registry in the world for top-level domain names since 1993, to express their fury. Some companies, known as domain name brokers, offered domain name registration to a public who was often unaware the firms simply registered the names with Network Solutions, charging extra for the privilege.

With over one million domain names registered by Network Solutions' InterNIC registry, in Herndon, Va., under a five-year contract with the National Science Foundation, a frequent grumble of Internet name-hunters is that all the good names are taken. After initially following a first-come, first-served policy, the company later adopted a policy protecting holders of Federal trademarks obtained before a domain name was registered to thwart the efforts of name speculators.

"The IRS has even declared a domain name to be an intangible asset, seizing and auctioning off some domain names because people didn't pay their taxes," says David Graves, director of business affairs at Network Solutions. "We've also had cases of marriages or business partnerships which fell apart fighting over domain names because they were pieces of property." In such cases, the company asked the people to resolve the issue among themselves or get a court order, and deactivated the Web site in the meantime so nobody could reach it.

Twelve-Year-Old David vs. Goliath

As a birthday gift from his father, a Bethlehem, Pennsylvania boy named Chris Van Allen—whose nickname was "Pokey"—received a Web site with the domain name www.pokey.org in 1997. The twelve-year-old promptly posted photos of his puppy and pages on favorite games and pastimes. A few months later, lawyers for Prema Toy Co., makers of the toys Gumby and Pokey, sent a letter claiming trademark infringement, and asked Chris to give up all rights to pokey.org.

The lawyers also notified Network Solutions, which placed the domain on hold and gave Chris another site. Chris began to get thousands of supportive e-mails from all over the world as Internet users championed his case. His family hired trademark lawyers to fight.

But all's well that ends well. Art Clokey, the creator of Pokey—a toy rubber horse—probably sensing a public relations disaster in the making, finally wrote to and called Chris in 1998, apologizing for the mess and allowing the child to keep pokey.org.

Grown Adults Fighting over Scrabble

The toy maker, Hasbro, owns trademark rights to the Scrabble name in the United States and Canada, but Mattel owns them in the rest of the world. When Hasbro registered www.scrabble.com, Mattel didn't feel like playing games—it sued. After the case was settled, the Web site now has links to both companies' sites.

This Lawsuit Stinks

Aircraft maker Lockheed Martin sued Network Solutions, offended because the registry gave out over a dozen domain names that were similar to "Skunk Works," the aircraft company's name for its high-security research and development division in California. A Federal judge absolved Network Solutions of all liability in a landmark decision in late 1997, saying it was not responsible for screening domain name applicants or making decisions on trademark rights.

Ironically, "Skunk Works"—where the U-2 spy plane was developed—was inspired by the *Li'l Abner* cartoon strip, where a still for making moonshine hidden in a hollow was called "Skonk Works." Cartoonist Al Capp complained. After mutual agreement, the aircraft maker was permitted to use the name, as long as it changed one letter.

Pimples.com?

Procter & Gamble is one of the record holders for the number of domain names held, with over 100, including products like charmin.com, and descriptions like diarrhea.com, underarms.com, babydiapers.com, and pimples.com. Kraft Foods also owns over 100, with hotdogs.com and velveeta.com.

A Rose By Any Other Name Is Worth $100,000

That's how much it cost Mecklermedia, a publisher of Internet trade magazines, like *Internet Week*, and host of hugely popular Internet trade shows worldwide, to buy www.internet.com from an Internet consulting company who registered it. (We hope they enjoy it.)

Some Enchanted Domain Name

The South Pacific islands of Tonga, Nieu, and Norfolk Island are among the nations who register their two-letter country domain names to noncitizens who pay a fee: $25 per year for ".nu" from Nieu (pronounced new-way), $1,000 per year for ".ni" from Norfolk Island. The majority of country names limit domain names to citizens. As a result, some Americans have domain names like "go.to" and "internet.nu."

Circus Animals?

It was a surprise to many people looking for Ringling Bros. and Barnum & Bailey Circus who typed the likely URL, www.ringlingbrothers.com, and found a site put up by PETA (People For Ethical Treatment of Animals), an organization that objects to the way circus animals are treated.

It certainly surprised—and displeased—Ringling Bros. (whose own Web site was at www.ringling.com). They complained to Network Solutions, and the PETA site is gone.

Snoopy Up for Grabs

A software designer in Sunnyvale, California, adored the Peanuts comic strip. He was also fond of a computer program to detect problems in networks called SNOOP. When he decided on a domain name, Johnson Wu didn't think twice; he registered snoopy.com, after the lovable beagle. The United Features Syndicate, which syndicates the comic strip, was less than amused. The name's gone, and Wu is not a happy puppy.

Copycat Site Tries to Dupe Public

Ironic, isn't it, but Network Solutions, which prevents more than one company from holding the same domain name through its InterNIC registry service, is itself the victim of a copycat domain name. Several thousand people have registered domain names with an Australian firm, Internic Software (www.internic.com)—paying over $200 for two years—thinking it was the real InterNIC (www.internic.net), which has charged $100 for the past few years.

After the United States Federal Trade Commission issued an opinion that the firm was deliberately misleading the global public,

the Australian consumer protection agency charged Internic Software with deceptive practices and asked a Federal judge to look into the issue in 1998.

"This is an excellent example of cooperation between law enforcers in different countries which benefit consumers in the international marketplace," said Jodie Bernstein, director of the Federal Trade Commission's Bureau of Consumer Protection.

I Scream, You Scream . . .

Bill Sweetman, a partner in HipHype, a Toronto public relations agency, decided on a whim to register scream2.com (and screamtwo.com) last year when he heard Miramax Films was going to release *Scream 2*. He then waited. Sure enough, a polite e-mail from the studio's vice president of interactive media and marketing asked sweetly if the domain name could be theirs. Delighted, Sweetman replied, for "a fair price."

Miramax, whose original *Scream* was one of the highest-grossing horror flicks ever, offered $300. Sweetman declined; he wanted to prove "how blind some major companies can be to the importance of the Internet in their overall marketing strategy." Miramax went on to choose the less catchy dimensionfilms.com/scream.2.

FAQs

FAQs (pronounced "faks") stands for frequently asked questions, and are lists of questions and answers on specific topics that appear all over the Internet, from company Web sites to newsgroups, to assist readers. Another example of the orderly, organizing genius behind the Internet, FAQs save the reader's and other people's time by answering likely questions and reducing the need for a telephone call or further research.

FAQs are very common in newsgroups, so common that a huge list of FAQs for thousands of newsgroups can be found at the Internet address "news.answers." FAQs can be found for each category of newsgroups, from recreation to computers, as well. The FAQs for recreation are found at "rec.answers." Those for computers are at "comp.answers." (See chapter 6 for more about newsgroups.)

For an example of a specific newsgroup FAQ, the newsgroup on current movies, "rec.arts.movies.current-films," includes common questions and advice on how users should handle them to save everyone's time. The FAQ even asks that people use spoiler warnings—include the word "spoiler" in the subject of a message or in its text if they are about to disclose the ending of a suspense film—to preserve others' enjoyment.

Here are some questions and the newsgroup's advice:

a) What movies has X appeared in/directed/written, etc.? Go to the Internet Movie Database (www.imdb.com), an encyclopedic source of cast, crew, studio, plot summary, running time, reviews, awards, and other facts, instead.

b) Does anyone know this movie (plot summary)? Ask people to e-mail messages to you directly.

c) What stories/movies/TV shows are about X? Ask people to e-mail messages to you directly.

d) How can I get the address or a phone number for (some famous star)? Call the Screen Artists Guild for an agent's or publicist's phone number.

e) Does anyone want to talk about X? Ask a more specific, substantive question.

At company Web sites, FAQs offer useful information and explain the whys, hows, and wheres of products from browsers, computers to mail programs. The FAQ for technical support for Navigator or Communicator on Netscape's site (http://help.netscape.com) lists every imaginable question.

For example, pick a product, such as the Netscape Communicator 4.0 browser package. You will see FAQ's organized by topics such as installation, configuration, connectivity and miscellaneous, which often solve specific problems. Click on the question to read the answer. Questions include:

:-) Uninstalling previous versions of Navigator in Windows 95
:-) How do I save a copy of every message I send out?
:-) Unable to find downloaded Communicator file
:-) Speeding up browsing by not loading images
:-) Preventing hangs and crashes when viewing a Web page which uses Java

:-) How do I send a Web page through e-mail?

:-) "The server does not have a DNS entry": what does it mean and how to fix it

The FAQ for Price Scan, a price comparison site for computers and equipment, includes questions like:

What is Price Scan?

Does Price Scan charge vendors to be listed in its database?

How do vendors get listed on Price Scan?

How can Price Scan offer this service for free?

How often is information in the Price Scan database updated?

It's helpful to print out some FAQ's that are especially helpful.

Plug-ins and ActiveX Control

A plug-in is an add-on software program that enhances the ability of your browser to do extra things, such as play music or interviews and display animation or video clips. While not indispensable—you don't really need your computer to sing, talk and shimmy around—these software programs can give you a fuller, more enriching (and noisier) multimedia experience.

Plug-ins come in especially handy at music, movie and television, news, game, sports, and general entertainment Web sites. But they are also found at many others, such as company sites and ads on Web sites. Strictly speaking, they can either be add-ons—programs which work within your browser—or helper applications—which work outside your browser. Many work with both Netscape Navigator and Internet Explorer browsers, but some with only one.

In most cases, plug-ins are free or cheap. Some may already be pre-installed with your browser, especially if you have a recent Netscape or Internet Explorer browser. They can also be downloaded from Web sites that require them—for example, a movie, television, or music site will often ask you to click to download the specific plug-in required. But to avoid delays, plug-ins can be installed in advance from their own Web sites or from group sites that list many plug-ins.

There are a great many plug-ins around, and new ones are being invented all the time. Don't think you need a whole bunch; it's best to play around on the Web first and see which tend to be needed at sites you often visit. They grab a lot of hard disk space and memory, and waiting for sound and images to kick in always limits your surfing speed.

The Windows 98 operating system, by the way, includes a "universal player" which plays many different sound and video files so you don't need a special plug-in for each one. Called the Windows Media Player, it plays RealAudio and RealVideo (versions 4.0 and below), QuickTime, NetShow (now called Windows Media), and other sound files, and works with both Netscape and Internet Explorer.

ActiveX controls are software programs that enhance and produce similar results for Internet Explorer the way plug-ins do for Netscape. However, the technology used to achieve these results is very different. If you have Explorer and are on a Web page with stuff intended to be viewed or heard with plug-ins, you'll be invited to download the proper ActiveX control from the Microsoft ActiveX gallery. If there is none, it can download the standard plug-in. If you have Navigator, you can add ActiveX abilities; just download a plug-in for ActiveX.

If you're a real text person, you may be able to live without plug-ins or ActiveX controls altogether. But the next time someone tells you about a terrific movie clip or music video, you may be jealous.

Some Popular Plug-ins

RealAudio

A high-quality, popular audio plug-in, this plays sound as soon as you start to download thanks to its use of streaming technology. (Streaming means compressed sounds and graphics are played during downloading and decompressed by a browser.) You don't have to waste precious time waiting for the whole file to download to hear it.

RealVideo

Another high-quality plug-in from RealNetworks, the makers of RealAudio, this plays video clips as soon as the download begins. Both are now part of the RealPlayer plug-in, which can stream near-CD-quality sound and newscast-type video from 28.8 modems.

QuickTime

This plug-in plays video clips, sound, and virtual reality worlds using fast-start, a feature akin to streaming, from Apple Inc.

Shockwave

If you hear a site is shocked—as opposed to shocking!—it simply means it uses this plug-in, popular in animation, games, and sound clips. Shockwave, which starts right after the file starts to download due to streaming technology, is from Macromedia.

Beatnik

This plays a variety of sound formats, such as WAV, AU, MIDI, MOD, and RMF. (See chapter 7 for more on sound formats.)

VDOLive

This plays video clips, and is often used to broadcast live events.

VXtreme

This also plays video clips, and is used for live events such as news broadcasts on the CNN site.

ichat

With this plug-in, you can take part in real-time chat sessions on the Web on sites such as Yahoo!, Pathfinder, and Entertainment Asylum.

Live 3D

This allows you to see 3-D graphics and experience a virtual world.

WIRL

Another virtual reality plug-in, this enables you to move smoothly through a 3-D environment.

CosmoPlayer

Another virtual reality plug-in, this hails from Silicon Graphics.

Chat means sending messages back and forth to people in real time, right after the messages are typed.

Lists of Plug-ins and ActiveX Controls

These helpful Web sites list and offer detailed descriptions of the many plug-ins and controls each browser can use. You can download them as well.

Netscape Navigator Components page
(http://www.netscape.com/comprod/products/navigator/
version_2.0 /plugins/index.html)
ActiveX Component page (for Internet Explorer)
(www.microsoft.com/activex/controls)

These Web sites list plug-ins and descriptions by popularity, category (sound, graphics, productivity), or operating system, and allow downloads.

CNET Browser page (see "plug-ins" link)
(www.download.com/Browsers)
BrowserWatch Plug-In Plaza
(http://browserwatch.internet.com/plug-in.html)

Web Sites Using Popular Plug-ins

Here are some music, movie, news and game Web sites and the plug-ins they require so users can hear sound clips, view video clips and chat to savor the full experience:

Broadcast.com www.broadcast.com
A huge variety of sound and video clips from live television and radio news, concerts, music CD's, author interviews, sports, public affairs and business.
RealPlayer, NetShow

National Public Radio www.npr.org
Public radio network with news and programs from "All Things Considered" to "Morning Edition."
Real Audio

CNN Interactive www.cnn.com
World, national and local news, including entertainment and business news.
RealPlayer, NetShow

Entertainment Asylum www.asylum.com
> Movie and television interviews, premieres, news and chats.
> RealPlayer, ichat

Classical Insites www.classicalinsites.com
> Composer and performer biographies and sound clips of classical music.
> RealAudio

Jazz Central Station www.jazzcentralstation.com
> News, articles about performers and sound clips of jazz.
> RealAudio

Rocktropolis www.rocktropolis.com
> News and sound clips of rock music.
> RealAudio

Hollywood Online www.hollywood.com
> Movie video clips, celebrity interview sound clips and news.
> QuickTime, QuickTime VR, MPEG PLayer, Microsoft Active Movie
> Player, Shockwave, RealAudio, ichat.

Live Concerts.com www.liveconcerts.com
> Concert, performer interview and press conference sound clips.
> RealAudio

C-SPAN Online www.c-span.org
> Video and sound clips of congressional hearings, Washington
> press conferences and speeches, and author interviews.

ABCNews.com www.abcnews.com
> Television and radio network news sound clips.
> RealPlayer

SonicNet www.sonic.com
> Concert clips, music news and chat.
> RealPlayer

CD-NOW www.cdnow.com
> Online music store with sound clips, articles and reviews for
> music from rock to classical.
> RealAudio

Volkswagen New Beetle www.beetle.de/starter/01logo.htm
Model of new car in 3-D with sound clips of description.
CosmoPlayer, Shockwave, RealAudio, RealVideo

Film.com www.film.com
Reviews of new and classic movies and sneak peeks of upcoming movies.
RealPlayer

Sony Music Online www.sonymusic.com
Sound and video clips of Sony artists, news about recordings, and chats.
RealPlayer, QuickTime

Sony PlayStation www.station.sony.com
Jeopardy!, Wheel of Fortune and other games can be played here.
QuickTime, RealAudio, Shockwave.

How to Install a Plug-in

If a Web page requires a plug-in not built into your browser, a box will pop up on your screen asking if you want it. You can decline and be on your merry way, or click the choice to get the plug-in. You will probably be taken to the Web site of the plug-in you need to download to hear or see the file. If the plug-in is built-in—for example, QuickTime, CosmoPlayer and Live Audio with Netscape Communicator—it will play the file automatically.

First, you need to create a temporary folder or directory on your hard drive where the plug-in will be after the download. Then, read the instructions and FAQ's on the plug-in's Web site to see if your operating system (Windows, Macintosh or UNIX) and browser version will support it. Then, click "download."

Next, choose the folder name you picked for the download when the directory window appears. Then, close your browser and any other applications you are using. Double-click the file name to run the file. Follow the instructions on the screen, and it should install automatically. If not, the file is compressed. Decompress it by finding the "setup.exe" or "install.exe" file, and double-click on that.

When done, re-launch your browser. To make sure all steps were followed correctly, click the "help" menu, then "about plug-ins," which lists all plus-ins your browser has. If your new plug-in is listed, you have succeeded.

A Sample Installation for Shockwave:

1. Name the temporary directory, for example C:\SHOCK.
2. Go to Shockwave's Web site (www.macromedia.com/shockwave).
3. Read its instructions.
4. Click "download Shockwave."
5. When the directory window appears, choose the temporary directory, C:\SHOCK.
6. Close Netscape and any other applications.
7. Double-click on the file name, for example C:\SHOCK/Shockwave.exe.
8. Follow the on-screen instructions.
9. After it is installed, re-launch Netscape.
10. Try it out. Your computer needs a sound card, of course, to hear the sound. On Shockwave's Web site, there are links to Web sites you can visit which use it for striking animation and sound effects.

Push Technology

Push means sending information to a user's computer on an automatic and regular basis, without effort on the user's part or an immediate request. In contrast to surfing the Web or doing a search—which is pull information to the user—the information pushed is customized to the user based on previously submitted preferences. In other words, the news or company information and updates come to you; you don't have to go looking for them.

Often called one of the most exciting developments on the Internet, push works through the use of intelligent agents, which scout around for information and forward it based on users' tastes.

A pioneer in push, the much talked about PointCast Network (www.pointcast.com) is free and delivers current news, stock market quotes, magazine articles, and weather to your computer when it is idle. Updated headlines, quotes, and scores appear on your screen like a screen saver during the course of the day, while you are talking on the telephone, deep in thought at your desk, or having a snack. PointCast can be personalized if you want to receive only local, national or international news, business news about a specific company or industry, a major newspaper such as Wall Street Journal Interactive or The New York Times, the sports scores, or weather for selected cities.

PointCast, which makes money by selling thirty-second animated ads that run on part of the screen and look something like TV commercials, needs fast modems, up-to-date hardware, and a speedy Internet connection.

Other companies have developed their own forms of push features, which do not require that a computer be connected to the Internet at the time, and so can save hourly connection costs. Push is inserted in some browsers, such as Netscape Communicator—which calls it Netcaster—and Internet Explorer—which calls it Channels. Both deliver information from a variety of news and entertainment Web sites straight to users' computers as often as they request it.

A much simpler, older, but very effective use of push is e-mail. As a result, countless company, news, and community Web sites are happy to add users to their e-mail newsletters. These advise about updates, new offerings, and tips and are delivered daily, weekly, or irregularly.

How to Set Up and Use PointCast

You can download PointCast free from its Web site (it takes about a half-hour for a 28.8K modem), or order a free diskette to be mailed to you by e-mail. This is what to do if you download:

1. Click "download" at PointCast's Web site.
2. Follow the instructions. First, choose your operating system (Windows or Macintosh), then U.S. edition, then region (East or West Coast, Midwest).
3. Save the installation file, "pcn32s01.exe" to your C:\ drive or your desktop.
4. Double-click the installation file to run it and install it.

If you think only young, technical types are on the Internet, guess again. Parent Soup (www.parentsoup.com), a Web site with separate communities for parents of babies, toddlers, school-age children, teenagers, and expectant parents, which is also on America Online, draws 56 million visits each month from parents eager to trade ideas and experiences.

"I was looking for support, and boy, did I ever find it," said Christine Schrodt, a mother of ten children from ages three to sixteen, in Mason City, Iowa. "I was also looking for other large families, and I found them, too."

She's now a community producer for the parents of teenagers section, which means she directs message boards and live chat areas hopping with topics like divorce and custody, children with attention deficit disorder, and raising healthy girls. She suggests ideas for the week's discussion through a weekly e-mail newsletter—such as teenagers with younger siblings, parents who are victims of domestic or sexual abuse and pressures on teenage athletes—but parents are always free to initiate topics.

She also offers a practical tip of the day. Past tips have included motivating your teenager by buying an organizer to track school assignments and holiday activities.

"It's made me a more confident parent," explains Schrodt. "You may have another idea you think no one else has, and then you get some immediate feedback that validates your idea. For example, disciplining teenagers. Some parents try to be friends with their children, but I simply do not tolerate disrespect. If my teenagers say something that's ha-ha funny, that's one thing. But if it's downright disrespectful, I'll call them to the mat on that. Other parents wrote in to say, 'good for you.'"

"The issues are so different depending on the age of the teenager. For young teens around 13, it's 'what happened to my sweet baby?' For mid-teens, it's when do they start dating, and how quickly do you let them drive on their own. When they're 17–19, it's about letting go, colleges, vocational training and the new set of rules because there's now an 'adult' in the house."

Each Parent Soup community also features live chats with pediatricians and other experts at scheduled times. Parent Soup is part of iVillage, which also offers communities on career issues (About Work, www.aboutwork.com) and health (Better Health and Medical, www.betterhealth.com).

5   Click "personalize PointCast."

6   Choose your dial-in connection (for example, Windows 95).

7   When the "personalize" box appears with a list of channels—from Boston Globe, CNN, Fortune, Miami Herald, Money, New York Times, Time, Wall Street Journal, Washington Post and Wired to general topics such as news, industries, companies, health, lifestyle, sports or weather—click the channels you want delivered.

8   When done, click "OK."

9   Click "update." In a few minutes, you will see the information on your computer. Click on a headline to read the full story. The timing will be faster if you have a speedy Internet connection and chose a minimum of channels, or slower if you chose many channels with a slower modem.

10 To tell PointCast how often to send updated information, click "options," then "update." If you have a dial-in con-

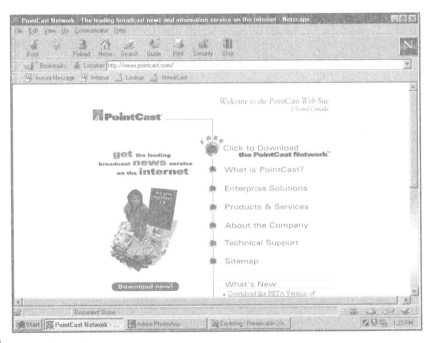

PointCast Network www.pointcast.com

nection, click "update only when I press update button." This means click "update" on the side of your screen when you are done reading information PointCast has sent. Business users with super-speedy direct Internet connections who want frequent updates can click "update with PointCast all-day schedule" or choose their own schedule.

A Sample Set Up for Netscape Communicator's Netcaster

1. Click "Communicator," then "Netcaster."
2. When the security box appears, click "grant." If another security box appears, click "grant" again.
3. The Netcaster Channel Finder window appears. A list of channels under the "in general" tab ranges from CBS SportsLine, Disney, HomeArts Network (from Hearst Magazines, including Good Housekeeping, Redbook and Town & Country) to TV Guide Online. A list of "business focus" channels ranges from ABC News, CNN to Travelocity. The "more channels" list shows other categories, such as entertainment, kids & family, personal finance, and home & leisure channels, each with its own offerings.
4. Click the tab for the broad category you want to view, for example, "business focus," "in general," or "more channels."
5. Click the channel you want to view. Information about this channel will appear. If you want this channel delivered automatically, click "add channel."
6. Click "continue" to add the channel. (If you have changed your mind, click "cancel.") A box asking you to register with Netscape will appear—click "sign me up," then "continue," and follow instructions. (Registration is free.)
7. A "channel properties" box will appear, which asks how often you want this channel updated.
8. Click the week, time and day options—for example, every week at 10:00 AM on Monday—then "OK."
9. Click the "display" tab, and pick the way you want the channel to look on your screen, for example, full-screen

(click "Webtop") or partial-screen so you can work on other things during viewing (click "Navigator window").

10. Click "cache." This show the maximum space the channel can use on your computer. Click "OK."

11. Any channels you have added will now appear in a list under the "my channels" tab in the Channel Finder window. When viewing one of your channels, you can always return to the main category list by clicking "Channel Finder" at the top of the window.

12. To create more space to view a channel, you can make the Channel Finder window disappear. Just click the tab on the left of the window. (The tab does not disappear, but moves to the right edge of your screen; click it, and the Channel Finder will reappear.

How Smart are Intelligent Agents?

Pretty smart, usually, but they're not mind-readers. These little software programs do whatever they are programmed to do, and can even make personalized recommendations to users—movies or music they may like—by learning their tastes and comparing them to others with similar likes and dislikes in their collective database. Some companies that make this kind of agent software are Firefly Network (www.firefly.com), Net Perceptions (www.netperceptions.com), and PersonaLogic (www.personalogic.com).

More companies on the Internet, such as bookseller and music store sites, are licensing this technology. This is why Amazon.com and Barnes & Noble can suggest that you may be interested in knowing that certain books are available, based on books you have bought in the past. Of course, intelligent agents are not geniuses, nor are they mind-readers. They have no way of knowing that the video game book was for your eleven-year-old nephew.

Cookies

Cookies are bits of information some Web sites collect from users and store on users' hard drives so they can be recognized on repeat visits. This means a shopping Web site can track patterns of purchases, other sites can learn consumer tastes, and registration-

Many singles are finding the Internet a fertile hunting ground to meet a lover. In fact, some marriages have resulted from matches formed over the warm glow of a computer screen. Some people are using matchmaking Web sites that charge a fee—the on-line equivalent of personal ads. But others are meeting in less formalized (and free) ways, such as newsgroups, bulletin boards, and Web communities based upon shared interests.

At Match.com (www.match.com), one of the biggest on-line matchmakers, thousands of profiles are available for the browsing. In an effort to maintain privacy, people contact others by anonymous e-mail. Match.com, which notes some weddings have resulted, offers a free trial.

Love@1st Site (www.1st-site.com) lets users search photographs and listings but doesn't let them contact each other directly. If someone is interested, the service will e-mail the other person asking if he or she wants to be contacted by that person. Also located on America Online's Digital City in about a dozen cities, Love@1st Site has a trial offer as well.

If you've met the mate of your dreams—online or not—you can make all kinds of wedding plans at The Knot (www.theknot.com), including searching through thousands of pictures of bridal gowns and bidding for a discounted travel package at auction. Wedding photographers, florists, caterers, and limousine services are some of the local vendor listings found at The Knot, which is also on America Online.

Available in book form, at a Web site, or on CD-ROM, *24 Hours in Cyberspace* (www.cyber24.com) is the first photographic essay that reveals how the Internet is changing people's lives worldwide. With over 200 striking photographs by well-known photojournalists and edited by Rick Smolan, who created the *Day in the Life* photography book series, this book truly gives the Internet a human face.

The project depicts the Internet's countless varied uses, from Buddhist monks to the rabbi of an online Orthodox Jewish synagogue and a Roman Catholic priest who is putting centuries-old rare books from the Vatican Library—such as the world's oldest Bible—on the Web.

Eskimo children in Canada whose tribe wants to promote its crafts and culture, a South African community project formed through joint black and white efforts, and students who are observing an archeological dig in Egypt in real time online are just a few of the ways in which geographic barriers are being broken down by the Internet.

In North America, the *24 Hours* project shows a Montana boy who is being home schooled through the Internet. It also depicts a Toronto woman, Carolyn Burke, whose Internet journal "Carolyn's Diary" landed her on the cover of *U.S. News & World Report*, as well as the project's home page. Cyber cafes, bars, and even ice cream parlors in Bangkok, Singapore, and Amsterdam show the Internet is not limited to those who own computers, but can be enjoyed for the price of a quick rental.

Many photographs and text excerpts from the book can be found on the Web site for the project, whose corporate sponsors included America Online, Kodak, Sun Microsystems, and Netscape Communications. This truly reflects the many human faces of the Internet.

required sites can identify users without requiring them to type in a user ID on each visit.

This is just dandy for the Web site, but—just like the real thing—cookies are not always good for you. Cookies are the reason why, after registering for a site once, you can be greeted by name on your next visit. Because of privacy concerns—not everyone is delighted by this show of warmth from a Web site and what it means—both the Netscape and Internet Explorer browsers give you the option of turning down cookies. (See more about protecting your privacy in chapter 8.)

Error Messages

It happens to everyone. You're having a fine time, surfing around and enjoying yourself, when one of those baffling, infuriating error messages appears on your screen. Your computer is misbehaving, telling you it can't connect to the Web site you want, or has never heard of it. What nerve.

The most common reason for an error message is simply that you typed in the wrong Internet address—misspelling it, leaving out a punctuation mark, using a back slash instead of a front slash (/), or omitting a capital letter. The exact address is needed without a slip-up, or else your browser can't find the site—one excellent reason to use bookmarks, so you just click an often-used Web site with no typing. So checking the Internet address carefully is the first thing to do when an error message appears.

Here are the most common, plus tips on what to do next.

401 Access Denied or Authorization Required

This means the person in charge of the site is limiting access to certain people, possibly through passwords. If you feel you should have access to the site—because you've used the password, for example—e-mail the person in charge to ask why you are being shut out. If you don't have the e-mail address, try "webmaster@" followed by the site's domain name.

403 Forbidden

This means the file was set up wrong by the person in charge. Nobody will be able to reach this site. Try later; maybe it will be fixed.

404 Not Found

This means there is no Web page with the name you typed, but a Web site exists at this address. The page may have been deleted or moved around by the person in charge. Type the address of the site's home page, then search through the site to see if the page has been relocated. Another explanation is that the person moved their entire site to a new location.

500 Server Error

This means the server has mechanical problems, or something was set up wrong. Try later; maybe it will be fixed.

The Requested URL Was Not Found (or, Cannot Open)

This means the Web site cannot be located. Click "reload" to try again. Another explanation is that your cache of already viewed Web sites may be too full. Clean it. In "options" or "preferences," click "advanced" or "browser," then click "empty cache" or something similar. See if you can reach other Web sites. If you can, there is a problem with this site; if not, the problem is with your computer or Internet connection.

Unable To Connect To

This means the site can't be reached. Perhaps the site was taken down or moved to another location and the person in charge didn't include a link to the new address. It may also be the server's fault—it's down or busy. Click "reload" to try again. Try to reach other sites; if you can, the problem is with this site.

Mail Call: E-mail and Internet Etiquette

Electronic mail, or e-mail, is a wildly popular service on the Internet and the major online services. So popular, in fact, that some people have turned away from all other forms of communication, such as regular mail—disdainfully called snail mail due to its pace of delivery—or even the telephone. It's easy, fast (usually, though sometimes messages are delayed just like snail mail), requires no paper, postage or pen, can be done at any hour, and—best of all, many users think—permits one-sided conversation without interruption.

The old-fashioned art of letter writing may be dead, but it's certainly been replaced by the short, snappy, casual missives, often crammed with abbreviations and odd punctuation, which generally passes for e-mail today. Thousands of users who would never think of sitting down to actually write a letter think nothing of dashing off twenty or thirty e-mails to people, many of whom they have never met face-to-face.

Your E-mail Address

Let's break down an e-mail address into its different pieces to understand it better. For example, in "marysmith@mindspring.com", "marysmith" is the user name or user ID. This is the name you have chosen or have been assigned by your ISP, online service, or company. Often, but not always, it is a version of your name. Sometimes, you can't get the exact name you want because it's already taken, so you pick something like marytsmith, msmith, mary, marys, or masmith.

The symbol after the user name, @, is pronounced "at." What comes afterward is the domain name, or host server—the system your e-mail address is on. In this case, "mindspring.com" is the name of Mary's ISP.

No spaces are used between parts of an e-mail address, and every letter, number, or punctuation mark must be typed exactly to reach the person. For example, "mary__smith7@mindspring.com" must be typed with the underline and the digit 7 (not the word); "m.smith@mindspring.com" must include that period (pronounced "dot"). Generally, e-mail addresses are lowercase—MarySmith is the same as marysmith—but sometimes addresses at companies are case-sensitive, meaning a capital letter really counts.

If you are corresponding with someone within the same online service, you can leave out the domain name. This means that America Online members can delete the "aol.com" among themselves, and Compuserve members can delete "compuserve.com," but the ending must be included if they are sending mail outside their online service. Otherwise, the mail will not arrive.

A Sample E-mail Message

An e-mail message looks something like this, allowing for different e-mail programs:

```
Subject: Meeting next week
Date: Mon., 15 May 1998 22:30 EDT
From: Laura Sheehan
To: Frank Lang
Hi Frank,
I'd like to attend the meeting next
Monday, if you still have room. I'll
bring one guest with me.
Thank you.
Laura Sheehan
```

Reply: Quick and Easy

If you want to send e-mail back to someone who sent you a message, click the message, then click "reply." This shortcut means you save time by not looking up and typing the person's name and e-mail address. You can rapidly dash off a whole string of e-mails this way in a few minutes.

When the person receives your reply, the e-mail will repeat his or her entire message plus the date and time, either at the top or bottom of your e-mail, depending on the e-mail program. It will look something like this:

In a message dated 98-05-04 10:14:17
EDT, you wrote:
Hi Kathy,
I'm taking my vacation in August. I'd
love to visit you in Arizona. Is the
second or third week good for you?
Love,
Sarah

This means Sarah sent a message on May 4, 1998 at 10:14 AM Eastern Daylight Time to Kathy, which is repeated in Kathy's response.

By the way, Sarah can also click "reply" to respond to Kathy's reply, and this can go on indefinitely. You're not entitled to just one reply.

E-mail Programs

If you have a browser, you may have a built-in e-mail program. If not, or if you prefer a different e-mail program, you can download one free from the Internet or buy one. If Internet Explorer 4.0 is your browser, Outlook Express is your e-mail program. If you have Netscape Communicator, Netscape Messenger is the name of its e-mail component.

You can send e-mail to groups or individuals. You can also keep track of people's e-mail addresses in an address book, so you don't have to keep looking them up on scraps of paper or their business cards. You can save messages you have received or sent, print out e-mail on paper, include part of an e-mail message in your own message, and, of course, discard e-mail.

There are many things you can do to organize your e-mail. It can be stored in different named folders (by subject, sender, or date), filtered by priority (high-priority, automatic deletion, etc.), and displayed grouped into threads (messages on the same subject). You can also encrypt your messages for privacy reasons if you wish. You can ask your program to check for new mail at regular intervals.

Messages can be sent in plain text or in HTML (great for sending Web pages), and you can change the look of your mail from drab to creative—boldface or underline it, pick a different or bigger printing font, use color, or include art—with these very popular browsers.

Think you can write whatever you want to your honey, co-worker or client in e-mail while at work? Think again.

Some companies are using software that can read their employees' e-mail and block access to objectionable Web sites. In some cases, deleted e-mail is even being retrieved and pored over. In fact, 35 percent of big and mid-sized companies admitted to snooping on their employees—by looking at e-mail and electronic files, recording phone calls and voice mail, or video-taping their work—in a 1997 survey by the American Management Association.

Software, such as SurfWatch, can censor access to undesirable Web sites, newsgroups, and chat areas, such as those dealing with sexually explicit material, violence or hate groups, gambling, and drugs. (See chapter 8 for how parents can use this software to protect their children.) A product called Assentor has some scary talents: it also screens all e-mail before it leaves a company, and it screens all incoming e-mail,

flagging messages that are offensive due to sexual, racist, religious, or threatening content—including jokes. Designed for use by financial services companies, Assentor also keeps a digital eye peeled for e-mail that seems to show insider trading, high pressure sales tactics, and other behavior that is against securities regulations.

In one lawsuit, a court upheld a company's right to fire an employee for nasty e-mail he sent to his boss. In another lawsuit, a court defended a company's right to read old e-mail by an ex-employee who had quit to join a competing firm.

There is no constitutional right to freedom of speech where private employers are involved, legal experts say. What the First Amendment forbids is government restrictions on free speech. Workplace experts at the American Civil Liberties Union warn employees that if they wouldn't want their bosses to read a message in their e-mail, they shouldn't type it.

Some e-mail programs show any URLs named in a message as links, so you can instantly get to that site, which is very handy.

Eudora, named after the writer Eudora Welty, and Pegasus are the names of some popular stand-alone e-mail programs. Some people prefer to use these even though an e-mail program is included with their browser. Both can be downloaded from the Internet (Eudora from www.eudora.com, Pegasus from www.download.com), obtained from your ISP, or purchased. The free version of Eudora, Eudora Light—which can be downloaded—has fewer features than Eudora Pro, its for-sale version. Popular features of Eudora Pro include its compatibility with many different mail programs and its ability to let you pick up or send mail from several different e-mail accounts, each for a different function, without restarting the program, which Eudora quaintly calls "multiple personalities." Other handy features are its ability to sort messages into folders by subject or sender automatically, as soon as they arrive, and understand "nicknames," which you can type instead of the recipient's e-mail address (or addresses for a group of recipients). Users who send and receive a lot of mail like such efficient mail management features.

Eudora can only be used with an ISP account, not with commercial online services, such as America Online or Compuserve, which have their own private mail systems.

Different e-mail programs announce that you have mail in different ways. You may hear a cheery computer voice say "you've got mail!" You may hear a song announcing a mail delivery. You may hear a horn blow and a picture of a mailman with a letter (if you have Eudora on a Macintosh). You may see a red light and hear just a ping sound (if you have WebTV).

Mail sometimes get returned, with a message that says "undeliverable." This is due either to a wrong e-mail address (just like the real post office) or because the person's mailbox is full. Check the address carefully and try again.

Let's look at how to start up and use e-mail in Internet Explorer 4.0, Netscape Communicator and Eudora Pro. If you have an older version or a different e-mail program, the basic process is more or less the same. Read the instructions in the help menu and the choices in the various windows carefully.

Internet Explorer 4.0: Starting Up Outlook Express

1. Click the mail icon (envelope and paper) on the toolbar. Then, click the "tools" menu, and choose "mail options."

2. On the "send" tab, you'll see four "mail sending settings." Click in the tiny box next to each if you want to save a copy of all messages you send (good idea), include the message you are responding to in your message (this reminds sender what he or she said; not really necessary), send your messages ASAP when you click "send" (good idea; avoids filling up your Outbox); and sets Outlook Express as your default e-mail program.

3. Choose the plain text option in the next section, the "mail sending format," because you may be dealing with other e-mail programs that are not the same as yours.

4. On the "read" tab, you'll see five "mail reading settings" plus "font settings." Click in the tiny box if you want to hear a sound each time you get mail (a cute idea, which grows less adorable as you get swamped with mail), consider a message read after it is previewed after a certain number of seconds (like throwing out your mail without opening it; of course, you would never do such a thing), and check for new mail at certain intervals (type in the number of minutes). Also, click the tiny box if you want to empty messages from your "deleted items folder" (good idea) and automatically add people you respond to in your address book (your call; you may not want to add everybody, just regulars). If you want to change your font size, width and so on, click "font settings."

5. On the "spelling" tab, click the tiny boxes so the spelling of your messages can be checked as per your wishes. For example, you can ask the program to always suggest corrections, ignore

Receiving E-mail

At least in the beginning, getting mail from the Internet postman can be an exciting event. That is, until all that spam—unsolicited or junk e-mail—starts to arrive. Or until everyone you know drops all other forms of communication and start e-mailing you like mad, then wondering why you don't respond immediately.

uppercase words (LIKE THIS), or words in messages you are responding to or Internet addresses. If you have certain unusual words you don't need spellchecked, click "edit custom dictionary."

6. On the "signature" tab, you can type a signature—a phrase or several phrases which will always appear at the end of your e-mail message. This can be descriptive—such as the name of your firm and even its address, telephone, and fax number—inspirational, humorous, or whatever.

7. On the "security" tab, you can choose to encrypt all your messages and add a digital ID so a recipient knows it's really you who sent that message.

8. You're done. Click "OK" to save all these choices.

Internet Explorer 4.0: How to Send E-mail

1. Click the mail icon to start Outlook Express.
2. Click the new message icon. (Or click the "file" menu, then click "new message").
3. Type the e-mail address of the recipient in the box after "to." If you want the same message to go to another person, click the tiny box next to "cc" and type this e-mail address. You can also send a copy to a person without others' knowledge by clicking "bcc."
4. Type a headline for your message after "subject."
5. Click in the big box and type your message. End with your name, even though your name will already appear as the sender.
6. Click the send icon (envelope) when done.

Internet Explorer 4.0: How to Pick Up E-mail

1. Click the mail icon.
2. Click the send and receive icon. (Or click the "tools" menu, then "receive, all accounts.")

3. The list of message subjects, senders, dates and times sent, if you have mail, will be in your inbox. Click on the one you want to read and its text will appear in the window.

Internet Explorer 4.0: How to Add Names to Your Address Book

So you won't have to scramble to find an e-mail address on a business card, scrap of paper, or saved e-mail message—or keep retyping names and addresses of your frequent correspondents— keep these names and addresses in an online address book.

1. Click the mail icon.
2. Click the address book icon. (Or click the "tools" menu, then "address book.")
3. Click the new contact icon. (Or click the "file" menu, then "new contact.")
4. Type the name, e-mail address, and—if you wish—any descriptive information about the person, such as job title, where you met, and what you discussed in the respective boxes on the "personal" tab.
5. Click "OK" when done. The home, business and other tabs offer space for more information on this person. When done, click "add." Repeat this process for each new name you want added. Then, click the "X" to close the window.

Internet Explorer 4.0: How to Delete E-mail

1. Click the message, then click "delete."
2. Now that your message is in the trash mailbox, click "empty trash" whenever you want to throw messages out.

Spam is unrequested junk commercial e-mail messages.

Netscape Communicator 4.0: Starting Up Messenger

1. Click the mail icon (envelope and paper) on the toolbar. Type your password, then hit your enter key.

2. To save a copy of all messages you send, click "edit," then "preferences," "mail and groups," "messages," then "automatically copy messages."

3. To set how often you want Messenger to check for new mail, click "edit," "preferences," "mail server," then more options. Click the tiny box if you want it to automatically check for mail, then click in the bigger box and type the number of minutes between mail checks. This means your mailbox icon will show a down arrow when you have new mail. If you want your password remembered so you don't need to type it every time you want to pick up your mail, click the tiny box next to this choice. Click "OK," then "OK" again when the Preferences box appears.

4. To mark messages as unread so you will remember to re-read them later, click the dot next to the sender name. This means the message will appear in boldface type with a closed envelope next to it. If you want to red-flag an important message, click the dot on the same line at the extreme right of your screen.

5. To find your folders for sent messages, drafts of messages you are still working on, trash for deleted messages, and typed but unsent messages, click "inbox," then the folder name to read messages inside.

6. To create a signature file, type it in a word processing program like Word and save it as a text-only file, or in a text editor, then click "edit," "preferences," then "identity." Click "choose" next to the box which shows the location of the file, then the file name, then "open," then "OK."

7. To change your font and size, click the second box from the left above the window where you typed message, then select the font you want from its pull-down menu. To

change font size, click the number box to the right of the font choice box, then select the size you want.

8 If you send a message with fancy formatting—such as boldface type, underlining or color text, each with an icon above the window where you typed your message—a dialog box may appear and ask the mail sending format you want. Choose plain text unless you know the recipient's mail program can read this formatting.

9 To check the spelling in your messages, click the spell icon after you type your message. The misspelled word will appear; so will suggestions to correct it. Click the right one.

10 If you want messages to be sent immediately after you create them—or want them sent slower than usual—click the message sending options icon directly above "subject" after typing your message. Click "priority" and choose from the pull-down menu—from low to highest priority, the Internet version of first-class or second-class mail.

11 To encrypt your message for security reasons, click the tiny box next to the encryption choice in the message sending options. To sign your message with a digital ID, click the tiny box next to the signed choice in the message sending options.

Netscape Communicator 4.0: How to Send E-Mail

1 Click the mailbox icon on your component toolbar to start up Netscape Messenger.

2 Type your password (unless you have asked that it be saved in the "mail and news preferences" menu under "options"), then hit your Enter key.

3 Click the new msg icon (pen and paper) in the toolbar.

4 Follow steps 3–6 in the Internet Explorer steps.

Netscape Communicator: How to Pick Up E-Mail

1. Click the mailbox icon on your component toolbar to start up Netscape Messenger and see your mail.
2. Type your password, then hit the Enter key.
3. The mailbox icon will have a down arrow on its left if you have new messages. The list of message subjects, senders, dates, and times sent will appear beneath your inbox. Each new message will be boldfaced, with a sealed envelope icon and a down arrow to its left. Click on a message you want to read and it will appear in the window.
3. Click the get msg icon (open envelope) to see any new messages that came during the day. The new mail is stored until you ask for it.

Netscape Communicator: How to Delete E-mail

1. Click the message, then click "delete."
2. Now that your message is in the trash mailbox, click "inbox," then "trash" whenever you want to throw messages out.
3. Click the file menu, then click "empty trash folder" when you are sure you want to discard messages.

Netscape Communicator: How to Add Names to Your Address Book

1. Click the Communicator icon.
2. Click "address book."
3. Click "new card."
4. Type the name, organization, title, e-mail address, and description of the person. If you want to add more information, such as telephone and fax number and home/business address, click the "contact" tab.
5. Click "OK," then the "X" to close the window.
6. If you want to add an entire list of people, click "new list." Then, type a name for your mail list, a nickname,

and description. (For example, People Met On Europe Vacation, Europals, and 1997 Vacation Italy and France.)

7. Type the name and address for each name on your list, hitting the Enter key each time.

8. Click "OK."

9. Type the name and e-mail address of each person you want to add, then hit your Enter key each time.

6. Click "OK."

Eudora Pro 4.0 for Windows— Installing

1. Insert the CD-ROM into your CD-ROM drive (or double-click on the file if you have downloaded), after exiting any other applications you are running, such as toolbars and anti-virus software.

2. Click the Eudora Pro icon when the Installer screen appears, then click "install."

3. Click "next," then "yes."

4. Type your user code, which is on the technical support sheet inside the product box (or in the message you received when you bought it for download), then click "next."

5. Click the boxes next to the items you want installed, such as the HTML viewer and QuickTime, which offer improved viewing of multimedia content in your e-mail, then click "next."

6. Choose a directory where you want Eudora Pro installed, then click "next."

7. Look over your settings to make sure they are correct, then click "next."

8. Click "agree" and follow online instructions when the QuickTime license agreement appears, if you chose this item.

9. If you want to read the "readme" help file, click "yes."

Eudora Pro 4.0 for Windows: Starting Up

1. Double-click the Eudora Pro icon. You may have needed to restart your computer after installation.

2. Click "next" when the New Account Wizard opens.

3. Choose the panel to create a new e-mail account, then click "next."

4. Type your name, e-mail address, login name, and incoming e-mail server (POP or IMAP), where Eudora needs to go to find your mail, each followed by "next." If your outgoing mail server (SMTP) is located on a different computer from your incoming mail server, you need to include this as well. (Ask your ISP what your POP, IMAP or SMTP servers are.) Click the "tools" menu, then "options," then "sending mail." Next, type your SMTP server—which often has a word before your ISP's domain name, such as "smtp," "mailhost," or "mail"—then "OK."

Eudora Pro 4.0 for Windows: How to Send E-mail

1. Click "new message" in the "message" menu.

2. Type the e-mail address (or a nickname you have chosen) of the recipient in the box after "to." If you want the same message to go to another person, click next to "cc" and type this e-mail address, or click next to "bcc" to send a blind copy.

3. Type your e-mail address.

4. Type a headline for your message after "subject."

5. Click in the big box and type your message.

6. Click the send icon (envelope) to send the message immediately. (Make sure the immediate send option is on in the sending mail options.) To send the message later, click the queue button. (Make sure the immediate send option is off in the sending mail options.) This way, when you are ready to send a batch of messages at one time, click the file menu, then "send queued messages."

Eudora Pro 4.0 for Windows: How to Pick Up E-mail

1. So that Eudora will automatically always check to see if you have new mail and transfer it to your computer, double-click "checking mail options," and type the number of minutes between mail checks in "check for mail every ? minutes." Do this for each alternate e-mail account as well. Click the personalities window, click the specific account, choose "modify," then "check mail" in the account settings.

2. Type your password for each e-mail account every time you open Eudora to check mail for the first time. If you want it to remember your password, click "save password" in "checking mail options."

3. When you are notified new mail has arrived, click the Eudora icon in your toolbar. You can be notified through a special sound, an alert box, or an open mailbox icon— or all three—depending on what you chose in the "getting attention options."

4. The list of message subjects, senders, dates and times sent will be in your inbox. Click on the one you want to read and its text will appear in the window.

Eudora Pro 4.0 for Windows: How to Delete E-mail

1. Click the message, then click "delete" on the message menu (or click "trash" from the transfer menu, or click the delete button).

2. Now that your message is in the trash mailbox, click "empty trash" from the special menu whenever you want to throw out a batch of messages.

3. If you want to look over messages in the trash mailbox before throwing them out, click the trash mailbox, choose only the messages you want to discard, then click "delete" from the message menu.

Eudora Pro 4.0 for Windows: How to Add Names to Your Address Book

1. Click the "tools" menu, then "address book."
2. Click "new."
3. Type a name for the file you are creating (for example, work or friends), then click box next to "make it an address book," then "OK."
4. To add a name to an existing file, click "new" in the address book, then type a nickname for the entry (a short, easy to remember substitute for the name or names, such as "college pals").
5. Choose the file for this entry, then click box next to "put it on the recipient list," then "OK."
6. Type the e-mail address of each person included in the nickname, separating addresses with commas. Type the real name of the person or people included in the nickname in "name" in the "info" tab.
7. Type descriptive information for the person or group, such as postal address, telephone, fax and where you met, in the "info" and "notes" tabs.
8. Click the "file" menu, then "save" to keep your changes in your address book.

Picking Up E-mail When You're Away From Home

If you're traveling, you can still pick up your e-mail from your home account. The rules are different if you take your own laptop computer with you—where all your personal account information is already signed on—versus using a strange computer. (Strange doesn't mean weird, but rather a computer at a computer rental center or a friend's or relative's home.)

With your own laptop, change the local access number in your modem's settings so it will dial up a local telephone number instead of the number you use at home. You can now pick up your e-mail and start Web surfing for the price of a local call. You can obtain the local access number from your ISP. Hopefully, if you travel often, you have a national ISP with hundreds of local access numbers nationwide.

If faced with a strange computer and you are an America Online user, ask if the computer has an AOL account as well—or check for its familiar icon on the screen. Because AOL has 10 million members, there's a good chance the computer center, home, or office you're visiting will have it. If so, sign on as a guest. Just click "select screen name," scroll down to click "guest," and type your screen name and password. That's it. If you want your e-mail saved on your home computer, click "keep as new."

It's a bit more complex if you don't have AOL. If the computer has Netscape, do this:

1. Click "options," click "mail and news preferences," then "servers."
2. For Outgoing Mail Server, type your ISP's domain name where it says "SMTP"—for example, "aol.com" or "webtv.net."
3. For Incoming Mail Server, type your ISP's domain name where it says "POP."
4. For POP3 User Name, type your user name—for example, "marysmith" or "msmith."
5. If you want e-mail saved on your home computer, check "left on the server."
6. Click "identity" in "mail and news preferences," and type your name in "your name" and your e-mail address in "your e-mail."
7. If you don't want to type your password every time you check mail, check "remember mail password" box in "organization." (This means anyone who uses this computer is also able to pick up your e-mail.)

If the computer has Internet Explorer, do this:

1. Click "mail," then "options," then "servers."
2. Type your name in "name" and your e-mail address in "e-mail address."

3. For Outgoing Mail Server, type "smtp." followed by your ISP's domain name.

4. For Incoming Mail Server, type "pop." followed by your ISP's domain name.

5. For POP3 Account, type your user name.

6. If you don't want to type your password every time, type it in "password."

7. If you want e-mail saved on your home computer, click "advanced," then "left on server."

How to Attach Files

Sometimes, you may want to send something along with your e-mail message. This can be an article, image, sound, video, or computer program as long as it is in the form of a computer file. Of course, the recipient's computer has to have the proper software to read and play the file, if not, a terrific music clip will not come across but will appear as a large unreadable file of gobbledygook.

To send a file attachment, you generally create the e-mail message first, then give a command noting a file will be attached, choose the file name, then send both. For example, in Netscape Communicator, after writing your message—maybe something like "article on health care attached" or "the enclosed photo may be of interest"—click "attach," click "file" (your other choices are to send a Web page or your address book card), click the name of the file, then click "open." End by clicking "send."

How to Open An Attached File

Click the e-mail message that has a file you want to open (it should have a subject like "article attached" so you know to look for an attachment, unless you are expecting it), then click the file name, which appears below the sender's message. Click "open it," then "OK" in the box warning you of possible security hazards, and the attached file appears. If you clicked "save it to disk" instead, click "save" and note the location where the file will be stored for future retrieval.

The warning appeared, by the way, because some nasty people sometimes send a computer program with a virus that can mess up

If you often travel beyond your ISP's local access numbers or are in a foreign country for a long trip but want to pick up your e-mail, surf the Internet, or get into your company's internal network on the road, there's a way to beat high long-distance or international telephone rates: use roaming Internet access.

Roaming allows you to borrow the services of a local ISP or a Point of Presence connection in hundreds of countries. You use your own password, log-in, and e-mail program to reach your home account, but your modem now dials up a local access number in the area where you are staying. A local number often means your telephone connection will be better than over long-distance lines. Your ISP needs to be a member of a global roaming network, however.

For example, if your ISP belongs to iPass Alliance, which means it agrees to use special software from iPass (415-237-7300 or www.ipass.com), you would pay anywhere from $2.50–$15 per hour plus $2–$3 per month to use roaming service. (ISP rates vary wildly worldwide.) But if your ISP is not a member, you can pay higher rates—but still less than many international calls—and still use iPass' network by using Homegate (310-533-3950 or www.home-gate.com). Homegate's rate is $.08–$.50 cents per minute plus $5–$15 per month.

Aimquest (408-955-1920 or www.aimquest.com), another roaming service, requires ISPs to belong to its Global Roaming Internet Connection, which includes big American ISPs like Netcom and SPRYNET. Its rate is $4–$6 per hour plus $.30–$1 for each successful dial-in. At eGlobe (888-345-6238 or www.eglobe.com), the rate is $8 per hour with a local access number, but a steep $1.25 per minute using a toll-free number. But you don't have to belong to a roaming network.

your computer. Thus, you should only open attached files from people you know. (See chapter 8 for more about computer viruses and how to prevent them.)

How to Send Electronic Postcards

Many Web sites offer free electronic greeting cards or postcards for many different occasions, including birthdays, holidays, anniversaries, new babies, or job promotions. You can choose from a wide selection of photographs (lots of cuddly teddy bears, cute kittens, art masterpieces, and travel scenes), cartoons, virtual flower bouquets, and even animation, and personalize the card with the recipient's name, your name, and your own message.

Animations include a birthday cake with flickering candles that plays "Happy Birthday," two polar bears hugging, and lips opening in a kiss. Some sites charge a small fee for these multimedia cards, and of course the recipient's computer must be able to handle animation.

The recipient gets an e-mail message noting he or she can pick up a card at the greeting card Web site with a special code. Some sites even offer free e-mail reminders, so you'll never miss that special day again. It's a nifty way to save time on trips to buy cards, as well as save money and tell that special someone you're thinking of them.

Instant E-mail

There are a couple of even faster ways to send messages than e-mail. When you see a message box pop up suddenly on your screen, demanding your attention—instead of piling up in your mailbox, waiting its turn like a patient little message—the sender is using instant messaging software. It's a bit unnerving the first time it happens, but it's a delightful way to send a message immediately to someone you know is online.

It's nice, too, to get an urgent—or friendly—message without repeatedly having to check your mailbox (and perhaps finding you've just gotten another piece of spam.)

Instant Messenger is one of the most popular free products. You can create a buddy list of friends, family, and colleagues, and see if they are online the same time you are. Although included with an America Online account, any Internet user can use Instant Messenger by downloading it from the AOL Web site (www.aol.com). Netscape's latest version, Communicator, also includes Instant Messenger. A privacy feature lets you control who sees you online, so only people who know your e-mail address can check. You can also ignore a message, if you wish.

Another popular free product with even more features is ICQ from Mirabilis (www.mirabilis.com), an Israeli company, which allows you to instantly send a message to a person or group, a file, or a Web page if they are online. ICQ (it stands for "I seek you"), which also can be downloaded from its Web site, alerts you if any of the people on the short list you created are online, and lets you signal your availability to others.

For example, if you don't want instant messages you can signal "do not disturb." If you want urgent messages only, you can indicate this. Even if you don't have ICQ, you can reach someone with ICQ by paging them with their ICQ number or paging them in other ways.

Some search engines, such as Yahoo! and Infoseek, also have instant messaging systems that are free to anyone who downloads them from their Web sites.

Using Mailing Lists

Mailing lists are discussions on certain topics conducted entirely by e-mail. A message generally goes to all the people who subscribe to the mail, which may be hundreds or thousands worldwide. Subscribers are usually passionate about the interest or hobby that is the subject under discussion. If you crave a full mailbox, you may want to join a mailing list or two. But be aware, many are not totally open to the public and may be local, regional, or screened by a moderator who may want to know more about you before you join. Some mailing lists from organizations also include events, jobs listings, and positions wanted.

The biggest list of mailing lists on the Internet is Liszt (named after the Romantic composer and pianist), which features more than 90,000 lists. At the wonderfully organized Liszt (www.liszt.com), you can search for a mailing list by name or by category. Categories

Heartwarming stories about people who use the Internet in various ways to help their families, a favorite cause, or achieve their dreams can be found at Folks Online (www.folksonline.com) in its true stories section.

A mother whose baby was born prematurely with pulmonary hypertension—his blood system could not get enough oxygen to his lungs—was sent gifts of food, books and art supplies for her older children, and frequent e-mails of love and support from friends she met in a mailing list for parents. Her mailing list pals even scheduled a Light a Candle Day of prayers and warm wishes for her newborn in the intensive care unit, and a friend posted updates when she was too busy and exhausted to do so.

An animal rescue group, Little Shelter in Long Island, New York, posts photographs of dozens of abandoned dogs and cats for adoption on its Web site in its virtual kennel and cyber cattery.

A mother of a child with Down syndrome notes she has received more support and learned more about medical treatments and educational opportunities for her child from a mailing list on Down syndrome than anywhere else. Disability-related mailing lists, where you can post messages about a child's accomplishments as well as ask questions and relate personal experiences, can be lifesavers for parents of afflicted children.

Mamma's Hands, a Seattle nonprofit that helps the homeless by supplying food, clothing, blankets, and help in rehabilitation has won donations, volunteers, and gifts as a result of its Web site.

A woman who loves Greece found a sailboat for rent thanks to a man met on a travel bulletin board she regularly uses for travel recommendations. She spent a glorious, but inexpensive, ten days sailing the Aegean Sea with her husband, cooking meals, sleeping on the boat, and docking at any island they found intriguing.

Folks Online also has message boards, chat, and a resources section listing recommended sites for beginners to the Internet, women, seniors, and families.

include arts—with subcategories like literature, movies, comics, and theater—business, politics, computers, culture, and more. Liszt shows short descriptions and how to obtain more information about the list.

For example, look up "humor" and find dozens of mailing lists, many of which are willing to e-mail you a new joke each day, and specialized lists like medical or psychology humor, offbeat humor, or funny things that happen on the Internet. Notice that Liszt thoughtfully includes links to related newsgroups, books, Web pages, and hardware or software at the top of the page. Click one to see the listings. (There may not be listings in every category for every topic you pick.)

If you look up the humor mailing list "aris-humor," you'll see the following:

```
Listname:          aris-humor
Hosted at:         mylistnet.net
Contact person:    owner-aris-
                   humor@mylist.net
Description:       Fully moderated, free
                   list, providing about
                   one joke a day to its
                   subscribers.
```

You now know whom to e-mail to join this mailing list. When you join a list, carefully follow the instructions you are given. Usually, you send an e-mail to the list manager with "subscribe" or something similar (sometimes, "subscribe" plus the name of the list) in the message body. If you later wish to be deleted, you send an "unsubscribe" message.

Minding Your P's and Q's On the Net

Here are some rules of proper etiquette for mailing lists, e-mail, and newsgroups.

1. Be short and concise in your messages.
2. Read for a while to absorb the kinds of topics discussed in the list or newsgroup, the tone of the messages, and any particular no-no's for which message writers are

scolded before you send a message of your own. (This is called lurking, by the way, but it's OK.)

3. Don't send an advertisement to a list or newsgroup. Indiscriminate sending of commercial messages is regarded as a form of Net abuse called spamming, and makes many list or newsgroup readers very angry. They often send flames—insulting messages impugning your intelligence or taste. For this reason, Liszt offers no more than 150 results for each search, and even has a special set of commercial mailing lists whose members welcome ads on certain topics.

4. Using capital letters is just like SHOUTING. You don't want to be SHOUTED at, so don't do it to others.

5. Don't make derogatory or prejudiced remarks. Bad manners are still bad manners, whether in person or in print. You'll see flames—the nature of e-mail seems to unleash people's dark moods and unhinge their manners—but try to remain above it all. Don't fan the flame, so to speak.

6. Don't send any sort of junk mail. "Make $$$ NOW" as well as joke e-mail fits in this category. Getting your mailbox stuffed with several junk e-mails each week is no laughing matter. It's polite to ask your intended recipients if they would like to receive such messages before you send them.

7. If your message only applies to one person on the list or in the newsgroup, send a personal e-mail instead a message to the whole group.

How to Prevent Spam

There it is, your official welcome as a new citizen (or Netizen) of cyberspace: "Make Lots of $$$," its header says. This unsolicited, often unwelcome commercial e-mail—the Internet equivalent of those telemarketing calls during dinner—will soon be joined by dozens like it.

You don't have to take it. Here are things experts recommend you can do to prevent being spammed:

:-) Reply to the sender, asking to be taken off their mailing list.
:-) Forward a copy of the message to your ISP's administrator.

:-) Automatically delete e-mail from certain addresses that have sent spam in the past by setting the filter in your e-mail program.

:-) Delete it as soon as you see the header, so it won't fill up your mailbox.

:-) When you fill out online forms—signing up for a newsletter, registering for an online publication, etc.—check "no" to the question asking if you would like to receive updates online. Perhaps you don't mind getting updates from some, but don't want further e-mail from others. It's your choice.

:-) Ask to unsubscribe from mailing lists or newsletters to stop further mail.

:-) Be sure to unsubscribe from mailing lists or newsletters using all your e-mail addresses. List them one after another in the body of the message. It's easy to forget you subscribed under more than one e-mail account.

:-) Use Spam Hater, a shareware product that tracks down the senders to notify them you don't want mail from them.

Showing Your Feelings Net Style: Emoticons and Abbreviations

Since e-mail lacks the intonations of people's voices and the expressions on their faces, people have tried to compensate. Some do funny little things with punctuation to express an emotion, called emoticons or smileys. (They kind of look like a face if you turn them around.) Others, to save time, use shortcuts for phrases.

Common emoticons:

:-)	smile
:-(	sad
:-0	surprise
:-I	frowning
:-c	disappointed
:-D	laughing
>:-<	angry
:-O	shocked/yelling

Networking for Women

Webgrrls (www.webgrrls.com), an international networking group for women interested in the Internet who meet regularly to exchange leads and information, and hear expert speakers on technology issues, has thousands of members. Webgrrls also holds inexpensive classes on HTML, Web site design, and selling products or services from your Web site, which non-members can also attend.

Chapters are located throughout the United States, and in Europe, Asia and Australia.

At a typical meeting, women tell others what they need—a job in Web design, a new computer, or contacts in a new city—and what they can give in return. Many have jobs outside the Internet industry but are eager to improve their skills and learn more about the field. The Webgrrls mailing list includes many upcoming events, such as trade shows and panel talks, and job opportunities in the Internet industry.

Its Web site, where you can join by e-mailing a local chapter, includes business articles and profiles of members who own Internet businesses.

Common abbreviations:

BFN	bye for now
BTW	by the way
FYI	for your information
G	grin
HTH	hope this helps
IMHO	in my humble opinion
LOL	laughing out loud
OTOH	on the other hand
ROTFL	rolling on the floor laughing

Free E-mail

Yes, free e-mail does exist. Sign up for free accounts with Juno (www.juno.com), HotMail (www.hotmail.com) or Eudora (www.eudora.com)—which simply ask that you view ads in exchange for the privilege of free mail service—or search engines such as Yahoo! and Excite, who want users to linger at their sites. In most cases, you pick up and send your mail at the company's Web site. (Juno, however, requires special free software, and can only be used on Windows.)

There's no catch. Free e-mail is a real bonanza if you don't want to pay for an Internet access account but would like to be in touch with friends, relatives, and others. You can check your mail at any Internet-connected computer at a library, at work, a computer center, or a friend's home (unless you have Juno). Just type in your password and login name at the e-mail provider's Web site.

Free e-mail accounts make it easy for people to find you when you change ISPs, or leave a company or school where you have an e-mail account. They also are handy if you travel a great deal.

Signing up is easy. To sign up for Hotmail, for example, go to its Web site and click "sign up here." Then, click "I accept" after reading its terms of service. Next, fill out the online registration form, choosing a login name—which can include letters, numbers or underlines or a mix, a password—so only you can pick up your mail, a reminder—to help you remember your password, and your first and last names. Your full name will appear with all e-mail you send. (This way, people will know that "cuddles@hotmail.com" is really you, Sarah Smith, instead of being mystified.)

Then, the form asks a bunch of nosy questions about your state, zip code, sex, occupation, household income, education, and interests. Nervy, yes, but this is so ads you see will be targeted, more or less, to people with similar demographic profiles. If any lines are left blank, Hotmail won't process the form. (If you are leery about divulging personal details, remember the data you type doesn't have to be true. It's a small price to pay for free e-mail.)

To use your free account, type your login name and password. Next, you will see a number of choices. Click "inbox" to pick up your e-mail, or "compose" to send e-mail. You can click "addresses" to add or view people's e-mail addresses in your online address book, "folders" to sort messages by saving some and discarding others, and "logout" when you are done.

To pick up e-mail, click the name of the sender. (Your first message will undoubtedly be from Hotmail staff, bragging about how many millions of people have their accounts.) After reading the message, click "delete" to discard, "reply" to answer, "forward" to send the message to someone else, "previous" to read the message before this, or "next" to read the next one. To delete a message when you are back at your list of messages, you can put a checkmark next to the sender name, then click "delete" at the bottom. To sort messages, click the pull-down menu next to "move to," which offers a choice of folders such as "drafts"—messages you are working on and have not sent yet—"sent messages," and "trash can"—yet another way to delete messages. Click the choice you want, then click "move to."

To send e-mail, type the recipient, subject and names of people who should get copies in the proper fields. To send an attached file, click "attachments," then specify the file name on the diskette you have inserted into the computer, next click the file type (such as plain text, word processing document, or other). When done, click "send." You will also notice a few other choices, which let you save the sent message, and even consult a dictionary and thesaurus for inspiration while composing your message.

In addition, Hotmail lets you find an e-mail message you have sent or received by typing the sender, recipient or subject name, or search for people's e-mail addresses. If you tend to forget important dates, such as birthdays, anniversaries or meetings, a handy e-mail reminder will alert you to these upcoming dates. Last but not least, if you don't want to bother reading e-mail from certain people—such as a "spammer" or ex-friend—you can block mail from their addresses, which means it will not appear on your screen.

The sign-up process is similar at Web-based e-mail services such as Yahoo, Excite, and Eudora, which also let you send attachments, set up address books and folders, and block unwanted messages.

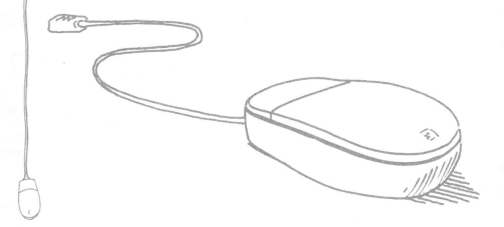

Meet and Greet:
Newsgroups, Bulletin Boards, and Chat

What Is a Newsgroup?

You're ready for some of that Internet community you've always heard about, and are eager to talk (well, type) and exchange ideas with your fellow Netizens. No matter what your interest or hobby is, you'll find a discussion group, called a newsgroup, already organized with tons of messages you can read and answer. These thousands of public bulletin boards, called Usenet (which stands for Users Network), post a user's name, e-mail address, headline, and date of message.

Newsgroups are divided into major categories, called hierarchies, each with many subcategories. The hierarchies, which are seen in the first part of a newsgroup's name, are rec (recreation), soc (society and culture), biz (business), sci (science), comp (computers), talk (controversial issues like politics), news (Internet and Usenet issues), misc (miscellaneous), and the famous alt (an alternative free-for-all with many unusual groups, many sexual in nature).

The subcategories are endless. There is often a second, third, and even fourth subcategory after the main hierarchy, marked off by periods, in a newsgroup's name.

For example, rec includes arts, antiques, travel, food, pets, humor, and skiing among many others. The rec.arts subcategory consists of books, movies, mystery, theater, and so on. The rec.arts.movies subcategory includes reviews, people, and announcements of events in the film industry. Often, more than one newsgroup serves a popular topic. For example, there are movie review newsgroups in the alt hierarchy—with one devoted solely to the critics Siskel and Ebert—and many alt newsgroups on specific directors and actors, such as Steven Spielberg, Martin Scorsese, Charlie Chaplin, and Sigourney Weaver, and movies such as *Jurassic Park* or *Titanic*.

Let's look at a few examples. The rec.travel subcategory includes newsgroups for many destinations and modes of travel, such as:

FOR	TRY
backpack budget travel	rec.travel.budget.backpack
hints and tips for travelers here and abroad	alt.discuss.travel.tips
places not to visit	alt.discuss.travel.avoid
travel in Europe	rec.travel.Europe

FOR	TRY
travel in Latin America	rec.travel.latin-america
travel in New Orleans	alt.travel.new-orleans
cruise travel	rec.travel.cruises
miscellaneous travel	rec.travel.misc

Interested in cooking, chocolate, or wine? Food newsgroups range from rec.food.chocolate, rec.food.cooking, rec.food.cuisine.Jewish, rec.food.drink.coffee, rec.food.recipes, rec.food.restaurants, rec.food.veg (for vegetarians), nyc.food (about dining out in the New York City area) and alt.food.chocolate. Some have moderators who guide the discussion so it doesn't fall off track.

Some post detailed lists of FAQs for common questions and their answers, so they won't get asked repeatedly and waste people's time.

For example, in alt.food.chocolate, French bakers ask for the history of brownies, a Hershey vs. Nestle debate rages, and folks ask for and share recipes. Its elaborate FAQ contains questions on everything from its history and naming—eighteenth century naturalist Carolus Linneaus named the tree *cacao theobroma*, or cacao, food of the gods, and the ancient Maya and Aztec Indians brewed chocolate beverages—and cooking tips to trivia, such as how much caffeine a chocolate bar contains. The FAQ gravely notes its goal is to serve as an answer to a question once posted in a newsgroup, which said: "I would be very much obliged if someone could tell me how a food that has been associated with acne, headaches, obesity, and many a trip to the dentist has managed to attract so much favorable attention."

No matter what your interest—if you're a cat lover, a fan of a certain automobile, a fisherman, a parent, classical music fan, suffer from depression or anxiety, interested in *Star Trek*, archeology, or Shakespeare—you can find a newsgroup where people with similar interests offer opinions and get advice.

You'll be struck by many things as you read newsgroup messages, such as the scoop offered by industry insiders, the willingness of many to answer questions or offer help or referrals, and the flames (insulting messages) that often erupt. Not to mention the sheer amount of time so many people seem to have on their hands to write messages!

A newsreader is a software program that lets you read and post messages to newsgroups. It may be part of your browser.

The online services, such as America Online and Compuserve, have their own version of discussion groups called forums or bulletin boards. These are organized by topic, have libraries of resources and FAQs, feature many subsections, and operate similarly to newsgroups. However, these are for members only.

How to Find Newsgroups

Before you look for newsgroups, you need software called a newsreader so you will be able to read and post newsgroup messages.

Luckily, both Netscape Communicator and Internet Explorer browsers include newsreaders. If you have Netscape Communicator, click on the newsgroup icon (balloons with messages inside) to launch Collabra. If you have Explorer, click the mail icon (mailbox) to launch Outlook Express and select the newsgroup option, or go to the "Go" menu, then select newsgroups.

You then click on different options to show the list of all newsgroups (a very long list appears, in alphabetical order), search for a newsgroup by keyword (all newsgroups that include the word appear), or look for brand new newsgroups (new ones are formed all the time). Clicking on any one newsgroup will display the headlines (or "headers") for the messages, the users' names, and posting dates.

Once you know a newsgroup's name, you can reach it if you type "news:" followed by the name in the Location or Address box of your browser. For example, to reach the movie review newsgroup called rec.arts.movies.reviews, type "news:rec.arts.movies.reviews." To reach a FAQ for a specific hierarchy, type "answers" after the hierarchy's name. For example, type "news:soc" for the society and culture FAQ. A list of FAQs for all newsgroup hierarchies is at "news.answers."

You can subscribe to newsgroups you want to read and respond to regularly, meaning they will automatically appear when you open your newsreader, so you don't have to hunt for them. Click "subscribe" or the relevant menu option, depending on your browser, then click the newsgroup.

Diana Dies, Thousands Mourn Online

When Diana, the Princess of Wales, was killed in a car crash in Paris on August 31, 1997, her death became one of the major Internet events of the year. Major news organizations began reporting details and chronicling her last few weeks just hours after the fatal crash. Of the tens of thousands of people around the world who mourned for "the people's princess," known for her active involvement in charities and her campaign against land mines, many did so online.

Much of the outpouring was in newsgroups, such as alt.talk.royalty. Others expressed their grief by setting up unofficial tribute pages within hours. Furious at the celebrity photographers who were chasing Princess Diana on motorcycles at the time, many posted protest banners or created Web sites denouncing the media and urging people to boycott tabloid newspapers.

Yahoo!'s Diana Index (www.yahoo.co.uk/headlines/news/diana.html) offers an extensive array of links to news stories and multimedia clips. Video clips of her wedding to Prince Charles, her funeral, and her candid 1995 BBC interview; sound clips of Elton John singing "Candle in the Wind" in her honor and Queen Elizabeth's statement; the official Web sites for the British Monarchy, the Memorial Fund and Princess Diana's will; and some unofficial tribute pages are included.

Mourners can even make an online contribution to her official Memorial Fund.

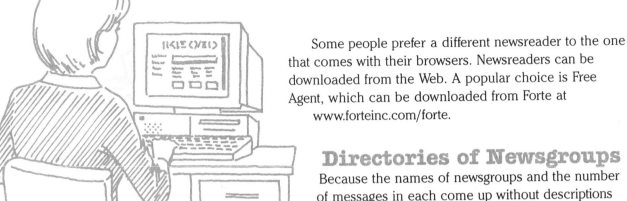

Some people prefer a different newsreader to the one that comes with their browsers. Newsreaders can be downloaded from the Web. A popular choice is Free Agent, which can be downloaded from Forte at www.forteinc.com/forte.

Directories of Newsgroups

Because the names of newsgroups and the number of messages in each come up without descriptions in newsreaders, many people use the very helpful newsgroup directories on the Web, which are grouped by category for easy reference and include links to enter the newsgroups. For example, Liszt (www.liszt.com/news) groups newsgroups by their hierarchies—rec, soc, biz, and so on—with many subcategories and descriptions. Liszt also shows which newsgroups have FAQs, with links to the questions. Deja News (www.dejanews.com), Reference.com (www.reference.com), and Cyber Fiber (www.cyber-fiber.com) use categories like "health/medicine," "business/money," "kids & parents" and "fan clubs and celebrities" and/or hierarchies. You can also do a search for newsgroups by typing a keyword in a box in all these directories.

How to Read and Answer Messages

After you click on a newsgroup, its list of short topic headlines will come up. Click on a headline to read the messages, which are called postings. You'll often see clusters of responses to the same headline grouped in what are called threads. For example, messages with the header "re:Spielberg" in a movie newsgroup are threads.

You'll notice the number of unread postings in each headline because your browser keeps track of which postings you have already read to save time. You'll also note the name of the writer and date of each posting.

For example, here's what the newsgroup on travel to Europe (rec.travel.europe) can look like:

rec.travel.europe	Total messages: 1000	Unread messages: 999
Subject	**Sender**	**Date**
Italy, Rome - Hotel Elite	Susan Strom	Fri. 23:58
Rome in October	James Lang	Fri. 23:50
Re: Florence	RBragman	Fri. 22:30
Re: Florence	John Finnegan	Fri. 22:22
Re: Florence	SKreer	Fri. 22:10
Best way to cross Alps?	LLKeane	Fri. 22:03
Re: Best way to cross Alps?	Nigel Smythe	Fri. 21:48
Renault Eurodrive in Frankfurt	Carol Davis	Thu. 21:05
Italy - our 18 day trip	RSantora	Thu. 21:01
Normandy-Brittany car route	Mark Callan	Thu. 20:30
Hiking in Ireland	Sam Elkins	Thu. 19:45
Re: Hiking in Ireland	Lisa Bain	Thu. 19:38
Re: Hiking in Ireland	BBGorman	Thu. 19:20
Police in Northern Ireland	Frank Peters	Wed. 22:15
Cheap hotels near underground station: London	CKent	Wed. 22:04
Best Hotel in Paris????	Mary Gallo	Wed. 21:47
Comments to my tourist guide to Lyons, France	LLurie	Wed. 20:02
Wanted: Swiss Bicycle Rental	David Hastings	Wed. 19:56
Re: Poland in May	Tom Jameson	Tue. 23:21
Looking for Paris apartment	FGNYC3	Tue. 22:13

If you want to read a particular message, click on it. You'll see something like this:

```
rec.travel.europe
Subject:  Best way to cross Alps?
Date:  Fri, 16 May 1998 22:03
From:  llkeane@hotmail.com
Newsgroups: rec.travel.Europe
I'm looking for a good, scenic train
route from Switzerland (Lucerne area) to
Italy this summer. Can anyone recommend one?
Thank you,
Larry L. Keane
```

It's a good idea to hang around a newsgroup for a while and just read its messages—called lurking—to get the flavor of the group and the topics discussed. Because many newsgroups have FAQs, it's also good to consult this before firing off a question about a topic which has already been discussed at great length.

When you decide you're ready to post a message in response to a message—or start a brand new topic and header—you can post it to the newsgroup at large, or you can send a private e-mail message to one person if your message refers only to them. You can print, delete, sort, and store messages, as well. Example: Reading and Answering Messages in rec.travel.europe:

Here's how Laura read and answered messages in the newsgroup rec.travel.europe mentioned earlier.

Laura clicks on the message "Italy, Rome—Hotel Elite" to read it. This was a hotel she and her husband found by accident a few years ago, and really enjoyed. She savors a bit of nostalgia at the memories. It sounds like nothing has changed, except the price. The poster of the message liked it, too, and recommends it to the newsgroup at large.

Laura then clicks on the "re: Florence" thread, reading each message. Uh-oh, a "flame war" is going on here: RBragman and John Finnegan are arguing strenuously about the merits of Florence versus Venice as Italy's most beautiful city, and are getting pretty insulting. John, passionately pro-Venice, says RBragman's opinions cannot be relied upon. He is still bitter about a hotel in Florence RBragman steered him to a few months ago, where he endured bad service and a noisy room facing the street where motorcycles kept him up all night. SKreer sides with RBragman, claiming Venice is crumbling, the canals are polluted, and "flames" John, making fun of John's past postings. Personally, Laura is on John's side, but wisely decides not to get involved.

Ah, here is some good, solid advice. In the "best way to cross Alps?" thread, Nigel recommends two magnificent train rides through Switzerland: the Zurich-Como route, and the "Glacier Express" from Zermatt to Chur. Laura sends him a private e-mail message, asking for recommendations of some choice small towns to spend the night in along the way. Laura also decides to print his response on the train rides to add to her collection of travel articles.

She can't resist another message about Italy, and scans "Italy - our 18 day trip" to see if she learns anything new. She does: the poster discusses high points of his visit to scenic towns in the Amalfi Drive area in great detail, in diary form. Laura opts to return to his posting later, when she has more time.

Briefly, however, she curiously scans the "hiking in Ireland" thread. She has never been to Ireland, although some friends absolutely raved about the countryside, and relatives have often invited her to stay with them. The posters are busy comparing favorite hiking routes and experiences meeting people in Galway in the western part of the country. Laura replies to the entire newsgroup, asking questions about what the Galway town where her relatives live is like, and what the weather is like in August.

Laura checks her e-mail. That was fast: Nigel already responded to her question about Swiss towns. She prints this message as well. It's getting late; time to go. Regretfully, Laura marks the messages she has read. She files others, in which she has no interest due to the headlines, in her trash folder to delete them. She stores the sheet of paper with Nigel's train ride messages in the travel folder in her desk.

Reading Newsgroups with Netscape Communicator 4.0

[1] Click the newsgroup icon (balloons with messages inside) to launch Collabra.

[2] Click the subscribe icon.

[3] Click "search for a group," then click the "search for" box and type a keyword to hunt for the newsgroups you want (for example, food) when you don't know their exact names.

[4] Click "search now."

[5] The list of newsgroups which include the keyword or are related to the keyword will appear in the big box, but with no descriptions. To subscribe to newsgroups, click the dots next to their names in the subscribe column, which turn into a checkmark, then click "OK."

[6] To subscribe to newsgroups when you know their exact names, click the newsgroup icon, then the subscribe icon. The alphabetical list of newsgroups and folders of related newsgroups will appear in the big box, but with no descriptions. To see the newsgroups within a folder, click the plus sign next to the folder. To subscribe, click the dots next to the newsgroup names in the subscribe column, then click "OK."

[7] To read messages in your subscribed newsgroups, click the plus sign next to your newsgroup server, which most likely starts with "news" and is listed in the Netscape Message Center window. The list of subscribed news-groups will appear, as well as the total number of mes-sages and unread messages in each newsgroup. If you are not already in Collabra, click the newsgroup icon to launch it.

[8] Double-click the newsgroup you want. The list of message headlines, senders, and posting dates will appear in the big box. The name of the newsgroup—for example, rec.food.cooking—will appear in the small box at the top, with the total number of messages and unread messages next to it. (The list will look like our list on p. 155.)

9 Click a specific message to read it. The message, headline, sender and date will appear in the big box.

10 To read other messages, click on a message in the small
   list of headlines, which includes the headline for the message you are reading, in the box above the message you
   are reading. To read other messages on the bigger message list, move along the list by clicking the down arrow
   or up arrow at the right of this box.

11 To show that you have already read certain messages,
   click a message you have read in the message list. Click
   the mark icon, then "read." To show you
   have read all messages before a certain date,
   click the mark icon, then "by date." This helps
   you keep track and saves time, because now you don't
   have to click each individual message; they will automatically be marked as read. Change the date in the box
   which appears if you want, then click "OK."

12 Unread messages in the message list now appear in boldfaced type, with a red tack next to each. Messages you
   have read, or marked as read by date, are in plain type.

13 To delete a message, click the message in the message
   list while the message is on the screen, then click the file
   icon. Click the trash folder.

14 To save a message on your computer, click the message
   in the message list while the message is on the screen,
   then click the folder where you want it stored. You may
   already have created personalized folders in the Netscape
   Message Center, such as "travel info" and "potential
   clients."

15 To sort messages in the message list by subject, sender or
   date so you can keep track easily, click "subject," "sender"
   or "date" below the newsgroup name in the small box.

16 To organize messages in the message list by thread, click
   the thread icon, next to the "subject," "sender" and "date"
   line under the small box showing the newsgroup name.
   Then, click a message you want grouped with others
   replying to it. Click the message icon, then click "watch

thread." A symbol will now appear next to messages in the same thread.

17. To unsubscribe from newsgroups, click the newsgroup name in your list of subscribed newsgroups. Press your "delete" key, then "OK" when the box appears asking if you want to unsubscribe from that specific newsgroup.

Posting Newsgroup Messages with Netscape Communicator 4.0

1. To reply to a message, click the reply icon. Decide if you want to reply to the entire newsgroup, send a private e-mail to the sender only, reply to the sender and all recipients of the message, or reply to the sender and the entire newsgroup. Then, click the reply choice you want.

2. Type your message. There is no need to type the recipient's e-mail address, name or message headline; this is automatically included, as well as the original message you are replying to.

3. Click the send icon.

4. To start a new message, click the new message icon. You need to be in a specific newsgroup with its messages displayed to send your message to that newsgroup.

5. Type your message. Also type a headline for your message. There is no need to type the newsgroup name; this is automatically included.

6. Click the send icon to send it to the entire newsgroup.

7. To forward a message to another person, click the message, then click the forward icon. Type the person's e-mail address in the small box, and type any e-mail message in the big box below it. Then, click the send icon.

8. To print a message, click the message, then click the print icon. Then, click "OK." If you want more than one copy, change the "number of copies" box.

What Are Bulletin Boards?

Bulletin boards, also known as message boards or forums, are discussion groups for reading and posting messages on specific topics very similar to newsgroups. However, they are found on certain Web sites, commercial online services such as America Online or Compuserve, and bulletin board systems, networks of connected computers which predated the Web. Although anyone can post a message on a Web site bulletin board, sites generally ask users to register first with their full names, e-mail and home addresses, jobs and interests because they hope to build steady audiences who will return and foster a sense of community. Some Web sites give users a trial run of their bulletin boards. On commercial online services, however, only paid subscribers can use the bulletin boards.

Bulletin boards are as varied as newsgroups. At iVillage (www.ivillage.com), a community site for women, bulletin board topics in the Career Channel include managing the tug of career and children, working and pregnancy, dealing with difficult people, the freelance life, job seekers, and sessions with career change, workplace and management experts. Its parenting channel, Parent Soup, discussed earlier in this book, and its fitness, food, money and other channels feature many bulletin boards.

A personal finance news and community site, The Motley Fool (www.fool.com), features serious bulletin boards—despite its silly name—which discuss retirement investing, women and investing, credit cards, international investing, and specific public companies.

At Idea Cafe (www.ideacafe.com), a small business owners' site, bulletin boards in its CyberSchmooze section range from working solo, starting a business, running a business to looking for financing. In its Coffee Talk with Experts section, guest experts answer certain questions posed in the board postings.

In the Mining Company's health/medicine area, bulletin boards topics include mental health issues,

such as abuse/incest support and panic/anxiety disorders; alternative medicine, such as herbs and healing; diseases, such as alcoholism, arthritis and heart disease; and nutrition, such as stopping smoking and nutrition. Its hundreds of other interest groups created by volunteer guides, including the Southern Cooking area discussed earlier, all have their own boards.

Among commercial online services, Compuserve is renowned for its thoughtful, informative "forums," which maintains libraries packed with reference materials, articles and photographs. In its Working From Home forum, work-at-home experts and authors Paul and Sarah Edwards lead study groups on topics like teaming up with other businesses or partners. Its sections range from marketing a business, running a business, office organizing, telecommuting, working at home with children, office hardware and software, to accounting/tax/legal questions.

Compuserve's Music/Arts forum sections include jazz/big band, blues, classical music, opera, and learning/playing. Reviews of concerts and music CD's are posted almost daily in certain sections, and later stored in section libraries. Recording labels from PolyGram, Virgin to Warner Brothers have sections to promote their latest releases in the Jazz Beat forum, which has sections on music festivals, collecting and musicians as well. News-related forums at Compuserve include forums for Time, Money and Fortune magazines, where readers can interact with their editors and writers, and CNN, where watchers can discuss world or national events. Its Journalism forum contains many sections for professionals with different specialties, including food/travel, investigative, business, science/medical and freelance writers, plus jobs/stringers, ethics, controversy, and a members-only area for an organization, the American Society of Journalists and Authors.

How to Search Newsgroups

You can search newsgroups in general, or a specific newsgroup, for a topic, writer, or posting date by using Liszt, Deja News, Reference.com, or Cyber Fiber—the easy-to-use newsgroup directories mentioned earlier—or search engines like Alta Vista, HotBot, and

Infoseek that search Usenet. Remember, these are public bulletin boards, so messages can be retrieved and collected.

Networking in Newsgroups and Mailing Lists: The Wrong Way

In 1994, two immigration lawyers in Arizona, Martha Siegel and Laurence Canter, decided to promote the United States green card lottery and their services in helping would-be citizens. Newsgroups were the ideal medium to communicate this message worldwide at a very low cost, they reasoned, and so they posted an ad to over 8,000 newsgroups in a few hours. Regardless of whether the topic was literature, politics, or computers, newsgroup readers were soon reading about Canter and Siegel.

The reaction the two lawyers received stunned them. Thousands of flames poured in, mail bombs—huge junk files intended to crash their computer system—hit their computers, their telephones rang off the hook with calls from outraged newsgroup users, and threats came in. They were denounced right and left on the Internet, where users regarded their ads as hideous spam. Some computer systems even crashed in different parts of the world due to the sudden volume of e-mail, and others experienced slowdowns.

The pair had been encouraged by their earlier success in posting messages in the alt.visa.us newsgroup and alt.culture newsgroups for many countries. But Usenet users, loud and clear, criticized them for what they called an unforgivable breach of Usenet etiquette: violating the noncommercial nature of these discussion groups.

Networking in Newsgroups and Mailing Lists: The Right Way

Diana Gabaldon, an Arizona author whose historical novel *Drums of Autumn* (Delacorte, 1997) zoomed to number one on the *Wall Street Journal*'s bestseller list and number two on the *New York Times*' hardcover fiction bestseller list in January 1997, credits on-line networking for much of her success. So does Nan McCarthy, a suburban Chicago author, whose three novels were published by Simon and Schuster's Pocket Books in the summer of 1998.

You've met, you've greeted, and now you're eager to talk to someone—REALLY chat, hearing a human voice, none of this typing malarkey.

You can, thanks to Internet telephony (pronounced tel-EFF-o-nee), a technology that makes telephone calls far cheaper than long-distance or international calls because they are routed over the Internet. Because companies who do telephony have so far eluded Federal government regulation, they've escaped the extra fees paid by long-distance telephone carriers.

It's an irresistible idea. But in an Alice-in-Wonderland twist, originally Internet telephony meant voice calls made from computer to computer without a telephone, but with a microphone and speakers. These calls were fairly poor in quality, however, with time delays before the other person spoke, and you would never mistake one for an ordinary telephone call.

But more and more, Internet telephony means telephone calls without an Internet connection—or even a computer—for either the caller or the recipient.

Some companies—like IDT, a New Jersey ISP, and Free World Dialup II—let users talk over regular telephones then route their calls, which have pretty good voice quality, over the Internet. In the case of Free World, the caller has to give the number being called to a gateway instead of dialing direct. But a special telephone invented by a French firm, the Aplio/Phone, calls you back, then allows unlimited use for the price of a one-minute telephone call.

Upstart Internet telephony companies are giving giant long-distance carriers a run for their money, who are now planning to route their calls over the Internet as well.

Gabaldon, a former scientist at Arizona State University and a technical writer, started writing her first novel, involving time travel to the eighteenth century Scottish Highlands and colonial America, when her children were small. A habitue of Compuserve since 1986, she once posted a passage from the book, *Outlander*, in a writer's forum about—of all things—what pregnancy feels like in answer to a discussion. Members liked it, and asked her to post more.

Through people met online, she was referred to a literary agent, who promptly won her a three-book deal from Bantam Doubleday Dell's Delacorte imprint. Gabaldon posted book excerpts in several Compuserve writer's forums. Eventually, as the buzz grew, one fan at the California Institute of Technology created a Web site for her series, which features titles to come, author appearances, a FAQ for plot and characters in the seven-hundred-page novels, even a map of Scottish clans. Another fan on America Online set up a reading group with weekly chats.

McCarthy, also a technical writer and avid Compuserve writer forum member, wrote *Chat*—a romance between a woman book editor and a male ad copywriter, which consists entirely of their e-mail exchanges—and self-published it, selling the book from her Web site, Rainwater Press (www.rainwater.com). Later, Peachpit Press, a computer book publisher, bought the rights. After she e-mailed a funny letter she wrote to Dave Barry, the syndicated columnist—a writer's complaint on never finding her book in bookstores—to a pal met online, the pal thoughtfully sent it to two humor mailing lists, HumourNet and Oracle, each of which has thousands of subscribers.

To her shock, she noted over fifty book orders the first day after her letter appeared, "more in one day than I've gotten from any publicity, including the *Wall Street Journal*," she recalls. A story on her Web site ran in *Publishers Weekly*, a trade journal, which led to the WSJ story. That spurred a story in *People*, which prompted a literary agent to contact her. The agent sold the rights to publish three paperbacks—*Connect*, *Crash*, and *Chat*—to Simon and Schuster's Pocket Books in late 1997.

On-line Magazines

Crave more news besides what you read in newsgroups? Many online magazines, or zines, offer a rich selection of articles on culture, politics, travel, books and arts reviews, essays, and news commentary. Some boast a heavier dose of attitude than others, while some are more intellectual, and others more popular culture-oriented. There is a great variety, and you'll recognize some bylines by well-known figures in the arts.

Here are a few. All are free unless specified otherwise.

Feed (www.feedmag.com) has articles on culture, politics, and technology, with an intellectual, often offbeat slant, and a strong dose of attitude. Discussion forums on stories, while a panel of four well-known people with diverse viewpoints debate issues. Free.

gURL (www.gurl.com) features articles for teenage girls that mince no words but have a dash of humor about topics including sex, friends, bodies, and feelings.

HotWired (www.hotwired.com) includes hip articles and columns about digital technology and culture; the online version of *Wired* magazine.

The Netly News (www.netlynews.com) has daily articles on technology trends and culture, on Time Warner's Pathfinder site.

Salon (www.salonmagazine.com) features fiction, as well as articles on arts, books, travel, politics, society, and arts reviews with a highbrow bent. The "Media Circus" column offers analysis and criticism of the news media.

Slate (www.slate.com) covers more Washington politics than other online publications, plus has articles on news and culture. Think of the *New Republic*, which Slate editor Michael Kinsley once edited. "Today's Papers" column compares front page stories in the nation's leading daily newspapers. The on-again, off-again subscription charge is now $19.95 annually.

Suck (www.suck.com) features daily, irreverent, super-cool rant with attitude to spare from anonymous writers.

Women's Wire (www.women.com) has articles on work, money, style, entertainment, and relationships for women; many profiles and how-to articles.

What Is Chat?

Chat takes a little getting used to, once you realize that chatting consists of typing messages back and forth in utter silence to people

After the first mention in the news of an alleged affair between President Clinton and a young White House intern—on the Drudge Report Web site in early 1998—the story flew into countless print, television, and radio outlets. Soon, it was the talk of the nation. But it was also absolute proof that a rumor, true or not, published on the Internet could be spread instantly, without waiting for a daily or weekly deadline, and had the power to influence mainstream news.

Here is a short timeline of the first week: January 17 (late at night): Drudge Report Web site runs an item about *Newsweek* refusing to print a story about the President's alleged affair with a White House intern.

January 18: The first newsgroup posting runs in alt.current-events.clinton.whitewater. In later weeks, hundreds follow in this and other newsgroups, like alt.politics.clinton.

January 20: The *Washington Post*, ABC News, and the Associated Press, a wire service, run stories about the alleged affair.

January 21: *Newsweek* runs the story its editors killed, which was scooped by the Drudge Report, on America Online.

January 22: *Time* runs a story on Time Warner's massive Pathfinder Web site, which turns into an ongoing feature.

January 25: Matthew Drudge appears on the television program "Meet the Press," with established journalists from the *New York Times* and the *Newsweek* reporter who wrote the original story about the alleged relationship.

January 26: *Dallas Morning News* runs a story on its Web site about a Secret Service agent's claims. It is later retracted.

The story is now everywhere in print, television, and radio. On-line news outlets like CNN Interactive are showing daily updates and photographs, and every imaginable tangent to the claimed story is front page news.

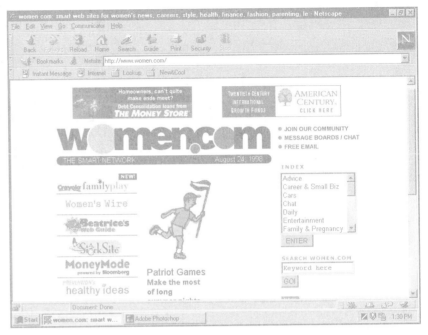

Women's Wire www.women.com

you can't see and often don't know. Chat is a way of meeting people on-line and talking to them in real time, faster than e-mail or newsgroups.

It can look a bit, well, chaotic. As you watch messages rapidly appear, almost by magic, in a box on your screen from a dizzying number of screen names, you'll have to scramble at first to keep track of who said what. In style and pace, live chat is different from the more organized world of newsgroups and bulletin boards, where you can read and answer messages at your leisure, often days after the original posting.

This often means people in newsgroups and bulletin boards, many of which have FAQs to create order, tend to think more before they type. The immediate nature of chat often means people blurt out the first thing that comes to mind.

But chat is very popular all over the world. Places to chat, called chat rooms—the room is virtual, as is everything else online—can be found on commercial online services, on Web sites ranging from some search engines to communities of common interests, and in

Internet Relay Chat (more about this soon). Chat rooms can be general or focused around one topic. Chats can be ongoing or scheduled at certain times featuring celebrities such as actors, television talk show hosts like Oprah Winfrey, authors like Robin Cook or Tom Clancy, or professional experts such as lawyers, psychologists, or business executives.

Chats can be held in a group or with one person—sometimes a person you meet invites you for a one-to-one chat; you can also arrange a private chat with a friend in a chat room you open just for the two of you. Chats can be with or without moderators, who lead the discussion and call on people who have questions or comments (it can remind you of school). On America Online, chat is found at "People Connection," as well as at individual areas centered on a topic, such as Entertainment Asylum, books, or the fitness area. Compuserve, always more formal about things, calls chats "conferences" in its various forums. Community sites, such as the Mining Company, Tripod, GeoCities, Parent Soup, Talk City, and the globe.com have chats for many different special interest areas.

At Talk City (www.talkcity.com), for example, which holds nightly chats with celebrities, chats and bulletin boards for interests ranging from business, family, spirituality, autos, entertainment to teens are offered. At theglobe.com (www.theglobe.com), users can instantly read short profiles prepared by members they meet in chat rooms, and view their home pages on its site, where interest areas include romance, life and infobahn (computers and the Internet). Its chatters can represent themselves by icons to assert their individuality.

Some companies, interestingly enough, are finding that chat need not just be casual banter. Chat is being used for customer service and technical support by companies like 1-800-Flowers, Mail Boxes Etc., and AT&T Worldnet, and by many universities, such as Yale and Cornell, for professor-student interaction.

A moderated chat featuring an expert, where users type symbols like "?" and "!" into the box on their screen and wait to be called on, can look like this:

```
Small Business Expert: It's a good idea
to set aside one day a week, or part of
each day, to market your services to
find new clients.
marysmith: ?
robert9: !
timsloan: ?
Moderator: Yes, marysmith? marysmith:
But how can you do this if you're so
busy working on your current project?
larryt: !
johnNY: !
susans: ?
Small Business Expert: Yes, it's diffi-
cult. But it's important to make time,
and avoid the "feast or famine" syndrome
many self-employed people face.
marlenec: !
Moderator: Yes, robert9?
robert9: I've found picking the same day
each week, or the same time every day,
helps. If I'm swamped, I promise myself
I'll do it tomorrow, no matter what.
marysmith: !
johnNY: What I do is...
Moderator: JohnNY, it's not your turn.
Yes, timsloan?
timsloan: My question was answered
already.
Moderator: Yes, larryt?
larryt: Uh, I forgot my question. Sorry.
```

Because you never know when you will be called on in a moderated chat, it's best to type your message in the box, then click "send." This way, you won't have to wait ten minutes twiddling your

In an interesting twist, new media is turning into old media as a variety of Web sites produce books based upon their content to reach a bigger audience.

"You can't just be online forever—you have a real life, too. It's important for online companies to realize people still read books and use traditional media," says Richard Turcott, a product manager for the search engine Lycos' publishing imprint, Lycos Press, which has teamed up to publish several books with Macmillan Computer Publishing.

These books, published mostly in 1997 and 1998, include:

The Motley Fool Investment Guide, by David and Tom Gardner
The Motley Fool Investment Workbook, by David and Tom Gardner
The Parent Soup Baby Name Finder
The Parent Soup A to Z Guide to Your New Baby
Cybergrrl! A Woman's Guide to the World Wide Web, by Aliza Sherman

Most Popular Web Sites: Best of the Net From A 2 Z, by Lycos Press
The Internet Games Directory, by Lycos Press
Tripod: The Book
The Best of nerve (erotic essays, fiction and photographs)

In at least one case, a Web site creator has landed his own television program.

Matthew Drudge, whose online gossip newsletter, the Drudge Report (www.drudgereport.com), has broken news about politics and entertainment—including allegations of President Clinton's affair with a White House intern—became the host of a talk show on cable television this year. The weekend show on the Fox News Channel, called simply "Drudge," features the Los Angeles scandal-seeker hosting a panel of gossip columnists and political pundits. His Web site, whose gossip items are also available by e-mail newsletter, includes many links to print, television, radio, and wire service outlets, plus specific gossip and opinion columnists.

thumbs, then be forced to gather your thoughts and type while everyone waits with bated breath for your question.

Many people think general chat rooms are filled with young people—often teen-agers or college students—with lots of time on their hands and rather aimless, silly, or X-rated talk because there is no common theme. Themed chats, community sites' special interest group chats, or the more structured newsgroups or bulletin boards offer more substantive discussion among adults. Of course, chat or newsgroups depend wholly on the stimulating qualities of the people who take part in them, unlike other Internet resources.

Internet Relay Chat, or IRC, is a medium where people choose among thousands of channels, or different topics, worldwide and chat with special software. Popular software includes mIRC for PCs, and Ircle for Macintoshes. Both can be downloaded free from the TUCOWS (www.tucows.com) Web site.

You need an IRC server, and many ISPs and commercial online services have them. If not, find the closest IRC to you through one of the biggest networks of IRC servers, such as EFnet (www.irchelp.org), Undernet (www.undernet.org) or DALnet (www.dal.net). Detailed information on using IRC, including lists of channels that you can search by topic—which show the names of chat rooms and numbers of chatters—and locations of servers can be found at their Web sites.

For example, searching EFnet for "books," only one came up —"#comicbooks"—and under "arts," only "#kungfu"—a martial arts chat room—appeared. (All IRC channels start with the symbol "#".) When you contact an IRC server, list the screen name you want to use for chats, and omit your full name and e-mail address if you want to remain anonymous. Many people do so for good reasons—to protect themselves from strangers in a no-man's land with no common theme—or bad—to pose as someone of a different age, occupation, or sex.

Once you connect to the server, a list of channels will appear in a window on your screen. Click on one you want and people's screen names will appear along the side. All chat networks have channels for newcomers called "#newbies" or something similar. General chat rooms are called "#chat," "#friendly," or something similar.

1. Go to Deja News' Web site, and click "browse groups" to see the hierarchies (rec, soc, alt, etc.).

2. Click the hierarchy you want. The list of newsgroups in that hierarchy will appear. Click the folder icon in the "browse" column to see the list of newsgroups in certain hierarchy subcategories (for example, rec.travel has several subcategories). Then, click "read" so the postings in the newsgroup you want will appear. If there is no folder icon, click "read" so the postings in the newsgroup listed will appear.

3. Click on the posting in the message list you want to read.

4. To move around to previous or later messages on the list, click "previous" or "next." Click on other choices to post a reply to the entire newsgroup, e-mail a private reply, view a thread, forward the message to another person, or mark a message as read. To read other postings the writer has made in this and other newsgroups, click "author profile."

5. If you don't know what hierarchy a newsgroup belongs to, instead of clicking "browse groups" in the beginning, you can click "interest finder," then type a keyword to find the newsgroups you want.

6. To read postings in a variety of newsgroups quickly, click a category channel on Deja News' home page. You will then see a couple of topics currently being discussed in newsgroups for that issue. Click a topic headline to read the postings.

7. To personalize Deja News by subscribing to newsgroups, which will appear on your own special page when you return, click "My Deja News" on its home page. Register by typing your name, e-mail address, and job on the online form. Choose one or more interests (for example, fashion or travel) listed to subscribe to these newsgroups. To change the newsgroups when their names appear, click "add/remove forums."

8. When you click on a subscribed newsgroup, its list of postings appears. Click "read," "post" or "unsubscribe," as you wish.

9. New newsgroups can be formed at Deja News by individuals, families, groups or businesses in a few minutes, if they already have a Web page of their own. Click "create new forum" to receive a URL link to this existing Web page, where the discussions will take place.

Games on the Internet

From shoot-'em-up action games to more sedate games like board games, card games, trivia, and even old standbys like television game shows such as Jeopardy!, you can have fun playing alone or with other players at countless Web sites. Many games are free, but some sites with fancier action/adventure games with multiple players charge a fee.

Game sites vary widely. At big gaming networks such as MPlayer and Kali, where many different types of games can be played, from action and combat simulation to board games, you need special software, which can be downloaded free from their Web sites. Many CD-ROM games let you connect with other players, either friends or strangers who also have the CD-ROM's, to play the games over the Internet. Some CD-ROM games even include gaming network's connection software. Their manuals include instructions on how to play with other players, which means connecting to their computers' IP (Internet Protocol) numbers. Some games, however, are online-only.

Internet games generally require fast, powerful computers with a lot of memory. Read the game's or gaming network's system requirements before you register at a site. Also read their fee structure carefully. Some game sites are entirely free; others charge a one-time fee, some a monthly fee, others a fee for premium features only. Some offer a specified number of hours of free play. At some game sites which rank players, they will find you other players at your skill level.

Some of the Most Popular Game Sites Are:

MPlayer

The variety of game categories ranges from combat simulation, such as Air Warrior; action games such as Quake, Red Alert, and games on international terrorism and corporate raiding from Tom Clancy's company, Red Storm Entertainment; classic board and card games such as Risk, Scrabble, poker, checkers and backgammon; and role-playing games such as Diablo, Underlight and Battlespire. Each category has links to newsgroups, bulletin boards, articles, demos and areas where players can download the games.

MPlayer's multi-player gaming network, which has about one million members, is free, although its premium service costs $30 per year, and lets players play games before they debut on the rest of its network.

Kali

Named after the Hindu goddess of death, Kali's home page sets the tone with a tongue-in-cheek Surgeon General's warning that its games are "highly addictive" and may cause loss of sleep. Offering action favorites such as Duke Nukem 3D, Doom, Star Craft, Quake and Red Alert, role-playing games such as Diablo, strategy, racing, combat simulation, pool and chess games, Kali can be searched by category or alphabetical game list. Bulletin boards, chat rooms and demos for most games are also included.

Charging a lifetime fee of $20, which includes free upgrades and one month's technical support by e-mail, this multi-player gaming network lets its over 200,000 players play in "ladders" or "leagues." Ladders are independent systems where individual players compete and are ranked against each other. Users can play in more than one ladder—the biggest, Case's Ladder, has over 70,000 players. In leagues, however, clans compete against other clans, and players can only belong to one league.

The Arena

Trivia, kids' games, and sports join action, combat simulation, strategy, role-playing, board and card games at Arena. Because Arena's multi-player network consists of several different gaming services, such as GameStorm and Bonus.com—some free, others with $10–$20 per month fees or a flat fee—players need to register with each service. Chat rooms are offered as well.

Players can download games, or buy a CD-ROM instead.

Microsoft Internet Gaming Zone

Particularly strong with board, card and word games from bridge, chess, checkers, and hearts to Monopoly and Scrabble, this multi-player network is the Web version of Microsoft Network's Internet Gaming Zone. Action, strategy, sports and combat simulation games from Jedi Knight: Dark Forces II for Star Wars fans to Microsoft's own Golf and Monster Truck Madness are included.

Happy Puppy

This site is a comprehensive resource where fans of computer and console games, including Nintendo 64 and Sega Saturn, can find demos, shareware, freeware and game tips, and meet each other in bulletin boards and chat rooms. Web games which need no downloads are also available. Game reviews and news are found at Pawpit Press; a weekly e-mail newsletter sends reviews from users and staff before they appear on the site.

Here are some of the hottest games in different categories:

Role-playing: Diablo

In this eerie Gothic fantasy world, choose the part you want to play—a warrior, sorcerer, or rogue. Then, pick up your sword to battle ferocious demons to the death with other members of your loyal team.

Trivia: You Don't Know Jack

This sassy trivia game, heavy on popular culture, uses a television game show format with an insulting host who delights in wrong answers. It's the free Web version of the popular CD-ROM. Although not a multi-player game, high-scoring players compete for prizes.

Combat simulation: Air Warrior

You can pretend to be the pilot of a World War I or II or Korean fighter plane or bomber, and get into dogfights to shoot down enemy pilots.

Action: Red Alert

Forget the Cold War is over: military fans can battle the Soviet Army, building tanks and other artillery, and play against one or more players.

Quake II

Humans war with aliens on a distant planet in this dark, futuristic world with spectacular special effects. The goal is to destroy the aliens' defense system, then battle the monsters one-on-one with machine guns, laser-splitting blasters, grenades and other weapons. A sequel to Quake, it is regarded as more realistic and gory than its predecessor.

It's easy for rumors to spread like wildfire on the Internet. If the rumor is about a company, it may damage its reputation, relationship with customers, or even its stock share price. As a result, some big companies are paying special firms to track what is being said about them in newsgroups, mailing lists, bulletin boards, and Web sites.

A false rumor accused Mrs. Field's Cookies of supplying free cookies to O.J. Simpson's victory party after his acquittal for double murder in 1995. The report aired on the TV program *Hard Copy* on a Thursday. Within eight minutes, a posting in the newsgroup alt.fan.ojsimpson urged people to boycott Mrs. Field's Cookies. CNN then picked up the rumor, which was retracted by *Hard Copy* the next night. Unfortunately, postings were already appearing in newsgroups from alt.cooking to other O.J. Simpson newsgroups to misc.investing, which discussed short-selling stock of companies which showed support for the former football star in any way. The rumor, supposedly based on a letter from a partygoer, also ran on anti-O.J. Web sites which urged boycotts of such companies.

Mrs. Field's Cookies posted an official response denying the rumors in the affected newsgroups on the following Monday. A flurry of supportive e-mails resulted, one of which read, "Thanks for whomping the rumors. It's nice when someone takes notice of us out here in cyberspace once in a while." Afterward, the company noted a single-digit drop in nationwide sales during those few days when the gossip was circulating on TV and the Internet.

"You can publish everything you want on the Internet, and there is no recourse. There are no editors in cyberspace," says James Alexander, president of eWatch Inc., the White Plains, New York firm Mrs. Field's Cookies used to track the Internet rumors.

Though the Internet at first seems to be a public relations dream for companies—due to the ease, speed and lack of paper and mailing costs in communicating information—it can quickly turn into a nightmare if a disgruntled customer, employee or dishonest person is involved. The inspiration for starting eWatch, Alexander said, was a math professor at Lynchburg College in Virginia, who found a flaw in Intel's microprocessor chip in 1994, and contacted Intel. Unhappy because Intel did not take his complaint seriously, the professor, Thomas Nicely, posted his finding in a newsgroup. Three weeks later, the *Wall Street Journal* ran a front-page story on the flaw, and the company took a $475 million loss later that year due to the problem.

"It's vitally important for companies to be aware of what the public, competitors, government, activists and others say about them," says Alexander, whose firm operates as an electronic clipping service.

In 1996, a false rumor on an AOL finance bulletin board that Syquest, a software maker, was removed from the NASDAQ list of high-tech stocks turned into a Reuters wire service story when the reporter failed to check facts. In 11 hours, the firm's stock plunged 32%.

Board games: ChessMaster

Turn your screen into a chess board, and feel like Garry Kasparov head-to-head with IBM's Deep Blue playing the game of kings against players who match your rank. Afterward, the software can analyze your strategy so you can do better next time.

Riddles: The Riddler

Not only riddles, but crossword puzzles, word and trivia games are found here. Players can compete for prizes.

Sports: Virtual Pool

Developed by a team of physicists aided by pool players, Virtual Pool claims novice players can learn, and even skilled players can improve their techniques, through this 3-D game.

Mysteries: TheCase.com

Short mysteries are presented here weekly, so players can read the clues and figure out who killed whom. A children's section offers magic trick how-to's, mysteries to solve, and scary stories. The MysteryNet section has biographies of famous mystery characters and authors, from Agatha Christie and Dashiell Hammett to Sherlock Holmes and The Saint, and articles on mystery genres and the history of mystery stories.

Game sites can be found at:

The Arena
(www.earthlink.com/thearena)

TheCase.com
(www.thecase.com)

Chess Master
(www.chessmaster.com)

Chess.net
(www.chess.net)

Engage Games Online
(www.engagegames.com)

Game Center
(www.gamecenter.com)

Games Domain
(www.gamesdomain.co.uk)

Gamesmania
(www.gamesmania.com)

Game Shows
(www.gameshows.com)

Gamespot
(www.gamespot.com)

Gamespot's Video Games
(www.nuke.com)

Happy Puppy
(www.happypuppy.com)

Jeopardy!
(www.station.sony.com/jeopardy)

Microsoft Internet Gaming Zone
(www.zone.com)

Mpath Interactive's MPlayer
(www.mplayer.com)

The Riddler
(www.riddler.com)

Total Entertainment Network
(www.ten.net)

Wheel of Fortune
(www.station.sony.com/wheel)

Yahoo! Games
(http://play.yahoo.com)

You Don't Know Jack
(www.bezerk.com/netshow

Creating Your Own Web Site Without Panicking

E nough surfing around other people's sites. You want your own to showcase your business, interests, and hobbies, and are eager to cast your net out into the sea—the Net, actually—and see what it brings back. But you are more than a little curious about cost and how hard it is. Some of those sites you've seen are pretty awesome.

A Web site can cost anywhere from nothing, a couple of hundred dollars—including domain name registration and hosting—or several million. It can be short, a page or two, or hundreds of pages, and it can be simple—text-only on a colored background—or elaborate, with images, animations, sound and video clips, toolbars, online payment capability, and many links within and outside the site. These factors influence the cost and complexity of building your site.

How to Design Your Own Page

If you have a basic knowledge of HTML and a graphic design background or flair, you may want to take the plunge and design it yourself with software tools you buy or download from the Web. If you

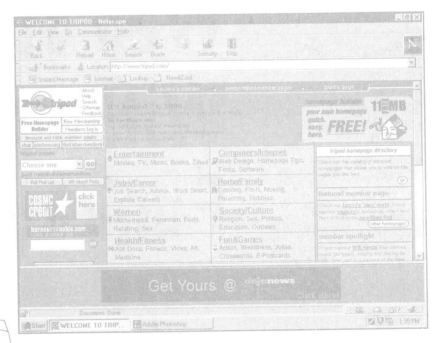

Tripod www.tripod.com

don't—and want this to be as simple and cheap as possible—take advantage of the free Web site creation services around. Let's look at these choices, starting with the free version.

For Free

Free home pages are available from some community-building sites on the Web, such as GeoCities, Tripod and theglobe.com, and from online services such as America Online and Compuserve and some ISPs. You'll be given free, easy-to-use tools and instructions to design your own Web site (without knowledge of HTML, if you choose), select images, background, and text colors, or upload those you already have from your hard drive. You can create and edit text, and create links within or outside your site. The community, online service or ISP will then publish your site, which will be hosted on its server, and your site's URL will include its domain name.

For example, GeoCities (www.geocities.com), the biggest such community on the Web, features over one million home pages in over forty neighborhoods centered around shared interests such as arts, family, sports, travel, and music. "Bourbon Street" is for fans of jazz, Cajun food, and Southern culture, while "Athens" is devoted to literature, writing, philosophy, and education. GeoCities will register your site, based on the keywords you select, within its community and in online directories of personal Web pages, which are segmented by geography and topic, so you can be found. GeoCities, a Santa Monica company, which has grown enormously since its launch in mid-1995, will throw in a free e-mail account to anyone who signs up for a home page.

Members, called homesteaders, must be willing to accept banner ads, which may promote an interest area or specific site in GeoCities or a sponsor. If they wish, they can have forum, search and e-mail functions on their sites. To encourage communication and cross-fertilization, descriptions and links to cool sites in GeoCities are featured daily. An exhibit of desert photos, classical piano solos, and a Cajun food site are among those that are offered.

Tripod (www.tripod.com), a community site geared mostly to people in their twenties and thirties, has over 800,000 members

Upload means to transfer files from your computer to another computer.

To take advantage of free Web site creation services, a Web-based e-mail account, and the chance to meet new people through chat or bulletin boards at theglobe.com, just click " " on its home page. Type your name, e-mail address and other information, and pick a user name for your new e-mail account.

That's it. You're a member now. Easiest group you ever joined, right? You will immediately get an e-mail welcoming you, which describes the features of your e-mail account. (You are able to send attached files, compile an address book, sort mail into folders, block unwanted mail from certain addresses, or send an automatic reply if you are on vacation.) The message suggests you log on to theglobe.com, where you are greeted by your user name (such as "beth95").

Over the next few days, you get a series of e-mails urging you to try out different features, which are described in detail and include links so you can immediately reach these parts of theglobe.com's site. You learn how to find chats by interest group, read more about members who are chatting and their home pages, find the most pop-

ular chats, read transcripts of celebrity chats with actors and comics, and how to "whisper"—or send a private message—to a chatter. To dress up the look of your chats, you learn you can use different font colors and sizes for your text.

If shopping interests you, you learn where to find merchants selling clothing, computer equipment, home and garden supplies, and toys and games (including The Disney Store, FAO Schwartz and Barnes & Noble) at its marketplace.

If you prefer the more thoughtful atmosphere of bulletin boards to chat, you are told there are many discussion groups grouped by interests you can join. You can post your own movie reviews, read music or movie reviews, place or respond to personal ads, send electronic greeting cards, or consult a romance advice expert. You can even read news headlines, to catch up on what's happening in the world outside theglobe.com. (Yes, some members of community sites may forget it exists.)

Members building their own sites have free access to over 250 multimedia files to add interactive and jazzy designs, plus a trial version of a simple Web authoring tool which requires no knowledge of HTML, Parable's ThingMaker.

in over thirty communities of interest (or pods) such as "Media" for movies, books, music, and television or "Funny Bone" for humor. Tripod members also get free e-mail accounts so they can pick up and send mail from its Web site.

At theglobe.com (www.theglobe.com), a community site with over one million members, about half under age thirty, there is a strong emphasis on meeting people through chat and bulletin boards. Interest groups, called cities, range from arts & entertainment, life, infobahn (Internet and computers) to romance, and members also get free Web-based e-mail accounts.

If you want to see what other people's home pages look like for inspiration, check out GeoCities, Tripod and theglobe.com. All offer additional storage space if you are planning a more elaborate Web site and other extra features, if you are willing to pay a small amount for Premium services.

To see what member home pages look like on some online services and ISP's, see Compuserve (http://ourworld.compuserve.com), Prodigy (http://pages.prodigy.com), and Mindspring (www.mindspring. com/dbase/index.html). Some make it very easy to look up member sites. At Compuserve, for example, where you can search by occupation, interests, full name, state, city or country, a search for "travel" turned up links to sites from members in Switzerland, Germany, Holland, New Zealand, the United Kingdom, France, Spain, Denmark and Canada, as well as states from Texas, Florida, Minnesota, Michigan, Florida, New York, Georgia, Hawaii to Oklahoma.

Some popular Web authoring tools come with your browser, like Netscape Communicator's Composer and Microsoft Explorer 4.0's FrontPage Express. Each shows you what your site looks like on the screen as you are composing. (This is called WYSIWYG, which stands for "what you see is what you get," and is a nice feature for an authoring tool to have).

Sample Web Site Design With Netscape Communicator's Composer

1. Click the Composer icon. A window appears, topped by a row of icons ranging from "images," "save," "boldface," "italicize" to "underline."

2 Type the words you want on your page inside the window, marked off by paragraphs.

3 Click "save" to keep the text you have typed. When the "save" box appears, type a file name, then click "save."

4 When the "page title" box appears, type a title for your Web page, then "OK." The title will appear at the top of the screen when people view your page, and should be listed in search engines so it can be found easily.

5 If you want certain text to have a different look, hold down your mouse and slide across this text. Then, click a "boldface," "italicize" or "underline" icon. If you change your mind, repeat these steps.

6 To add color to certain text, hold down your mouse and slide across this text. Click the "color" icon, a down arrow next to a black box, then click the color you want when the color chart appears.

7 To change the print font of certain text, hold down your mouse and slide across this text. Click the pull-down menu named "variable width," the click the font you want.

8 To change the size of certain text, hold down your mouse and slide across this text. Click the "size" icon, a down arrow next to a number, then click the font size you want.

9 To move or indent certain text, hold down your mouse and slide across this text. Click the "align" icon, which looks like a page of text, then click the "left," "center" or "right" icon to move text. Click the "indent" icon, which looks like a page of text with a right or left arrow, to index text to the right or left, respectively.

10 To see how your page looks so far and add changes, click "open," then click its file name when the window appears, then "open."

11 Click "save" to keep the page, then "preview" to admire how your page will look to others.

12 After you are done viewing your page, click "X" to close the window.

13 To add images to your page which you have stored on your computer, first click the area on your screen where you want the image to be. Then, click "image."

14. When the "image" box appears, click "choose file" to view your images. Click the file name of the image you want, then "open," then "OK."

15. To create a link to another Web page, hold your mouse down and slide across the word or phrase you want to connect to another Web page.

16. Click "link." When the "character" box appears, type the Internet address of the exact page you want linked, then "OK."

17. To create a link within the same Web page, click the area on your screen where the link will connect to. Click "target."

18. When the "target" box appears, type a name for the target, then press "enter."

19. Hold your mouse down and slide across the word or phrase you want to link to the target area, then click "link."

20. When the "character" box appears, click the target you want the word or phrase to connect to, then "OK."

21. To publish your Web page, click "save" to keep the final version of your page, then click "publish."

22. When the "publish" box appears, click the "HTTP or FTP Location to publish in" box, then type the location where your page will be stored on your Web server. Ask your ISP for the location.

23. Click the "user name" and "password" boxes, and type in your information.

24. Click "OK." When the "security" box appears, click "continue," then "OK."

Too many steps? The fast, easy way to design a Web page with Netscape Communicator's Composer is to use its already-designed templates or Page Wizard. Its templates are skeleton Web pages where you simply fill in the content, without bothering about design and layout decisions. There are special templates for individuals, companies and products. Its Page Wizard offers boxes where you type your choices for color, links, introduction and so on, skipping behind-the-scenes steps.

Nonprofit Web Sites With Strong Points of View

Nine proposed Web sites with strong points of view won a total of $150,000 in grants from the newly formed Web Development Fund in mid-1998.

The noncommercial Web sites include Adoption (a gathering place for those affected by adoption), After Suicide (a gathering place for survivors), PostWar Central America (political issues), Working Stiff (resources and viewpoints about workplace issues), and Teen Screen (teenagers on economic and cultural differences).

Funding for the Web Development Fund comes from the PBS Network, Ford Foundation, and other foundations.

Here is what to do:

1. Click "new."
2. To use a template, click "from template." Click "Netscape templates." Then, read about templates, then pick one from its list.
3. To use the Page Wizard, click "from Page Wizard." Then, read about what to do, then click "start."

Some makers of Web authoring tools offer free demos for a trial period from their Web sites.

You don't need to know HTML nowadays to design a site with databases, searches, animations, bulletin boards, toolbars and all kinds of advanced features. As interest in the Internet grows, Web authoring products are getting easier to use, offering more complex features, and cheaper. Different tools have their fans. Detailed descriptions and system requirements can be found on their makers' Web sites.

Here are some popular WYSIWYG editor Web authoring products, which need no knowledge of HTML. You pick the layouts and style elements you want from the choices they give you, and the coding is done in the background. While easy and quick to use, you give up total control of your site by using their systems.

Filemaker Home Page 3.0 (formerly Claris Home Page) www.filemaker.com

Very simple to use, producing a site within minutes for beginners, and very cheap (about $100). You can even include a searchable database on your site if you also have another product from the company, a subsidiary of Apple Computer, Filemaker Pro 4.0, installed.

NetObjects Fusion 3.0 www.netobjects.com

An artistically striking and carefully-crafted collection of design templates will make your site look like it was done by professional designers. More expensive (about $300), requires more effort, and more hard drive space than Filemaker, but quickly creates detailed layouts which would take hours of work elsewhere.

CREATING YOUR OWN WEB SITE

Elemental Software Drumbeat 1.01 www.elementalsoftware.com

More expensive than NetObjects Fusion and Filemaker (about $700). While a variety of design templates let you build a page, then vary it so other pages will match its look for consistency, you can't borrow Web pages from the Internet or use existing HTML files you may have on your computer.

Here are some popular code-based editor Web authoring products, which do need knowledge of HTML:

Allaire HomeSite 3.0 www.allaire.com

Easy to use, quick, very cheap (under $100) and regarded as one of the best code-based editors. Wizards help simplify site design by reducing the number of steps.

Luckman Interactive WebEdit Pro 3.0

Easy to use, very cheap (under $100) and helpful wizards, but with fewer features than HomeSite.

Sausage Software HotDog Pro 4.0 www.sausage.com

Lacks a variety of design templates for easy site building, and requires HTML skills to add all kinds of sophisticated features like Java and push technology channels (about $100).

Here are some hybrid Web authoring tools. These let you do most things in WYSIWYG, but allow you to see the HTML code and change it if you wish.

Microsoft Front Page Express 98 www.microsoft.com/frontpage

Easy to use, flexible—whether you prefer to use its themed design templates and 2,000 images or build an original site from scratch—cheap (about $150), and able to produce a stylish look, it is regarded as one of the best WYSIWYG editors. However, some features work only if you have Internet Explorer as your browser, not Netscape. You change from an editing window to a view of the HTML code to alter what you have created.

How I Designed My Own Web Site: Donna Dee

Donna Dee, thirty-eight, a computer industry manager and the mother of two children ages five and eleven, in Bremerton, Washington, is a Tripod member who enjoyed using its free page-building tools for her site (http://members.tripod.com/~DonnaDee).

"You can pick the format you want your page to look like. You're given a choice of layouts, then asked if you want to add links or pictures in different areas—just check the box," says Ms. Dee, a member of the Funny Bone humor pod, Writers Block and Poetry pods. "It even has a paint chip—there's a color chart, which makes it easy because you don't have to know the color code number. You can see what the colors look like right away without having to publish the site."

"It's something a novice can do without knowing HTML. Once you know HTML, you can edit your site without beginning from scratch," says Ms. Dee, who has added music and extra pages to her site since learning HTML. It began simply as a list of favorite links, from children's sites to resources for Web site graphics.

"I don't care for Web authoring kits. They're either extremely complicated—which defeats the purpose—or too simple and don't do what you want them to do."

"Tripod is a place where I go to play," says Ms. Dee, now a premium member, paying $36 a year for more disk space and a bigger selection of graphics and colors for her site. "There's always new content, and I've never felt out of place. There's even a 'toy box,' with games and all kinds of funny stuff."

SoftQuad HoTMetaL PRO 4.0 www.softquad.com

Needs more familiarity with HTML tags than Microsoft Front Page Express, but lets you build complex sites with helpful wizards in a choice of three ways and cheaply (about $130). You can pick WYSIWYG, viewing HTML code to modify pages you have created, or a graphical view of your pages which includes HTML tags.

Macromedia Dreamweaver 1.0 www.macromedia.com

A sophisticated product from the maker of the Shockwave plug-in, but not for beginners, this can create beautifully-designed, pre-cisely-done pages with advanced features like Java or plug-ins in WYSIWYG or raw HTML code format.

On the Cheap

If you really want to create your own site from scratch, you'll need a Web authoring tool. Many Web authoring tools include collections of images you can use, design templates to follow, and toolbars or menus that are fairly easy to use. Many are geared to amateurs and are $100 or less, but can range up to about $700.

Shareware Web authoring tools are even cheaper, often requiring a registration fee of less than $50. Shareware is software that is free for a trial period, often thirty days. If you plan to keep using it, you are expected to pay a registration fee to the developer and you are entitled to free upgrades. It's found in many places on the Web, and sometimes is available on CD-ROMs or floppy disks.

Classes in basic and advanced HTML and Web design are held by universities, continuing education programs, art schools, organizations and some ISP's. Some are as low as $10–$25 per course.

You can also take Web design classes online at ZDNet's ZD University (www.zdu.com). The classes, which are taught by instructors or self-study—your choice—also range from using browsers like Netscape or Internet Explorer to programs like Word and Excel. The cost is $4.95 per month to take as many classes as you want.

A Short Lesson in HTML

The programming code used to create Web pages, which your Web browser is able to read so you can view them properly, is called HTML (hypertext markup language). Pages written in HTML are nothing more than words typed in standard English, accompanied by instructions that tell your browser to do many nifty things. For example, HTML can add colors, pictures, sounds, animations, and links to other parts of the same Web page or another Web page, either on or off the site, in response to commands. It can print words in boldface, italics, or underline, change the font size and look of your text, and arrange the layout of everything on the page.

This is what the HTML code for our last screen shot of a Web page looks like:

Each individual command is called a tag. Each tag is enclosed within the symbols for smaller than and greater than—"<" and ">"— and there are lots of equals signs (=), quotation marks (") and spacing that must be followed exactly. One crucial thing to remember is how to end a command, because otherwise the command keeps chugging along like an Eveready bunny, boldfacing or underlining everything in sight. You end a command with a slash symbol. For example, to start boldfacing, the command is . To stop boldfacing, the command is .

HTML is fairly simple once you get used to it, although it can look like frightening gibberish the first time you see it. It can even be used in e-mail to add colors, pictures, sounds, and changes in the look of the text in your message. But not all e-mail programs understand HTML. Unfortunately, some recipients may not see all the dazzling effects you've created, but just the code itself or a blank page. Because of this, it's best to ask the recipient if they can receive e-mail in HTML.

Here are a batch of commands (or HTML tags) to start with:

Start and end HTML passages   `<html>`

Boldface   `<b>`

Change font size   `<font size="X">`
(The number of the font size
of your text goes where "X" is.
For example, "7" is very large text;
"1" is very small.)

Center text or picture on the page   `<center>`

Italics   `<i>`

Moving text (This will look like a news ticker across the page.)	`<marquee>`
Create a link to a page	`<a href="URL">linked word</a>`

(Insert the full URL of the page you want to link to, plus the slash sign at the end, within quotation marks. For example, "http://www.enews.com/" if you want to link to Electronic Newsstand, a magazine lovers' site with summaries of top stories in many magazines. Then, insert the word or phrase where the link starts where "linked word" appears; for example, ">Electronic Newsstand<".)

Insert a link to a picture	`<img src="URL GIF name">`

(Insert the full URL of the page where the picture is located, plus the slash sign at the end. Then, insert the name of the picture, which in this case is a GIF, and ends in ".gif".)

Insert a link to a sound file	`<embed src="URL WAV file name">`

(Insert the full URL of the page where the sound file is located, plus the slash sign at the end. Then, insert the name of the sound file, which in this case is a WAV file, ending in ".wav".)

Change font color (Insert the Netscape color name or the color's RGB hex code	`<font color="color name">`

Where Is Shareware?

There are some huge repositories of shareware software on the Web, each of which has many thousands of products for free downloading such as plug-ins, e-mail and news-reader programs, games, filtering and blocking software, and screen savers. Some products on these sites, called freeware, are entirely free. But if a product is called shareware, you're supposed to pay if you want to keep using it after its trial period expires.

Here are some sites that are all easily searchable.

CNET's Download.com (www.download.com) has reviews and weekly picks as well as downloads.

CNET's Shareware.com (www.shareware.com) has file names and downloads.

Jumbo! (www.jumbo.com) has downloads for over 250,000 shareware products.

ZDNet's Software Library (www.hotfiles.com) contains reviews and downloads for shareware products.

number; for example, hotpink, royalblue, or orchid. There are many color resource pages on the Web that list the colors and hex code numbers.)

Change background color Color is also assigned using a numerical value	`<body bg color="red">`
Change background design (Perhaps you want a wallpaper effect with pictures in the background.)	`<body background="someGIF.gif">`
Line break	` `
New paragraph (This adds a blank line.)	`<p>`
horizontal rule (This is useful to break up a page visually.)	`<hr>`
Create a column of bulleted items	`<ul>`
List each item in the column (For example, to create a list of flowers set off by bullets, start with "<ul>." The column underneath would look like:	`<li>`

```
<li>rose
<li>daisy
<li>petunia
```

There, that was pretty painless, wasn't it? Of course, HTML has many more commands and gets more complicated. These are just the basics. But there are excellent lessons on HTML, at both simple and advanced levels, on the Web, and many books on the topic. We've included some in the resource list that follows. As with anything, it takes practice, involves many mistakes at first, then quickly picks up speed and skill.

A homesteader in GeoCities, Kim Berry, a mother of three in rural Hertford, North Carolina, built Web sites in the community site's Yosemite and South Beach neighborhoods entirely with the help of its free page building tools.

The Yosemite area in GeoCities is intended for outdoor lovers, so Ms. Berry's 130-page site (www.geocities.com/Yosemite/Gorge/1038) teems with camping and scouting experiences, links to related sites, and a Smokey-the-Bear graphic. A pull-down menu on her colorful home page lists her pages for easy navigation, and a welcome marquee (a message which scrolls across the screen) and guest book greet visitors.

In contrast, her site in South Beach (www.geocities.com/SouthBeach/docks/3642)—a more open-ended neighborhood centered around meeting people and communications—features links for chat areas, Web site building reference tools, and friends' and family pages. Music from the songs "I'll Always Love You" and "Time In A Bottle" plays as a welcome.

"The tools are laid out so neatly. If you know how to copy and paste, boom—it's there," says Ms. Berry, thirty-eight, who knew no HTML when she started creating her sites. "A guest book with up to nine questions to ask visitors, links to sites with free graphics, a color chart to look up the codes for the colors, everything. You can click 'preview' to see what your site looks like so far, then save it so it won't be erased and continue working on it."

"I finished my first page in less than an hour," adds Ms. Berry. As for the HTML she has since learned, "Once you understand the basic concept—this is how you talk to your browser—it's not hard. In the beginning, I printed out pages from the Internet on HTML and always used them as a reference. It was like getting behind the wheel of a car for the first time."

She also praises the convenience of the free e-mail forwarding account from GeoCities. "You never have to worry again about leaving your ISP and losing mail. This is like a Post Office box on wheels that follows you around anywhere in the world, sending your mail wherever you are at the time."

Resources for Web Page Design

Books

Complete Teach Yourself HTML Kit (Sams, 1996), by Laura Lemay
Creating Killer Web Sites 2nd edition, (Hayden, 1997), by David Siegel
Designing Web Graphics 2 2nd edition, (New Riders, 1997), by Lynda Weinman
Graphics & Web Page Design (Sams, 1996), by Laura Lemay et al.
Web Concept and Design (New Riders, 1996), Crystal Waters
Web Pages That Suck: Learn Good Design by Looking at Bad Design (Sybex, 1998), by Vincent Flanders, Michael Wills, and Michael Willis

Web Sites

These offer clear lessons on learning HTML or are terrific resources for pictures and colors.

A Beginner's Guide to HTML (www.ncsa.uiuc.edu/General/Internet/ WWW/HTMLPrimer.html)

The Clip Art Collection (www.ist.net/clipart/uwa/bkgs/bkg_menu.html)

CNET's Builder.com (www.builder.com)

Color Resources (www.geocities.com/ResearchTriangle/8795/colors. links.html)

Creating Killer Web Sites Online (www.killersites.com)

How Do They Do That With HTML? (www.nashville.net/~carl/htmlguide/index.html)

Introduction to HTML (www.cwru.edu/help/introHTML/toc.html)

Introduction to HTML and URLs (www.utoronto.ca/webdocs/HTMLdocs/NewHTML/intro.html)

Lynda's Homegurrlpage (www.lynda.com)

WebMaster Resource List (www.adultlist.com/resource.htm)

WebPage Authoring Reference/Resource Listing
(www.uh.edu/www_resources/web_authoring.html)

Awards for Best Web Sites

Cool Site of the Day Awards (http://cool.infi.net/csoty/index.htm)

High Five Awards (www.highfive.com) Weekly design awards
from David Siegel, author of *Creating Killer Web Sites*, with articles
and interviews with designers.

The Webby Awards (www.webbyawards.com) Annual awards,
originally from *The Web* magazine, now defunct.

How to Find Someone to Design a Web Page

You can hire a Web design firm or even your ISP to design a site,
but first ask their prices and see if you will be charged a project fee
or hourly rate. Web designers want to design high-paying Web sites
for corporate clients, not small, $1,000 jobs. Many people recom-
mend that the way to find a low-cost designer is to ask a local university or continuing education program that offers classes in
multimedia design to suggest some quality, inexpensive Web site
designers. These may be college students or recent graduates who
are skilled and perhaps designing sites part-time or full-
time. Grab them now before they are out in the real
world and commanding market rates in this very
popular field.

Twenty Design Tips To A Cool Web Page

1. Think about your reason for having a Web
site. Do you want to sell products like your
handmade sweaters or your childhood
comics collection? Do you want to sell
your services, including your resume and
perhaps samples of your work? Do you want to
showcase your hobby or interests, hoping to find like-
minded fans? Or a combination? Keeping your purpose

It's the most private of communications in the most public of media, but that hasn't stopped many people from writing diaries on the Web, exposing their thoughts, feelings, personal experiences, and artwork to millions of strangers.

A surprisingly diverse crew write on-line diaries: lawyers, chemists, secretaries, artists, and consultants, and people in their thirties and forties to college students and teenagers. Some have written daily, or almost daily, entries for two years. Some keep searchable archives of past entries and mailing lists for fans, and all invite e-mail.

Many are grouped into Web rings, which are linked collections of related Web sites on many different topics that let users easily jump from one to another. A Web ring that includes hundreds of diaries is Open Pages (http://diary.base.org).

Recommended diaries, each with its own distinctive voice, are:

The Daily Epiphany
(http://members.aol.com/ chancew1/epiphany/index.html)
The diary of Bill Chance, a Texas environmental chemist and father of two, offers thoughtful observations on family life and detailed descriptions of places visited, such as the Oklahoma City bombing site.

Willa's Journal
(www.willa.com)
The diary of Willa Cline, a Kansas legal assistant, homespun and sincere, has monthly reflections on subjects like keeping friends' secrets and a dream journal.

The Mighty Kymm
(www.inet-images.com/mightykymm/ index.htm)
The diary of Kymm Zuckert, a New York area off-off-Broadway actress, theater director, and medical lab employee by day is funny and self-disparaging.

Tracing
(www.ounce.com/301a/tracing)
This diary of an anonymous British-born Chinese woman architect in New York is analytical and thoughtful.

Terrapin Dream
(www.asan.com/users/terrapin/wshit8.htm)
The diary of Terry Baker, a New York digital artist who is HIV-positive is life-affirming, touching, and candid, with a strong Beat influence.

and your audience in mind will help focus your content. Your purpose and audience will also influence the design of your site. Form follows function, as the expression goes.

2. Organize your content clearly with a logic that makes sense. Make it easy for people to find different types of information in different areas. If they're struggling to find information, they may feel frustrated and leave. A Web site should be like a department store, with clothing on one floor, appliances on another, and so on. Many company sites have "about us," "products," "what's new," "search" and "contact us" sections for clarity. Yours may have "personal pages" in addition to a more business-like section.

3. Do an outline or flow chart. Plan a balance of content and graphics, which pages follow other pages, how users can skip ahead to sections of interest or go back easily to the home page or other sections, and which links are internal (within the site) or external (outside of the site). Don't expect to get this right on your first draft; expect many revisions. But planning now will pay off later.

4. Don't overwhelm users with too many choices at once. There's no need for your home page to describe every nugget of information your site contains. It'll look a bit "busy" if it does. Instead, group content into broad categories with subcategories, following the example of Yahoo! or newsgroup hierarchies (remember rec and soc?). This way, exploring your site will be like peeling layers of an onion.

5. Create a handy navigation device so users can find information in different areas fast. Design a toolbar with icons and descriptions (for example, an envelope for e-mail, coffee cup for a forum, and a magnifying glass for a search are some common icons), or a menu with text-only words or short phrases (search, e-mail, etc.). Place this in an obvious spot, like at the top or on the left of your home page. A good idea, by the way, is to use both icons and a text menu—the text menu can go at the bottom—or a text menu only if you want as many users as possible to reach your site. Some users may have slow modems and will have a longer wait to download images, some users

may not be loading images for a speedier surf, and some may be using a text-only browser like Lynx.

6 Make your site work with different hardware or software. Your Web site, which looks fantastic on your machine, may not look so great elsewhere. Test by viewing your site on another operating platform (PC or Macintosh), with other browsers or their earlier versions, or at slower modem speeds. Don't be a technology snob. Gear your site to the lowest common denominator to reach the biggest possible audience (unless this is not your goal).

7 Offer useful or interesting information. Users will be eager to return (and maybe even buy something if you are selling a product or service) if you offer free tips, an extensive collection of links or articles on a specific topic, or include relevant trade associations and news. This also offers a publicity hook for your site, so it may attract coverage in the news media or encourage others to link to you. Some sites with great links in a specialty area have even been acquired by companies who desired their comprehensive resources.

8 Don't get carried away with the technology. Some designers get so enchanted with the bells and whistles of Web technology that their sites require plug-ins right and left. These dazzling displays overshadow and make it hard for some users to reach the content. Keep the file size of each page down. If a graphic with a fairly big file is coming up, it's polite to note the file size so a user can decide whether to take the time to download or not. Remember that content is king, a mantra you'll hear with ghastly frequency in cyberspace.

9 Include contact information. List your e-mail address, although some Web sites also include telephone numbers. Users may want to buy from you, feature you in articles and books, inform you that certain parts of your site are not working or are inaccurate, or offer you all kinds of dandy opportunities. They may also want to say you're being nominated for worst site of the day. But why do you want a site if not to reach the outside world?

10 Read books, articles, and Web tutorials about site design. Look at award-winning sites for creative inspiration as well.

It's best to learn at least a basic working knowledge of HTML. Because the Web is such a different medium from print or television, the more you know about the limitations of Web technology tools, the better. A sample list of books and Web resources is included in this chapter.

11 Borrow graphics from online libraries. You don't have to create all those twirling images and fancy designs from scratch. Many icons, backgrounds, and animations are in the public domain, available for free and ready to use from various Web sites with big collections. Many images on Web sites are copyrighted, however, and you cannot reproduce these without permission. Check with the Web site owner if you are not sure.

12 View your site with the graphics turned off. Does it still make sense? Make your site interesting to plug-in have-nots and those who turn off graphics for speedy surfing as well.

13 Update your site regularly. It doesn't inspire credibility if your information is outdated, or if you are still touting an event that occurred a year ago. It's a good idea to note the date of the update on your site—helpful to your visitors and a motivator to you to keep current!.

14 Observe Web writing style. It's short and snappy and has lots of headlines and subheads, many paragraphs, and links to other pages for more detailed explanations. Long passages of text don't cut it since they're hard on the eyes to read online. In the immortal words of a former editor of mine, it's "granular, nonlinear and organic." At the time, I thought it was California-speak, but it's true.

15 Make sure your links work. The Web is a graveyard of dead sites and sites that have moved. Hard to keep up with, but do your best.

16 Understand the differences between GIFs (Graphics Interchange Format) and JPEGs (Joint Photographic Experts Group), the two main graphics formats for

Measuring a Web Site's Popularity

These are three different ways of measuring the popularity of a Web page based on the amount of traffic coming to the page.

A page view means each time a page is displayed at the request of a user. For example, when a Web site boasts it has one million page views per month, this means its pages have been looked at one million times. It does not necessarily mean one million people came to the site (although it can).

A visitor means a unique user. A Web site that claims one million visitors per month means it has counted one million different people. A visit refers to the total number of pages a single user has looked at during a distinct time period.

A hit (or impression) is tallied each time a computer file is displayed. Because a Web page can consist of several different files—text files, picture files, and sound files, including those pictures used in ads—one page view can mean four or five hits. For this reason, the number of hits for a Web site is much higher than the number of page views or visitors.

How I Designed My Own Web Site: Bill Chance

Bill Chance, an environmental chemist living in the Dallas suburb of Mesquite and the doting dad of two small sons, describes how he designed his Web site (http://members.aol.com/chancew1/index.html) on his own. His site includes a thoughtfully written diary, "The Daily Epiphany," which is included later in this chapter, plus favorite links to camping, backpacking, bicycling, self-help, movies, and books sites.

"I'm an America Online user. I used to use its own page-building tools—just go to "My Home Page"—which is fine if you want a dirt-simple site to put up your name, some information, and a picture to the world. You don't need any HTML tags for a simple Web site. But not any more.

"Since my site has grown, I bought Adobe Photoshop, and now don't want to use anything else. I've also found shareware called LView Pro—only $25 to register it—which is great, really the best, to convert from one graphics format to another, such as change the size of an image or make something brighter.

"I've tried many HTML editors, but I've been unhappy with them and prefer to write my own HTML. I use Microsoft Word and write my own macros to create a template—a design layout with the necessary commands—so I can just plunk in new material without doing all the commands from scratch. A really good way to learn HTML, I've found, is to look at the "view source" option in the "view" command on my screen, which shows the raw code behind what you're seeing on a Web site. This way, if you notice a snazzy effect, you can figure out how the person did it. After you try it yourself five or six times, you get the hang of it. It's not hard.

"The biggest mistake beginners make with HTML is to leave off the closing tags—for example, </b> to end bold-face text—which can cause all sorts of problems.

His final tip on Web site design: "Keep it as simple as you can, and make it do what you want it to do."

Web pages. Know which is appropriate for the type of images you prefer (photographs, line art, animations, etc.).

17 Ask for people's e-mail or home addresses, or possibly their demographics (occupation, age, sex). You can build a mailing list this way. Just tell people what it's for—to alert them to special sales on your products or service, winners of a contest or game on your site, or issues of your newsletter. Don't sell these names and addresses. People already get more "junk mail" than they can handle. If people ask to be removed from your list, do so promptly.

18 Set up an autoresponder. This is an automated software program that sends a file by e-mail—text, graphics, or sound—in response to an e-mail request. In other words, people can automatically receive information by e-mail without you doing anything. Companies such as Hartley's (www.hartley.on.ca/grabber3.html) sell them.

19 Proofread your site. Misspellings and grammatical errors can diminish the content. Have a trusted colleague or friend proofread as well, offering a fresh perspective.

20 Track the number of visitors. Your ISP can give you a report, but these are confusing. Use a good, inexpensive traffic-tracking software.

Graphics, Sound, and Video Formats

GIFs and JPEGs are the most common graphics file formats by far on the Web. If the image is a GIF (Graphics Interchange Format), its file name ends in ".gif," and can range from 256 colors to monochrome. A GIF is used often in logos, banner ads, and computer-generated art.

A JPEG, a graphics tile format created by the Joint Photographic Experts Group, has a file name ending in ".jpeg," and is often used for photographs and complex images.

PNG is the third, up and coming, graphics format. It has just been recently supported.

You'll often see tiny images, called thumbnails, which you can click to see a full-screen image. This can be quite striking if it's a beautiful artwork or scenic photograph. Image maps are images that

How Do Web Sites Make Money?

One question which seems to baffle people the most as they cruise the Web is how all these millions of elaborate pages make money. It's pretty baffling to many Web site owners as well, but sites try to make money through one (or more) of three ways: advertising, electronic commerce (selling products or services), and subscriptions.

are broken down into sections, each of which you can click to see a particular section. For example, you'll often see a map of the United States and be able to click on a certain state, region, or city.

The most common sound files are Audio Player (which end in ".au"), Wave (".wav"), MIDI (".mid" or ".midi"), and AIFF (".aif" or ".aiff"). You might even see ".au" files, very common in the early days of the web, and still available today. The Web page will note a link is for a sound and often describe the sound type and file size, so you can decide to hear it or not.

Your browser will often play a sound if you click on the link without your needing to do anything else. But in some cases, your browser will show a message noting it cannot play the file because you need a plug-in, and will note the name of the plug-in. Many Web sites allow users to download a sound file on the spot.

Generally, a sound file will not play until the whole file is transferred to your computer. But in some cases, such as RealAudio—which plays high-quality sound and whose files end in ".ra"—the sound starts to play when the download starts thanks to streaming audio technology.

You don't really need to know too much more about graphics and sound files unless you want to include them in the Web site you are creating.

Common video files on the Web, which play movie clips, celebrity interviews, and cartoons, are AVI (Audio Video Interleaved), MPEG (Motion Picture Experts Group) and QuickTime, whose file names end in ".avi," ".mpeg" or ".mpg," and ".mov," respectively. The link to the video generally says the file size and the estimated download time. Videos take a long time to download, often fifteen minutes to a half-hour or more, because so much graphics, sound, and motion information is crammed into the file.

No-No's in Web Site Design

Here are nine don'ts, courtesy of Jeffrey M. Glover, a Web designer in Minneapolis and Webmaster of Glover.com. The "Sucky to Savvy" section of his dandy site (www.glover.com) offers clear, easy-to-follow instructions with a humorous touch on how NOT to design an effective site.

His pet peeves are:

1. Blink
   You may love a page which is blinking, flashing, shimmying, rocking and rolling, but others find this annoying and distracting.

2. Background music
   Ever been greeted by a site that starts playing music or emitting sounds immediately? Just the thing to let your boss know you're hard at work preparing for today's meeting, right? Offering users a choice in playing music is good manners.

3. Loud backgrounds
   Loud, neon, or overly fancy backgrounds overlaid with text can make it hard to read the words or make users' eyes hurt, which kind of defeats the purpose of your site. A light, easy-on-the-eyes background so your text stands out is better.

4. Gratuitous use of frames
   Some browsers don't support frames, which divide a Web page into at least two different sections that are independent of each other. Frames also take longer to download. Many Web pages offer the choice of frame and no frame versions.

5. Overuse of image maps
   Big images, with many different spots to click that link to other pages, take a lot longer to download. If you're going to do an image map—for example, a map of a country with different regions to click—offer another way to access these links, such as a text-only menu at the bottom.

6. Construction signs
   Those Site Under Construction signs are silly, Glover says, since all Web sites in theory are still under construction and should be updated, with dates noted, regularly.

7. Scrolling marquees
   These are rapidly moving lines of text, like a news ticker, which can be hard to read and irritating. If the text is important, it should be stationary and easy to read. If it's not important, why include it at all?

8   Personalized alerts
These bulletins pop up on the screen during your visit, or bid you farewell by name when you leave. Unnecessary and smart-alecky, in Glover's opinion.

9   Ticker tape status bars
These rapidly moving lines of text, like scrolling marquees, appear at the bottom of your screen, and are annoying and unnecessary.

Glover also warns against link lunacy, or the foolishness of including too many links on the page and encouraging users to leave the page as soon as they enter it.

Secrets to Successful Web Site Promotion

1   Register your site with search engines. Click on the "add URL" button on the home page or relevant category page of most popular search engines for this free service. Fill in the title of your site, URL, short description, and keywords. The length of time before your site appears in the database varies by search engine, but often takes a few weeks.

2   Follow the golden rule. Offering free links to others' sites if they link to your sites or carry banner ads promoting your site is the Internet way of do unto others as you would they do unto you. This can be done either informally, asking people, or formally, through a service. LinkExchange is the best-known of these reciprocal services, but there are others, such as Banner Swap and Burst!. Some operate by giving you a certain number of credits, others by giving you cash, which reflects a percentage of the ad revenue. Some specialize in certain types of sites.

3   Link to high-traffic sites. One of the best ways to drive users to your site is for a popular site to include a link to yours. This is not easy, but a shared interest or mission gives you a better shot.

Java, With Cream and Sugar, Please

Maybe you've heard about Java—Web designers often get excited talking about it—or seen the message on some Web sites that a Java-enabled browser is required to experience the full effect.

Java is a programming language developed by Sun Microsystems in 1995, which sends small programs over the Web to run on your computer and make the Web site do fancy things. The small programs, called applets, make the site interactive in some way and have many uses, from chat, ads, stock tickers, to games. Java can run on any operating platform, such as Windows 95, Macintosh, and UNIX, which accounts for some of its popularity.

Originally called oak, the language was renamed by its product team—coffee lovers, every one—to evoke its potential

to "wake up the Web" to be more stimulating and dynamic, notes Kim Polese, the former Java product manager who now heads her own firm, Marimba.

The directory for all things Java is Gamelan (www.gamelan.com), which offers descriptions, news, links to Java software developers, and much more. Gamelan is the name of an orchestra of percussion instruments in Java, the Indonesian island that is one of the world's great coffee producers, and became a synonym for the brew.

Recent versions of Netscape Navigator and Internet Explorer are Java-enabled. If you wish, it is easy to turn off Java. For example, in Netscape Navigator 4.0, go to the "edit" menu, then "preferences," then "advanced," and uncheck the box that notes Java is on.

Twelve Things to Do While You Wait

They don't call it the World Wide Wait for nothing—the standard joke that this is what www really stands for.

Instead of staring with glazed eyes at your computer screen, which seems to doing none of the tasks you politely asked it to perform, here are some useful things you can do while waiting for a download, search, or image-packed page to load.

1. Get up and stretch; you can probably use it. Tighten your pelvic or stomach muscles, do facial exercises to release tension, or wring your hands, which have probably been typing a long time.

2. Walk around to re-acquaint yourself with your home or the rest of your office.

3. Rest your eyes; you need it from all that staring at the screen with fur-rowed brow. Look out the window and gaze at the wonders of the nat-ural world.

4. Pat the family pets, if you are at home. They can probably use the affection. Check their food and water supply.

5. Pay a few bills. Keep bills, your checkbook, stamps, and a pen close by, so you can use a few minutes productively.

6. Straighten up your office. Take a few minutes to organize some of your papers into piles, remove clutter, glance through your in box, or sweep clear the surface of your desk.

7. Sort your mail. Mail certainly does accumulate—both the paper and electronic kind—so sort it into urgent, less urgent and junk piles.

8. Sift through business cards you're received recently. If you have a Rolodex, add some cards.

9. Grab a snack. We're thinking fruit juice, a piece of fruit, or another healthy snack here, not junk food.

10. Review your to-do list for the next day. If you don't have one, make one, ranking items by importance.

11. Glance at your calendar for the week. Remind yourself of any upcoming meetings, family events and get-togethers.

12. Water the plants. Remove dead leaves, or repot if it's overflowing the pot.

4. Pay for Web site announcement services. These companies will register your site with hundreds of search engines, yellow pages, major directories, and What's New sites for a fairly low fee. This saves the time of filling out all those online forms one by one. Some of these are Submit-It (www.submit-it.com) and WebPromote (www.webpromote.com).

5. Add your URL to all promotional materials. Your URL should appear on your business card, brochure, print, television or radio ad, and packaging, just like your telephone number, so potential customers can reach you.

6. Use newsgroups, chat forums, and online mailing lists. Join discussions and make relevant or instructive points, alluding to your site in passing. Observe Net etiquette of the site or list first, so you don't get flamed for tooting your horn too loudly.

7. Add your URL to your e-mail signature. A link to your site others can click on after your name is an easy, painless way to promotion.

8. Be selective about placing banner ads for your site. Research sites your audience will want to visit. Weigh the higher costs of high-traffic sites with lower costs of more closely targeted sites.

9. If you use an advertising agency to create your Web site or banner ad promoting your site, make sure you get a tracking report. This report tracks the number of impressions the site or ad receives, plus the click-through rate—how many people click on your ad to access your site.

What Makes A Good Web Site?

"Value," says Larry Chase, president of Chase Online Marketing Strategies, a New York firm, and author of *Essential Business Tactics for the Net* (Wiley, 1998). People visit Web sites in search of three types of value, he says:

:-) financial incentive—to save money or make money

:-) utility—to find useful or interesting content

:-) interactivity—to connect with fellow humans in playing games, chatting, etc.

"Give something of value away for free—not the whole farm, but a few acres," advises Chase to keep people coming back. He practices what he preaches. He is also publisher of a bi-weekly newsletter on noteworthy Web sites, Web Digest for Marketers (www.wdfm.com), available free by e-mail or on its Web site. But he licenses the newsletter's use in print, accepts ads, and over 60 percent of his speaking gigs and consulting work in the past year have been generated by WDFM, which has thousands of subscribers.

"Spend less money on your Web site and more money on marketing it. Companies hate when I say that, but it's true," says Chase. First, target your audience as narrowly as possible, and offer something of intense interest. Maybe a fan site with lots of links and information on a much-loved television show, musical comedy composer, or actor, Or photographs, articles, and recipes for a certain country or region. "If you're marketing to everyone, you're not marketing to anyone. The mistake most people make is that their sites are a mile wide and a half-inch deep. Instead, make your site a mile deep."

Chase has many favorite Web sites—click the "Don't Click Here If You Want A Life" link on WDFM to find an eclectic assortment. But he has a soft spot for the detergent Tide's site (www.clothesline.com), which features a Stain Detective with step-by-step help on how to remove stubborn stains—just select the stain type, fabric and color. "It's a wonderful free service that comes right out of the product, and a great example of branding a product. "Other sites are flashing, buzzing and gyrating, but this is really helpful."

The challenge to get noticed in an ever-widening sea of sites is "to establish an obvious, up-front point of difference," Chase says.

Address http://chapter_eight.com **Links**

GETTING AROUND

Introduction

Chapter One

Chapter Two

Chapter Three

Chapter Four

Chapter Five

Chapter Six

Chapter Seven

Chapter Eight

Chapter Nine

Chapter Ten

Appendices

Protect Yourself and Your Kids: Viruses, Snoops, Perverts, and Other Nuisances

Protecting Your Children

If you're a parent, you probably worry about what your children may find or whom they may meet on the Internet. Who can blame you? There are pornographic pictures, sexually explicit newsgroups and chat rooms, gory photographs, and racist remarks. Some sexual abusers who prey on children have been known to pose as children in chat rooms, win a child's friendship, and eventually try to set up a face-to-face meeting with the child. Advertisers who prey on children (and their parents' wallets) try to entice children with cute cartoons into revealing their home addresses and family credit card numbers.

Of course, this happens in the real world, too, and to some extent fears about what may happen to youngsters on the Internet are exaggerated. It would be a shame for your children to miss out on all the educational, fun, and wonderful things online because of some rotten apples. After all, you probably don't want to ban your child from all newsstands because they sell some magazines with nude photographs, all television watching because some shows are for adults, and school because of conversations he or she may overhear or teachers who may seduce them.

Still, parents should be cautious and teach their children not to take everything at face value on the Internet, especially now that the Communications Decency Act was declared unconstitutional. This law would have made sexually explicit content online, which was easily accessible to minors under eighteen, a crime.

Here are some commonsense tips on safe surfing for children that experts recommend.

:-) Watch your child's Internet activities. This doesn't mean standing guard like a grim sentinel, but dropping in from time to time, and sometimes asking pleasantly if the child has found anything interesting.

:-) Surf with your child. Explore family-friendly sites together, help with homework, or e-mail a relative or friend on occasion. This way, your child learns surfing need not be a solitary pastime but an activity the family can enjoy together.

:-) Encourage your child to tell you about online pals he or she has made and share knowledge and skills he or she has gained. Your child may well be more Internet savvy than you are. Learn from each other!

:-) Warn your child not to reveal a home address, telephone number, or credit card numbers online.

:-) Warn your child against online pals who offer to send gifts, candy, or money. Just like the real world variety, unusually generous on-line strangers are often up to no good, trying to buy a child's trust.

:-) Warn your child that everyone is not whom they claim to be online. That eleven-year-old trying to meet your child may actually be a fifty-year-old exconvict.

:-) Don't let your child set up a meeting with an online pal without your knowledge.

:-) Tell your child not to respond to e-mail that is frightening, threatening, or obscene.

:-) Tell your child that not everything they see on the Internet is true. Inform them that anyone, not just reliable sources, can publish information.

:-) Set time limits so your child is not spending too much time online. He or she should be out in the sunshine and fresh air playing with real world friends, engaging in hobbies, and having a variety of experiences. Sex abusers prey upon needy children who aren't getting enough emotional strokes at home or in their social lives.

:-) If your child is on America Online's "Kids Only" site, tell them how to use the on-site pager to reach a monitor if they feel uneasy that you are not around.

:-) If you find child pornography or a sex abuser online, report it to the National Center for Missing and Exploited Children at 800-843-5678.

:-) Don't let your child use unmoderated chat rooms.

:-) Use filtering software to screen out objectionable material.

Childproof Your Computer

A variety of software products will censor the Internet for you, with varying degrees of secrecy. Filtering software works by blocking access to not just Web sites, but also newsgroups, chat forums, and e-mail messages with objectionable content, or by deleting offensive words. Objectionable can mean sexual content or pictures, profanity, violence, hate groups such as the Ku Klux Klan, drug culture, or gambling. These software products come with their own preset lists of topics to be censored, which you can generally edit to your liking by allowing some categories but forbidding others.

For example, you can block sexual content and pictures and hate groups, but allow gambling, profanity, and drug culture, if you prefer. A few products even show you their exact list of unsuitable sites and areas, so you don't have to take their word for it, which can be edited as well. Lists are updated often as new adult-oriented sites appear.

Some software products also give detailed reports on your child's Internet activities, logging sites, newsgroups, and chat rooms visited. Some products can be tailored to several members of the household. In other words, a parent can have separate no-no lists for a seven-year-old, eleven-year-old, and thirteen-year-old. Those ever-present Web ads can be blocked by certain products. (Some of you may wish this product was invented for television and radio commercials.) While some excel at catching incoming or outgoing information, others capture both.

Shareware versions of filtering software, which sell for about $30–$40 once the trial ends, are available from the software makers' Web sites and from encyclopedic shareware sites like Jumbo! and CNET's Shareware.com and Download.com. In case you're wondering, filtering software tends to be more sweeping than not, because it searches for keywords, without judging if the intent is educational or hardcore pornography. This sometimes means harmless sites are blocked, such as an AIDS awareness site or even the National Organization for Women site—because it contains links to sites for homosexuals—and so they have provoked strong feelings on both sides of the issue.

Here are some filtering software products:

Cyber Snoop
(www.pearlsw.com)
800-732-7596

A handy feature of this software allows you to view its entire list of nearly 2,000 objectionable sites, and add or delete sites. This product, from Pearl Software, also records all Web site, newsgroup, and chat room visits plus e-mail messages, with links to the Web sites so you can reach them instantly.

Depending on the version you have, Cyber Snoop can show attempts your child has made to visit blocked sites, block the release of personal information, such as last names and credit card numbers, and record the entire content of Internet Relay Chat (IRC) and Web-based chat. (These features are in 3.0, the more expensive version, which takes about five minutes to set up, as opposed to five-ten minutes for 2.0.)

Sample Set-up and Use for Cyber Snoop 3.0

1. Insert the CD-ROM in the CD-ROM drive.
2. Follow the online instructions after it starts automatically, including naming the program file C:\PROGRAM FILES\SNOOP3.0.
3. When done, click "start," then "programs," then "cyber snoop 3.0" folder and "cyber snoop 3.0" file name. Type the software's serial number and a password.
4. Cyber Snoop is now ready to "snoop." If you want to read the list of objectionable sites—which are automatically blocked unless you decide otherwise—you need to request it. This no-no list will be e-mailed to you as a text file. If you want to delete or add sites, click "list manager," then click "delete" or "add."
5. Cyber Snoop runs by "stealth," unless you decide to change it. This means a child will simply be unable to reach certain sites, with no warning posted and no hint activity is being observed. To change this, click "security menu," then "set warning message." If you don't like the mild warning which comes automatically—which notes activity is being monitored by Cyber Snoop—you can

invent your own. (From "you naughty child!" to "no!"—it's your choice.)

6 Whenever you run Cyber Snoop, type your password. A log of visits your child has made to Web sites, news-groups and chat rooms since the last time you cleared the log will appear. The entire content of two-way dia-logues held by your child in Internet Relay Chat (IRC), Web-based chat, newsgroups and e-mail will show up as well.

Net Nanny
(www.netnanny.com)
800-340-7177
You can also view the restricted list from Net Nanny Ltd., which blocks the release of personal information—credit card numbers and addresses—as well. This product can be tailored to several users.

You can add or delete from Net Nanny's no-no list, which can be downloaded free from its Web site. Web sites, words, news-groups, chat, e-mail, even violent CD-ROM games can be monitored. You can choose if you want it to block access, display a warning message, hide certain words, shut down, or merely post a log of visits and activity. If you wish, Net Nanny can also restrict access to only certain sites you have approved.

Cyber Patrol
(www.cyberpatrol.com)
617-494-1200
You can't view the no-no list, but can add or delete categories. The screen will say "blocked by Cyber Patrol" if anyone tries to access a forbidden site. From The Learning Company, this software also blocks the release of personal information, as well as restricting the number of hours spent on-line.

CYBERsitter
(www.cybersitter.com)
800-388-2761
Probably the strictest filtering software, this comes with a restricted list that even includes sports and recreation sites in addition

to sex and violence. You can't view this list, either, but you can turn off categories and block all newsgroups—not just the offensive ones.

Net Shepherd
(www.netshepherd.com)
This software has a rating system for Web sites by age group and by quality, and works with the Internet Explorer 3.0 or 4.0 browser's Content Advisor feature to block sites. In other words, you can tailor its settings so whatever is viewed is appropriate for children ages six–nine, ten–twelve, thirteen–seventeen, over eighteen, or objectionable to all groups. From Net Shepherd, it claims the world's biggest Internet ratings database, with over 500,000 sites.

A Web Site for Cautious Parents

At Smart Parent.com (www.smartparent.com), you'll find not only information on filtering software, but many links to Web sites of interest to parents and children. (See the Children's and Parenting sections in chapter 9 as well.)

Viruses: When Bad Things Happen to Good Computers

Computer viruses are nasty things. Like their medical counterparts, these viruses can produce miserable symptoms such as making your files disappear, turning data on your files into unintelligible garbage, slowing your computer down to a snail's pace, or causing it to freeze up. Some can glue themselves to perfectly normal programs on your hard disk or floppy disk and infect them, causing havoc when you open up an infected file. Other viruses cling to the part of your hard disk that keeps operating instructions, causing problems when you start up your computer.

Some do silly stuff, like pop up on your screen with a message on a certain date. Others, meant to be practical jokes, warn you all your data will vanish if you open an e-mail message or hit a certain key, but—surprise!—it was only fooling. (This type of

Is Your Child's School Connected to the Internet?

Net Day 2000 (www.netday.org) is a grassroots organization which invites parents, teachers, and others to be volunteers in wiring grade schools and high schools in the United States to the Internet.

Volunteers, who can be with or without technical skills, are given wiring kits with enough equipment to connect computers in six classrooms. Companies are invited to sponsor the wiring of a school or group of schools.

States and cities vary widely in the percentage of grade schools and high schools that have Internet connections. If you are interested, check the list of K–12 schools on the group's Web site, which also includes a state-by-state list of technology funding for public schools and the latest news on this subject.

A virus is a computer program that runs unexpectedly on a computer, often when a certain action is performed or on a certain date. It is a nuisance bit of code written by programmers who get their jollies from playing tricks on other people and disrupting computer systems. (We sincerely hope these folks start applying their considerable talents elsewhere.) If not detected and stamped out, they can hobble your computer's ability to perform and make you want to tear out your hair.

joke can give you a heart attack. We don't think it's funny, and neither will you if it happens.)

There are thousands of viruses roaming the computers of the world—new ones are being discovered all the time—often with exotic names like Michelangelo, Maltese Amoeba, MadSatan, and Marauder (and these are just the Ms!) If you download lots of files from the Internet or receive many e-mail attachments from unknown sources, chances are you'll meet up with a virus at some point—the majority are transmitted in these ways. If you have a UNIX system, viruses are much less common; if you have WebTV, they're nonexistent.

What to Do About Viruses

Luckily, "flu shots" are available, which can lessen the chance your computer will catch a virus, as well as detect and cure them. Experts advise these tips:

:-) Get an antivirus software program. They are sold at retailers, generally for $50–$70, and available in shareware and freeware versions.

:-) Scan all Internet downloads, e-mail attachments, and disks and games obtained from other people with an antivirus program before you run them.

:-) Don't let someone you don't know use your computer.

:-) Be alert to virus-like symptoms, such as noticeably slower computer performance, an unexplainable decrease in available memory, modifying program files, or suddenly renaming files.

:-) If your antivirus program spots a virus, turn your computer off. Start it up again with a clean floppy disk containing the anti-virus software. Clean your hard disk with this software.

Antivirus Software

Norton Anti-Virus
(www.symantec.com/nav/index.html
800-441-7234

This old standby from Symantec detects all known and unknown viruses and is easy to install and use. The handy auto-protect feature allows it to scan all documents and programs on a continual basis. However, you may prefer the on-command feature, which will scan regularly on a day and time of your choice—for example, every Monday at 9:00 A.M. If a virus is found, click the "delete" button to remove it. The LiveUpdate feature connects you to the Symantec Web site for automatic updates. There are also four helpful videos.

McAfee Virus Scan
(www.network.com)
800-338-8754

This software prevents and removes all known and unknown viruses, with free automatic updates for the life of the product. From Network Associates, this virus scanner has a choice of three interfaces with different features and is easy to use.

McAfee also offers a free demo.

Dr. Solomon's Anti-Virus Deluxe
(www.drsolomon.com)
888-377-6566

More expensive than others but high-quality and easy to use. Free updates for one year, free unlimited upgrades, and the ability to schedule scans at certain regular times are included.

How Can I Protect Myself From Snoops?

It's an alarming thought, but you may not be alone as you are sitting at home at night or during the workday, happily surfing the Web or sending romantic e-mails (a contradiction in terms?). Others may be poring over your Web activities, e-mail messages, and newsgroup postings with fascination, trying to figure out exactly what kind of person you are—often trying to uncovering your buying habits so they can sell you stuff.

Here are some ways that people can gather information about you.

Only Fooling: Virus Hoaxes

Virus hoaxes—warnings often circulated by e-mail, that some dire event will occur if you open an e-mail message with a certain subject header—are as annoying, or more so, than the viruses they pretend to warn against. Many are nothing more than an online version of the chain letter.

You can read an informative and amusing site about virus hoaxes, including classics like "AOL4FREE," "WIN A HOLIDAY," and "PENPAL GREETINGS" at Computer Virus Myths (www.kumite.com/myths/home.htm).

:-) online registration forms
:-) Internet directories
:-) your browser talks
:-) newsgroup postings
:-) e-mail
:-) credit card numbers

What I Can Do To Protect My Privacy

Let's look, one by one, at the ways information can be gathered and how to prevent it:

Online registration forms

Many Web sites ask you to register before you can browse the site or access special parts of the site, even though the site is free. An online form asks your name, address, telephone number, e-mail address, and possibly more personal details, such as occupation, household income, industry, and age.

This is helpful information the site can use for marketing purposes, such as attracting advertisers or e-mailing you news of special sales or features in the future. Sometimes, this data can be sold to marketing and mailing list companies, who note that you are interested in certain hobbies or products.

You don't have to divulge these facts. In many cases, you can release what you are comfortable with releasing and leave some questions blank, or even (really) fib about truly personal questions. You should weigh the importance of viewing the Web site against disclosing personal information, and realize that maybe a very similar site exists which isn't so nosy. If you fill out many on-line forms, expect lots of E-mail from those sites.

Here's an example of what an online registration form looks like to buy a product:

```
Account Information
First Name (long box)
Last Name
Password
```

```
Shipping Information
Recipient Name
Address
Line 1
Address
Line 2
City,
State
Zip/Postal Code
Country (pull-down menu—often starts
with USA)
Day Phone
Night Phone
E-mail
Credit Card Information
Address
Line 1
Address
Line 2
City, State
Zip
Country (pull-down menu—often starts
with USA)
Account Options
(yes) (no) We have a personalized bi-
weekly E-mail newsletter. Do you want to
receive the update?
(yes) (no) Would you like to receive
announcements about contests and special
deals?
Create New Account (press this button to
submit)
```

People-Finder Directories

There are popular people-finder directories on the Web, such as Four11, Switchboard, Bigfoot, WhoWhere, Infospace, and Internet Address Finder where you can look up people's telephone numbers, addresses, and e-mail addresses nationwide. (Just for a thrill, find

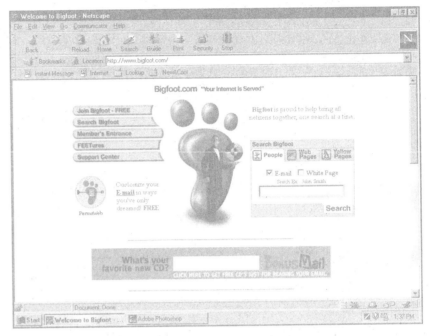

Bigfoot www.bigfoot.com

out how many people in the United States have your same name.) Information is gathered from public sources, such as telephone directories and newsgroup postings—if you're listed in the telephone directory, you'll most likely turn up in these listings; if you're unlisted, you won't—but you may appear in some, not others. In some people finders, you can look up the person and telephone number behind the e-mail address. The latest Netscape Navigator and Internet Explorer browsers include some of these people finders.

While it may be delightful tracking down old friends, relatives, and people who owe you money, it may not feel so delightful on the receiving end, especially if the sender is a spammer or someone who takes offense at your writing on the Web. However, you can delete your telephone number, address, and e-mail address—just go to the directories' Web sites—if you wish. You'll need to do it for each directory where you appear, since they are independent from each other. Of course, if you don't mind being found, you may want to keep or add your listing.

How to Look for People in a People-Finder

Type in a person's name and address at a people-finder's Web site, and the telephone number will often appear. If you type in just the person's name, many addresses and telephone numbers nationwide will show up, or only people in a certain state or city if you add this in as well. To expand the list of results, type in just the initial of the person's first name plus their last name, because many people are listed under their first initial in telephone books for privacy reasons.

To look up people when you just have a telephone number, address or e-mail address—let's say you found a piece of paper in your spouse's pocket, for example—go to InfoSpace's Reverse Lookup in its White Pages section. Type in the residential or business telephone number or residential address (United States only), or the e-mail address (worldwide), and the person's name may appear, which is pretty impressive. InfoSpace also has a Celebrity Search, where typing in a name will often land a business mailing address, e-mail address and/or Web site, which often is a fan tribute site.

How to Delete, Change or Add Your Listing in a People-Finder

If you are less than thrilled your address and telephone number is there for the world to see, follow the instructions at the people-finder directory's Web site to delete your listing. There are also instructions to update your listing if it is wrong because you have moved, or add a listing.

At Switchboard, for example, do this:

1. At the bottom of its home page, click "create/modify listing."
2. Click "get a password."
3. Click "find my current listing" (to delete or change) or "add new listing."
4. Type your first and last name, e-mail address and zip code. (Typing your address and telephone number is optional, but will speed up finding your listing if your name is fairly common.)

Finding Lost Friends and Relatives Online

Helpful Web sites with addresses, telephone numbers, and e-mail addresses of people and businesses nationwide are:

Four11
(www.four11.com)

Switchboard
(www.switchboard.com)

Bigfoot
(www.bigfoot.com)

WhoWhere?
(www.whowhere.com)

Infospace
(www.infospace.com)

Internet Address Finder
(www.iaf.com)

555-1212.com
(www.555-1212.com)

5   Click "submit." When the listings appear (to delete or change), click on the correct one.

6   A password will be e-mailed to you within five days with instructions to change or delete your listing. Click "reply" to the message, which verifies your e-mail address. Then, go to Switchboard again, click "my corner," then "modify main listing."

7   Type your e-mail address and the password given to you.

8   When your listing appears, change it if you wish. You can add extra details, such as fax, page or cell phone numbers, home page URL, employer name, address and telephone number, college attended, interests and group affiliations. Your e-mail address can appear with your listing, if you wish. A privacy feature, called "knock-knock," allows you to receive e-mails without divulging your e-mail address in your listing. After making changes, click "modify my listing."

9   To delete your listing, click "please do not show my listing or my e-mail address."

10   Click "submit changes."

Many colleges also post e-mail alumni directories. The American School Directory (www.asd.com), which lists public, parochial, and private K–12 schools nationwide also has alumni sections where graduates of each school can post their e-mail addresses and other information.

Your Browser Talks

Your browser leaks information about you every time you surf the Web. The brand of browser you have, your ISP, whether you have a PC or Macintosh, and the last Web page you saw are happily provided, if the site asks.

Those clever little cookies are bits of information certain Web sites make your browser store on your hard drive, so you will be recognized on later visits. The path you traveled through the site, products you purchased, ads you saw, and files you downloaded can be recorded. This way, the site builds a stronger profile of you each time you visit, and can tailor its content or ads to match your interests. If you are also registered at a site for which you hold a cookie, the site can tie your name and e-mail address to your surfing patterns. This is why a site may greet you by name on your very next visit, always disconcerting the first few times this happens—particularly when it's not even your computer, as happened to me the first time I registered for a site.

You can disable cookies entirely with the latest versions of Netscape Communicator and Internet Explorer. Or if you want, you can receive an alert when you are about to be given a cookie and can choose to accept or decline. (There's nothing like this alert feature to show you how common cookies really are.) You can search for cookie files and delete them—look for cookies.txt or MagicCookie—or pick a software program that will clean them out automatically, like NSClean or IEClean from Privacy Software, a firm with a vacuum cleaner logo. If you clean up yourself, you'll need to do it often, since new cookie files will be created and replenished in the twinkling of an eye. For more than you ever wanted to know about cookies, visit CookieCentral (www.cookiecentral.com).

To surf anonymously without Web sites tracking your footsteps, you can use something called The Anonymizer (www.theanonoymizer.com), whose motto is "On today's Internet, people do know you're a dog!" after the famous cartoon with a dog gazing at a computer, pondering the wondrous fact that nobody else knew he was a dog. This acts as a screen between you and Web sites you visit, scouting for the sites you want and then bringing them to your browser. It's about $60 per year, or free for a trial version, which is slower.

Newsgroup Postings

Newsgroups are public bulletin boards for airing opinions, trading information, and gossip. Yet many people are surprised, even alarmed, to hear their collective wisdom can easily be searched by the person's name in Deja News or Alta Vista. If you don't want your likes, dislikes, favorite newsgroups, and rantings to be read and collected by the curious, you can prevent your postings from reaching these search engines' archives by typing "x-no-archive: yes" in the header of each message. If you can't do this with your e-mail program or newsreader, typing this as the first line of your message will do.

The most famous anonymous remailer, Penet, located in Finland, shut down in 1996. After trouble with the Church of Scientology, the Finnish police, and the Government of Singapore—as well as threats against himself and huge e-mail bombs of junk intended to crash his computer—Johan (Julf) Helsingius quit.

Inflammatory newspaper articles, the murky legal status of the confidentiality of e-mail amid law enforcement efforts, and recurring e-mail bombs finally led Helsingius to close anon.penet.fi for good.

Offering free, untraceable, two-way e-mail to a motley international crew of about 500,000 privacy seekers, Helsingius drew the wrath of the Scientologists when someone posted confidential documents to the newsgroup alt.religion.scientology. The Finnish police insisted Helsingius cough up the name of the poster, and demanded he release his entire database. Then the Singapore government took offense at irreverent postings which appeared in newsgroups, and demanded the person's identity.

E-mail

You can encrypt (encode) your e-mail messages so they can be read by the recipient, but no one else along the way. Don't worry, you don't have to study any code books or learn some elaborate spy technique. The popular software product from Pretty Good Privacy, PGP, makes it easy and automatic by simply adding some extra icons to your toolbar. Click a lock to encode, and click a pen to give a digital signature, which verifies to the recipient you are who you claim to be.

Both sender and recipient have to use PGP, which uses public key encryption, meaning each person has two keys and the key that unlocks the coded message you receive is not the same key that encodes a message you send. People's public keys, in fact, can be found on the Web, so that messages can be encoded and sent to them. But their secret keys to unencode their mail are known only to them alone. This is considered much safer than other types of encryption, where if the code-breaking tool that encodes and deciphers is discovered, all secrecy is lost.

You can also send e-mail anonymously through services called anonymous remailers. These services receive your message, remove your name and e-mail address, and resend it, usually for free. Of course, the body of your message should contain no identifying information. With some anonymous remailers, you can also receive responses.

You may wonder why you would bother writing a message without attaching your name to it, and why would anyone pay attention to it? But in the peculiar blend of intimacy and distance that is the Internet, many people prefer to be untraceable. Political dissidents, people exposing scandals in their companies, people embarrassed about sexual abuse they have endured or committed, and unsavory types who are dishonest or who bother people online have all used remailers.

A list of anonymous remailers, with articles and resources on the topic, has been posted by a University of California at Berkeley graduate student at www.cs.berkeley.edu/~raph/remailer-list.html.

Credit Card Numbers

Paying by credit card over the Internet is much safer than the public generally believes, and less risky than handing a credit card to a merchant or waiter or reciting it over the telephone, according to Internet security and electronic commerce experts. Still, hackers have invented all kinds of techniques to break into computer systems, and dishonest people have collected and sold batches of credit card numbers or diverted traffic from other Web sites to themselves.

It may surprise many to hear that more than 60 percent of Internet fraud victims pay by check, cash, or money orders and only 19 percent pay by credit card, according to the National Consumer League, a nonprofit organization in Washington, D.C. A person who disputes an unauthorized charge on a credit card bill will have, at most, a $50 liability if the charge is not reported to the credit card company right away, just as if a wallet were stolen. The real risk is to the merchant in sales where the credit card is not physically handed over, like paying by telephone or online. (In a card-present transaction, where the card is handed over, the issuing bank holds the risk, by the way.)

Ten Tips to Safe Buying on the Internet

The National Fraud Information Center, a nonprofit organization that is a partnership of the National Consumer League and the National Association of Attorneys General, says the key issue to buying safety is not how you pay, but who you pay on the Internet. Here are some of their tips:

1. Know who the merchant is. If it's the on-line store of a real world company, such as Eddie Bauer, Dell Computers or The Gap, not to worry. If it's an on-line merchant you've never heard of, particularly one who has contacted you by e-mail, do your homework first to see if the firm is legitimate. Ask for its telephone number and address if it's not offered, and call the telephone company to see if the number is registered to the firm so you have recourse if trouble occurs. Do a search to see if articles on the firm pop up, and see if they're

positive stories. Dishonest people have set up Web sites purely to collect credit card numbers.

2. Understand the sale terms. This means total price, including shipping charge, delivery date, guarantee, and return policy. By federal law, delivery is in thirty days unless otherwise specified.

3. Print out the online order form. This way, you have a record of your order if the Web site vanishes or if your purchase is defective or never arrives. Be sure you have the merchant's e-mail and Internet address and order date for tracking purposes.

4. Check if the Web site is secure. Recent Netscape Navigator and Internet Explorer browsers actually have an icon that shows if a Web site you are on is secure, meaning credit card data is scrambled. A closed padlock or key means it's secure, an open padlock or key means it's not. If your browser lacks this built-in feature, ask the merchant if high forms of security such as SSL (Secure Sockets Layer) or SET (Secure Electronic Transaction), which is newer, is used. If not, pay by telephone, mail, or fax. Many merchants have these options.

   Online merchants who use SSL include Amazon.com, Music Boulevard, Barnes & Noble, MovieLink, Travelocity, Preview Travel and e*Trade.

5. Consult state or local consumer protection agencies and the Better Business Bureau. Ask if the merchant needs to be registered. If so, check with that agency and ask if there are any complaints.

6. Never give your password or Social Security Number to any merchant. Merchants don't need them, and it's like giving out your bank ATM number to passers-by.

7. Avoid offers with lots of capital letters that promise you can MAKE BIG $$$ or urge you to BUY RIGHT NOW!!! Need I say more? Good merchants rely on quality products and responsive service, not flamboyant punctuation and high-pressure gambits.

8. Ask the merchant for background material or customer references before buying if it's an online merchant. An honest merchant will be able to supply these to you.

[9] Avoid merchants with post office addresses and anonymous e-mail addresses. Knowing that the merchant's e-
mail address is "user@xxx.com" and their real world
address is unknown means the person is not eager to be
traced and does not inspire confidence.

If you are a victim of Internet fraud, call NFIC's Internet Fraud
Watch at (800) 876-7060 or contact them on-line at www.fraud.org.

How to Avoid the Technical
Support Blues

When you are dealing with telephone or e-mail technical support
from a computer hardware or software maker about a problem, here
are some tips to save time and prevent frustration:

:-) have your computer on, as well as your Internet connection,
when you call so you can easily follow the advice the repre-
sentative gives you. Hopefully, you have a second telephone
line or a super-speedy Internet connection which allows you
to call while you use the Internet. If not, write the advice
down carefully so you can follow it when off the telephone.

:-) give the make and model number of your computer, your
operating system, the amount of memory (RAM), and the
version number (3.0, 4.0 etc.) of your software

:-) describe the problem clearly. Instead of wailing "it isn't
working," is your screen blank, what was the last action you
performed, did your computer freeze up with all your work
on the screen?

:-) if an error message is on your screen, what does it say?

:-) remain calm and coherent. Shouting will not help, and the
more excitable you get, the less you are able to describe the
problem and follow instructions.
Unfortunately, the telephone waits for technical support can
be lengthy, and e-mail questions are often not answered
promptly. Technical support costs are often hefty after a free
time period. The voice mail menus can give you the run-
around, and the quality of help—especially if you have an
older system—can leave much to be desired. (Wait until you

hear "I have no idea why it's doing that" at $2.95 per minute.) Before you plunge in, follow these steps:

:-) if the problem seems to be with your monitor, mouse, external modem or printer, check the cable cords to make sure nothing has gotten disconnected. A pet, a child, or even you may have accidentally loosened the cords.

:-) read your print manual and any help files to see if they cover your problem.

:-) go to ZDNet's HealthyPC.com (www.healthypc.com), which offers a alphabetical database of computer hardware and software technical support Web sites under "Support Finder." Tips on troubleshooting, computer care and maintenance and virus protection are also included (Symantec, the maker of Norton Anti-Virus, is a sponsor).

:-) go straight to the computer hardware or software maker's Web site, and look for the technical support section. Some offer excellent detailed help. You may want to bookmark the page for future reference.

:-) look for the FAQ's in the site's technical support section; often they are organized by topic

:-) if there are many FAQ's or they don't seem to cover your problem, look for a trouble-shooting section which addresses specific problems, or a database where you can search by product, version or phrase. Some databases are called Knowledge Bases, and can be treasure troves of useful information.

:-) go to the newsgroups which cover your operating system or product (look under the ".comp" hierarchy) and post a question. Often, you will get helpful answers from experienced users.

The Top Ten Internet Scams

Internet Fraud Watch, a service of the National Fraud Information Center, in Washington, DC. lists the following top ten Internet scams. (This means a high number of complaints received fall into these categories and that consumers should be careful—not that everyone offering these services is dishonest!)

1. sale of Internet services
2. sale of general merchandise
3. auctions
4. pyramid schemes
5. business opportunities
6. work-at-home scams
7. prizes
8. credit card offers
9. book sales
10. magazine subscriptions

Other Safety Tips

Be Careful At Work

Your company generally has the right to read the e-mail you write and receive and examine your Web surfing activities, because this is happening on computers they own and on company time. A handful of short, unrevealing personal messages probably won't get you into trouble. But I've heard of at least one case where a person was fired due to an e-mail. (He disclosed to people in a division that it would be downsized, before the company was ready to release this information. Guess who became the first to be downsized.) Remember, some employers use products like SurfWatch and Assentor to snoop on employees, and it's perfectly legal, although it may seem unsavory.

Find Out Privacy Policies

Your ISP or online service probably has a written policy on privacy. Ask what it is. So do many Web sites; read what it says. For example, the policy on Time Warner's Pathfinder Web site, which includes articles from *People*, *Money*, *Time*, *Fortune*, and other magazines, notes that it may place cookies on your hard drive to track your activities, and gives information you have released to it to marketing companies. However, you may request to be removed by sending an e-mail to Pathfinder.

Putting the World's Classic Books Online

At Project Gutenberg, volunteers all over the world work diligently to transfer the world's great books—from Shakespeare to *Madame Bovary*, children's classics like *Alice in Wonderland* and *Peter Pan*, and poetry such as T.S. Eliot's *The Wasteland*—to the Internet so anyone can read them, free.

Project Gutenberg, named after the founder of the printing press, is currently supported by Carnegie-Mellon University in Pittsburgh.

How to Survive A Computer Crash

It's bound to happen sometime. Your computer freezes and refuses to budge in response to your commands. For some odd reason, pressing an increasingly desperate number of keys, yelling, even cursing has no effect whatsoever. Your computer just sits there—mute, stubborn, utterly unresponsive.

What to do? If you call technical support you're probably be placed on eternal hold, making you even more frantic. You can't seek help online because your computer is locked, which should have occurred to those people writing online help tips, you think to yourself. Of course, it would have been helpful to read those tips before this happened.

First, it's best to save work you do to your hard disk very often, so if your computer locks up you've only lost new material added since the last time you saved. For example, if you don't save work for an hour, you're at risk of losing an hour's worth of work. Most computer programs now have an autosave feature. This automatically saves your work as you do it, based on the time settings you selected. If you have this autosave feature, set it so your work is saved at very small intervals.

Perhaps your computer is occupied writing to or reading your hard disk, and you're a bit too fast for it. Most computers will have a light on to show the hard disk is working. If no light is on, listen for reassuring sounds that it's busy. When it's done, try your commands again.

Press the escape key a couple of times, which often produces results. Then, hold down the alt key and press escape again. Try holding down the control key and pressing escape. Try pressing the break key, or control and break.

If those key combinations don't work, it's time to re-start the computer. Exit the program you're in if you can. Then, try a soft boot—hold down the control, alt, and delete keys. You can press the reset button if your computer has one. You'll lose some work since you're restarting, but hopefully not much.

If all fails, shut the computer off entirely. Wait for it to cool off a bit—at least ten seconds—and restart it.

If your computer crashes often, notice which programs are running at the time it happens. Perhaps files involved with the program are messed up in some way. Try to fix it by re-installing the program software with the add/remove software utility listed in control panel. Choose "remove program," then click on what you would like removed. Warning: if you see a notice that says removing it will affect other programs, your computer is probably not joking. Let things alone.

Now, reinstall the program. Restart your computer and try doing the same things you were doing when things usually crashed. If it still doesn't work, you'll probably have to install Windows again for a fresh start, if this is your system.

Top Web Addresses You Need to Know

All the sites, listed alphabetically by subject, are free unless noted otherwise at the end of listing.

Antiques and Collectibles

Learn About Antiques and Collectibles

http://willow.internet-connections.net/web/antiques

Advice on how to pick and deal with antiques dealers, plus information on a broad range of collectibles, from china, furniture, and quilts to dolls, can be found at this site.

Art

Louvre

http://mistral.culture.fr/louvre

View paintings, sculpture, and other masterpieces from the famous Paris museum.

National Gallery of Art

www.nga.gov

View 100,000 paintings and sculptures from the Washington, D.C. museum, which you can search by artist or title.

Web Museum

http://sunsite/unc/edu/wm

Browse famous paintings, organized by artist and type of art—from Impressionism and medieval to contemporary—then click on the image to enlarge it screen-size. Biographies of artists and descriptions of types of art are at this twenty-four-hour, free museum as well.

Auctions

OnSale

www.onsale.com

Bid on computers and equipment, sporting goods, and consumer electronics at the Web's biggest auction site.

Web Auction

www.webauction.com

Bid on variety of products, starting at only $1.

Books

Amazon.com

www.amazon.com

This online bookstore with over 2 million titles, is searchable by title, author, or topic and offers deep discounts. The site has reviews and recommendations, plus free e-mail reminders of books you may like.

Barnes & Noble

www.barnesandnoble.com

The big chain's online store is searchable by title, author, or topic and offers deep discounts on purchases, many live author chats, reviews and interviews from print, television, and radio outlets, and recommendations.

BookSearch

www.booksearch.com

This site offers a free search service for out-of-print and rare books. It actually hunts for books instead of just checking its own database.

Bookwire

www.bookwire.com

A comprehensive resource about books and the publishing industry, with links to author Web sites, author appearances, reviews, and resources for writers.

The Independent Reader

www.independentreader.com

A guide to independent bookstores nationwide, this site offers monthly reviews of recommended books, with links to the stores' sites.

The Romance Reader

www.theromancereader.com

Hundreds of romance novel reviews, plus articles, author interviews, book signings calendar, and freebies (newsletters, bookmarks, even books) from the novelists.

Business and Finance

BusinessTown

www.BusinessTown.com

Over 1,000 pages packed with savvy advice on all aspects of starting and running a small business. Includes instructional articles, interactive forums, downloadable letters and forms, sample business plans, ideas for new businesses, and much more.

EDGAR Online

www.edgar-online.com

Corporate filings by public companies to the Securities and Exchange Commission are searchable by company name, filing type or date. Full financial statements of companies are available to paid subscribers.

E Trade

www.etrade.com

Buy stocks, mutual funds and options online, plus track market indexes and favorite stocks.

Hoover s Online

www.hoovers.com

This site features company profiles, addresses and telephone numbers, key executives, statistics such as annual sales, number of employees and recent stock price, and job openings. It is searchable by company name, industry, region, or amount of sales. Extra services are available to paid subscribers, such as archives of company news stories and historical financial details.

Idea Cafe

www.ideacafe.com

Information, quizzes, and resources for small business owners are provided with a light, humorous touch. Profiles, message boards, and handy tips are included as well.

The Motley Fool

www.fool.com/index.htm

David and Tom Gardner, authors of several investment guides, offer advice on investing in stocks, financial news and analysis for the individual investor. The site also has bulletin boards and a searchable database by topic, and is also on America Online.

The Quote

www.quote.com

This site features stock quotes, breaking financial news, and overall performance for specific industries and cities; fee for real-time stock chart action.

Small Office

www.smalloffice.com

Articles and tips for small businesses, from sales and marketing, creating a Web site, saving money, and increasing efficiency, from *Home Office Computing* and *Small Office Computing* magazines.

The Street.com

www.thestreet.com

Stock quotes, breaking financial news, and commentary are included on this site. A fee is charged for stock and mutual fund tracking and other special features.

Cars

Auto-By-Tel

www.autobytel.com

Buy a new or used car, easily searchable by model type, with information on leases, reviews, and other resources.

Catalogs

CatalogLink

www.cataloglink.com

Browse offerings or order catalogs from many retailers, selling everything from clothing and home and gift items to sports, business, and computer equipment.

Catalog Mart

http://catalog.savvy.com

Browse or order from over 10,000 catalogs on over 800 subjects, from clothing to business and computer equipment.

The Gap

www.gap.com

The casual clothing chain's site has a mix-and-match feature to show how different styles, types, and colors go together with varying hair color and skin types, plus catalog listings, pictures, and a store locator.

J. Crew

www.jcrew.com

This site has catalog listings and pictures plus a store locator.

Lands' End

www.landsend.com

This site features catalog listings for clothing, luggage, and bed linens, plus an overstock section with discounts of up to 75 percent off.

Spiegel

www.spiegel.com

The Spiegel site has catalog listings for intimate apparel, electronics, and a deep discount section.

Children's Interest

Bedtime-Story

http://the-office.com/bedtime-story

Featured at this site are beautifully illustrated stories for children, searchable by topic, such as magical or humorous, and age group, plus plot summaries and estimated reading times.

Bonus.com

www.bonus.com

Over 1,000 activities for children, including quizzes, games, puzzles, educational material and surfing to child-safe Web sites are included at this site.

Children's Express

www.ce.org

Monthly magazine with serious articles written by, and for, teenagers and preteens, largely on culture or politics.

Disney Books

www.disney.com/DisneyBooks

Read *Bambi*, *The Lion King*, and other beloved stories with colorful illustrations and sound clips.

Disney's Daily Blast

www.disneyblast.com

This site has daily games, activities, on-line crafts projects, and jokes for children. Read regular interactive stories and animated comics, and learn the alphabet and numbers with famous Disney characters.

Getting Real

www.gettingreal.com

A teenagers' site, this has weekly diary entries from teenagers, each focused on choosing a career, finding a college, arts, sports, or technology. Games, activities, message boards, and links to sites of teenage interest are included.

Kidnews

www.vsa.cape.com/~powens/Kidnews3.html

Articles written by children or classrooms include news, features, fiction, sports, and poetry.

Yahooligans!

www.yahooligans.com

From the search engine Yahoo!, articles and news on this site range from science, world geography, cultures, and history to art, entertainment, sports, plus games and bulletin boards.

City Guides

CitySearch

www.citysearch.com

Extensive listings are included for nightlife, restaurants, music, art, talks, hotels, and shopping in about a dozen cities in the United States, including New York, San Francisco, Washington, D.C., Nashville, and Raleigh/Durham. Searchable by category—for example, restaurants can be searched by gardens, fireplaces, singles, and live music.

Lycos CityGuides

http://cityguide.lycos.com

Included are short guides to 400 cities in the United States, including maps, business listings, news, and description, plus Web links and descriptions for certain cities worldwide, especially Europe and North America.

In 1995, the first company that went public by placing its financial documents on the Web to draw investors was Spring Street Brewing Company, a small New York brewery that made a Belgian-style beer. Headed by a former Wall Street securities lawyer, Andrew Klein, the firm sold over 860,000 shares of stock to 3,500 investors through its initial public offering, which was also advertised in print.

Because of a few quirks—the stock could not be traded on a standard exchange such as the New York Stock Exchange or NASDAQ—Spring Street Brewing later allowed prospective buyers and sellers to contact each other by e-mail through a bulletin board on its Web site. After deals were struck, money and stock certificates were sent to the company, which forwarded them to the investors. The trading was later modified at the request of the Securities and Exchange Commission (SEC), which asked that a bank or escrow agent handle the funds.

Because the Spring Street Brewing offering generated such strong interest—inquiries were still coming in months after the initial public offering period ended—allowed investors to buy stock without brokers or commissions, and the firm to save considerable print and postage costs, Klein got a brainstorm to start a business helping other companies go public on the Web. He formed Wit Capital Corporation, named after his wheat-based beer, in 1997.

Today, many people do Web-based stock trading, using stock brokerages such as DLJdirect (the online version of Donaldson Lufkin & Jenrette), eSchwab (discount broker Charles Schwab's on-line counterpart), Fidelity Web Xpress, and E*Trade. By the year 2002, $688 billion will be managed in on-line trading accounts—five times the amount in 1997—according to Forrester Research, the market research firm in Cambridge, Mass.

Sidewalk

www.sidewalk.com

At this site you'll find extensive listings and many reviews for restaurants, movies, theater, nightlife, art, music, and shopping for nine cities in the United States, including New York, San Francisco, and Seattle; searchable by category.

Yahoo! Metros

www.yahoo.com/promotions/metros

Yahoo's city guide features web links to resources and businesses in a dozen cities, including New York, Boston, Chicago, Miami, and Austin. You can also make your own local guide by typing in your zip code at local.yahoo.com.

Boston.com

www.boston.com

From the *Boston Globe* and *Boston Magazine*, this site is a travel guide to New England, plus restaurants, arts, nightlife for Boston.

At Hand

www.athand.com

A guide to California, this site includes sightseeing, real estate, and arts, plus local guides for San Francisco, Los Angeles, Silicon Valley, and San Diego.

New York Magazine

www.newyorkmag.com

This site has restaurant, movie, theater, music and art reviews, plus articles and personal ads.

Washington, DC City Pages

www.dcpages.com

Restaurant, music, theater, and art reviews, plus a DC top 10 feature are included at this site.

Consumer Safety/Privacy

The Anonymizer

www.anonymizer.com

Surf Web sites without being tracked or send e-mail anonymously through this site.

Better Business Bureau

www.bbb.org

Learn how to recognize common scams, plus tips on buying safely and descriptions of the bureau's dispute resolution programs.

Computer Virus Hoaxes

www.kumite.com/myths

Learn to spot virus hoaxes on the Internet and read about well-known cases.

Cookie Central

www.cookiecentral.com

The last word on cookies, which allow Web sites to track your habits and preferences on the Web, this site also includes privacy protection tips and pros vs. cons of cookies.

CyberPatrol

www.cyberpatrol.com

This site has child-protection software to block objectionable on-line material.

CyberSitter

www.cybersitter.com

Child-protection software to block objectionable on-line material is available at this site.

National Foundation for Consumer Credit

www.nfcc.org

Locate authorized budget counseling and debt management services—searchable by city—plus information on credit reports, bankruptcy, and a debt quiz from this network of nonprofit community budget counseling groups.

National Fraud Information Center

www.fraud.org

Learn how to recognize common scams, especially in telemarketing and against seniors, and know your rights under the law. This site from the National Consumers League also has an Internet Fraud Watch section.

NetNanny

www.netnanny.com

This site has child-protection software to block objectionable online material.

Pretty Good Privacy

www.pgp.com

Software to scramble your e-mail for privacy protection is available at this site.

Scambusters

www.scambusters.com

This site features a newsletter with tips on recognizing and preventing Internet scams, spam, and hoaxes.

SurfWatch

www.surfwatch.com

Child-protection software to block objectionable online material is available at this site.

Cosmetics

Cover Girl

www.covergirl.com

Makeup tips for face, eyes, lips, and nails, plus advice for quick makeovers can be found on this site.

Revlon

www.revlon.com

This site has information on cosmetics, hair, and fragrance products. A virtual face feature lets you pick a makeup look and offers detailed advice.

Crafts

Craftsearch

www.craftsearch.com

Search stores and suppliers for hobby, craft, sewing, and quilting by zip code. Plus, there are almost 5,000 links for these topics.

Dating

Love@1st Site

www.love@1st-site.com

This matchmaking service offers profiles and photographs, plus a privacy feature. It costs to join, but there is a free trial offer.

Match.com

www.match.com

Matchmaking service, with profiles and a privacy feature, charges a fee, but there is a free trial offer.

Education

American School Directory

www.asd.com

Basic facts on all public, private, and parochial grade and high schools in the United States, with links to their Web sites, can be found at this site.

FastWeb

www.fastweb.com

This site is a free college and graduate scholarship search service. Type in your profile and likely matches from the thousands in FastWeb's database will be sent by e-mail. Federal and local financial aid information, such as grants and loans, is also available.

Kids Web

www.npac.syr.edu/textbook/kidsweb

A library of information and links for children, from kindergarten through high school, is offered at this site. The site is searchable by subjects such as science (divided into biology, astronomy, chemistry and so on), social studies, and the arts.

ScholarStuff

www.scholarstuff.com

This site is a directory of thousands of college and university Web sites in the United States and abroad.

Entertainment

ABC

www.abc.com

Look for plot summaries, cast biographies, and trivia quizzes of popular ABC shows such as "Ellen," "NYPD Blue," daytime soap operas, plus news shows at this site.

Ain't It Cool News

www.aint-it-cool-news.com

Gossip, advance news, and reviews (by amateurs) of test screenings of movies in production are featured at this site.

Blockbuster Video

www.blockbuster.com

Movie videos for sale or rental, music CDs and CD-ROM games for sale, plus some entertainment news can be found at this site.

CBS

http://marketing.cbs.com

Look for David Letterman's "Top 10 Lists," plus information on shows such as "60 Minutes," "Murphy Brown," daytime soap operas, and news shows.

Cinemachine

www.cinemachine.com

This site has movie reviews from print and online publications nationwide, searchable by title or keyword.

Dilbert

www.unitedmedia/comics/dilbert

This the official site of Dilbert, the famous comic strip, by Scott Adams, which spoofs office life.

The Dominion

www.scifi.com

From the Sci-Fi cable television channel, this site offers science fiction galore, from movie clips and trailers, classic radio dramas (including Orson Welles), celebrity chats, games, and an on-line store.

Entertainment Asylum

www.asylum.com

This site has movie and television news, celebrity interviews, events coverage, and chat Included are sound and video clips (requiring RealPlayer) in genres from science fiction to drama. Also accessible on America Online.

Entertainment News Daily

http://entertainmentnewsdaily.com

Featured on this site are book, theater, movie, music, and television news from major newspapers and trade publications distributed by the New York Times Syndicate.

E! Online

www.eonline.com

This site from the E! entertainment cable channel has movie and television news, gossip, sound and video clips of movie premieres, and chat.

Girls On Film

www.girlsonfilm.com

Offering movie reviews from four women in their twenties, this site also has movie news, celebrity interviews, gossip, and articles from readers.

GIST TV

www.gist.com

This site has local TV listings by zip code, which can be customized by time, channel, and show type, also included are articles, video previews of television programs, and chat forums.

Hollywood Online

www.hollywood.com

A guide to official movie Web sites and reviews, this site also has sound clips of celebrity interviews, entertainment news, and games.

Internet Movie Database

www.imdb.com

This vast resource has facts about over 100,000 movies, including cast, crew, plot summaries, reviews, film studios, running time, press releases, and more.

MovieLink

www.movielink.com

An online version of MovieFone, you can check movie times and buy tickets at local theaters, Search by title, star, time, type, and zip code.

MovieWeb

www.movieweb.com

Featured are video clips of trailers, photographs, plot summaries, and production notes from upcoming, current, and past movies, plus links to the movies' and studios' official sites.

Mr. Cranky's Guide to This Week at the Movies

http://internet-plaza.net/zone/mrcranky/thisweek.html

Unusually opinionated but often wildly amusing, this site has current movie reviews, with message boards for each film.

Mr. Showbiz

www.showbiz.com

Here you will find movie and television news, celebrity interviews, gossip, reviews, searchable database, games, and chat.

NBC TV Central

www.nbc.com/tvcentral/index.html

Look for plot summaries, cast biographies, trivia quizzes, and awards for favorite shows like *Seinfeld*, *ER*, *Frasier*, *Mad About You*, *Friends*, and daytime soap operas.

The Oscars

www.oscar.com

The official Academy Awards site, it has current winners, interviews and photographs, plus a searchable database for past winners.

PBS

www.pbs.org

Information and schedule dates for many public television programs on science, travel, nature, talk, mystery, children's shows (such as *Sesame Street*), and games.

Playbill

www.playbill.com

A comprehensive theater lovers' site, you will find reviews, articles, theater listings nationwide, ticket purchases, plus tons of links to Web sites of Broadway shows, Tony Awards, musical comedy, history, etc.

Reel.com

www.reel.com

Rent or buy movie videos at this site, including thousands of classic, art house, foreign, and rare films. If you're having a tough time deciding, the delightful Movie Map feature lists movie categories with many subdivisions, such as Suspense/Thriller/Psychological/Mind Games, and suggests a long list of sleeper gems you may not have heard of.

Roger Ebert on Movies

www.suntimes.com/ebert/ebert.html

Read movie reviews and learn about favorite movies from the *Chicago Sun-Times* critic of "Siskel & Ebert" fame.

Telerama

www.cinema.pgh.pa.us/movie/reviews

This movie review search engine has links to reviews in print and on-line publications (more extensive than Internet Movie Database's reviews) and is searchable by title or keyword.

Ticketmaster Online

www.ticketmaster.com

Buy concert or theater tickets, searchable by keyword or state.

Tony Awards Online

www.tonys.org

This official Tony Award site has articles, interviews, Tony Award nominations and winners from Broadway shows—past and present—a theater locator for shows, plus video and sound clips of the award ceremony.

TVgen

www.tvguide.com

TV Guide's site offers television listings by zip code, soap opera and science fiction sections, movie reviews and times, entertainment news, gossip, and games.

Food/Drink/Restaurants

Coffee Journal

www.tigeroak.com/coffeejournal

Articles and recipes about coffee and cafe culture worldwide are available at this site from the print magazine *Coffee Journal*.

Cuisinenet

www.cuisinenet.com

This site has thousands of restaurant reviews in a limited number of cities, but offers helpful price and opening hours facts.

CyberMeals

www.cybermeals.com

A free take-out and delivery service from thousands of restaurants in certain cities nationwide, menus are available in cuisines from Asian, European, and American.

Epicurious

http://food.epicurious.com

Recipes from great chefs worldwide, articles from *Gourmet* and *Bon Appetit* magazines, a limited number of restaurant reviews, and a searchable database of food articles from Conde Nast Publications are all available at this site.

Fodor's Restaurant Index

www.fodors.com/ri.cgi

A thorough guide from the Fodor's travel guidebooks, this site has restaurant reviews for dozens of cities worldwide.

Food TV

www.foodtv.com

This site from the TV Food Network offers recipes from its many shows, from "Too Hot Tamales" to "Essence of Emeril," answers to cooking questions, and a glossary of cooking terms and tips.

Godiva Chocolatier

www.godiva.com

Buy Godiva chocolates online, browse recipes, and find out where stores are located.

Good Cooking!

www.goodcooking.com

A gigantic collection of recipes, many submitted by readers, this site also has articles about types of food, ethnic cuisines, and facts, but not especially well-organized.

Hot! Hot! Hot!

www.hothothot.com

Giant list of international spicy sauces for sale, this site is searchable by heat level, country of origin, ingredient, or name.

Meals for You

www.mealsforyou.com

Find many recipes, well-organized by type of food (seafood, meat, vegetarian), ingredients, diets, ethnic cuisines, and nutritional content.

NetGrocer

www.netgrocer.com

The first national online supermarket delivers non-perishables—from baby food and care items, beverages, canned goods, pet food, and pasta to staples like paper products—by Federal Express.

Once A Month Cooking

http://members.aol.com/OAMCLoop/index.html

Learn how to cook one month's worth of meals in one day, with tips on planning, buying in bulk, cooking and freezing, plus recipes.

Over the Coffee

www.cappuccino.com

A complete resource on coffee history, health, cyber and real-world cafes, literature, health, and home roasting, this site also lists retailers for coffee beans and equipment.

Sally's Place

www.bpe.com

This site has restaurant reviews for several dozen cities plus detailed articles on specific foods, ethnic cuisines, and beverages.

Virtual Vineyards

www.virtualvin.com

Wines, food, and gourmet gifts are available at this online store.

Waiters on Wheels

www.waitersonwheels.com

This site offers a delivery service from restaurants in California, Washington, and Nevada. Various cuisines are available, with online menus. A fee is charged for each order.

The Webtender

www.webtender.com

This handy online bartending service offers instructions on mixing drinks and is searchable by drink name, ingredients, alcohol, and glass type.

Zagat Restaurant Survey

http://cgi.pathfinder.com:80/cgi-bin/zagat/homepage

From the *Zagat* print guides, this site offers reviews of top restaurants in several dozen U.S. cities that are compiled from reader comments.

Foreign Languages

Travlang Foreign Languages for Travelers

www.travlang.com/languages

This site offers common phrases in dozens of foreign languages, plus sound clips to hear correct pronunciations.

Free Stuff

Club FreeShop

www.freeshop.com

Free products and trial offers, from magazines and software to catalogs, are all available at this site.

Games

Gamespot

www.gamespot.com

Featured at this site are computer game reviews, downloads, and tips.

Happy Puppy

www.happypuppy.com

This site is a gathering place for computer game fans, with news, reviews, game downloads, and message boards.

Jeopardy!

www.station.sony.com/jeopardy

Play the famous television trivia game show here.

The Riddler

www.riddler.com

Many trivia quizzes and puzzles are available here, plus the chance to win prizes.

Suspect

www.electrastudios.com/suspect

Play detective and search for clues in this online murder mystery.

You Don't Know Jack

www.bezerk.com/netshow/index.html

Popular culture trivia quizzes are presented in a television game show-style, with sound clips and the chance to win prizes. Based on the popular CD-ROM.

Gardening

Gardening.com

www.gardening.com

An encyclopedia of over 1,500 plants, a plant problem-solver, and directory of related Web sites, searchable by subject, region, or keyword are found at this site.

Virtual Garden

http://vg.com

This gardener's best friend is on the Pathfinder site and features an encyclopedia of about 3,000 plants and trees, articles on gardening advice, seasonal tips and weather forecasts searchable by time zone, and answers to questions.

Genealogy

Ancestry.com

www.ancestry.com

This site offers free lessons on how to trace your family tree through birth, marriage, and death certificates and other records such as the Social Security Death Index. An online store sells genealogy software, books, and supplies.

Cyndi's List of Genealogy Sites

www.cyndislist.com

This site offers over 28,000 links in over 90 categories, from different countries to libraries, publications, military sources, mailing lists, and newsgroups.

Gifts

Cybershop.com

www.cybershop.com

Gourmet cookware, foods, electronics, and home furnishings products purchased at this site are shipped gift-wrapped within twenty-four hours. The directory is easily searchable.

1-800-FLOWERS

www.1800flowers.com

This online delivery service offers bouquets, plants, food and gift baskets can be searched by item, price range, or special occasion.

The Virtual Florist

www.virtualflorist.com

An online delivery service for bouquets and gift baskets, this site also offers free floral electronic greeting cards if your budget is tight.

Government

Census Bureau

www.census.gov

Oodles of statistics are available this site on everything from population numbers, household income, age, ethnic group, housing starts, and businesses, to computer ownership. Many reports as well.

Department of Education

www.ed.gov

Useful information at this site includes publications for parents on helping children learn various school subjects, using a library and preparing for tests, Federal financial aid

for college students, plus Federal efforts to improve technology in schools.

Federal Trade Commission's Consumerline

www.ftc.gov/bcp/conline/conline.htm

This site from the commission's Bureau of Consumer Protection offers publications on all types of frauds including real estate, cars, credit, health and fitness, and the Internet. A separate section details how to report fraud.

Fedworld

www.fedworld.gov

A huge Federal government site, you can find or buy reports or publications, find specific agency sites, browse databases with tax form information and Federal jobs.

Food and Drug Administration

www.fda.gov

This site offers detailed descriptions of approved drugs for humans and animals, diet supplements, food, and cosmetics, plus drug news and consumer advice.

Healthfinder

www.healthfinder.gov

This encyclopedic site from the U.S. Department of Health and Human Services offers the latest government health news: choosing quality care—from health insurance plans, hospitals, long-term care to medical treatment—hot topics from cancer, AIDS, to food safety; sections on seniors and children; support groups; and publications.

Internal Revenue Service

www.irs.ustreas.gov/prod/cover.html

This useful site has information on filing tax returns electronically, frequently asked tax preparation questions, regulations in plain English, downloadable forms and publications, and telephone/fax numbers for tax tips.

National Aeronautics & Space Administration

www.nasa.gov

At this site you will find the latest news, research findings, and history of the NASA space program. A multimedia gallery offers fascinating photographs and video of the Mars landing and space shuttle launches.

PubMed

www.ncbi.nlm.nih/gov/PubMed

This site gives you free access to MED-LINE with its nine million articles in medical journals from the National Institute of Health's National Library of Medicine database that feature the most recent research findings.

Small Business Administration

www.sbaonline.sba.gov

Featured on this site are extensive FAQs on starting, financing, and growing a business, plus a directory of offices and resource centers by state and a library of shareware for running a business.

Social Security Administration

www.ssa.gov

Find out your estimated retirement benefit based on your lifetime earnings, learn about retirement, survivors, disability and Supplemental Security Income benefits, and find the closest Social Security office by typing in your zip code.

White House

www.whitehouse.gov

Read Presidential speeches, news releases, and achievements of the current Administration, plus learn how the Federal government works and the history of the White House. There is also an easy-to-read children's section.

Health/Fitness

American Psychological Association

www.apa.org/pubinfo

This site has online booklets on mental health issues (from memories of childhood abuse and depression to sexual harassment) plus tips on how to choose a therapist.

CyberDiet

www.cyberdiet.com

Get tips on proper eating and exercise, with a database of calories and nutrients for common foods, nutritional profiles (based on age, sex, build, and activity level), and daily food planners.

The Doctor Directory

www.doctordirectory.com

Search this site for addresses, telephone numbers, specialties, medical school attended, and board memberships of physicians. You can search by state and city.

FitnessLink

www.fitnesslink.com

A comprehensive resources on fitness, this site has exercise, nutrition, diet and stress-busting tips, news, mailing lists and publications, plus message boards.

GriefNet

www.rivendell.org

This site offers support groups for the bereaved, from the widowed to parents whose children have died to women who have given up babies for adoption.

InteliHealth

www.intelihealth.com

From the Johns Hopkins Medical Center, this site has information on adult health by topic, medical journal article summaries, a nutrition database, and a nationwide doctor finder.

Internet Mental Health

www.mentalhealth.com

This site has descriptions and treatments for over fifty mental health problems, a directory of dozens of psychiatric drugs (with information and side effects), and medical journal articles.

KidsHealth.org

www.kidshealth.org

From pediatric experts at The Nemours Foundation, funded by the duPont family, this site has resources on children's physical and mental health, first aid emergency tips, treatment, and support groups for parents. A children's section contains games, recipes, and animations on how the human body works.

Mayo Health Oasis

www.mayo.ivi.com

Extensive medical and health information from the world-famous Mayo Clinic includes drug and disease directories, and resources on women's and children's health, heart disease, cancer, allergies, and Alzheimer's. Medical and diet questions are answered by e-mail.

MedHelp

www.medhelp.org/index.htm

This nonprofit organization offers thousands of medical journal articles, support group listings, a patient network to find others with the same illness, and medical questions answered by e-mail.

Medscape

www.medscape.com

This comprehensive medical and health resource includes thousands of medical journal articles and daily medical news, searchable by topic, from surgery to women's health to managed care, drug name, or medical term.

Fan Tribute Sites

Because the democratic nature of the Web means anyone can be a publisher—as long as you create or have someone else create a Web site—many fans have lovingly built sites to pay tribute to their favorite television shows, actors, plays, or heroes.

Some fan sites are:

- The Seinfeldiest Site on the Web
www.seinfeldiest.com
    The NBC comedy beloved by many may have moved on, but over 300 video clips, sound clips, photographs, quotations (from "yada, yada, yada" to "master of my domain"), and trivia quizzes perpetuate the memory at this colorful site.

- X-Files Resources for X-Philes
www.concentric.net/~gwacie/index.shtml
    A huge list of links, including plot summaries, sound clips, newsgroups, mailing lists, and merchandise are featured at this site.

- Xena: the Warrior Princess
http://plaza.interport.net/logomanc/XENA/index.html
    Photographs, newsgroups, mailing lists, fan clubs, biographies, plus Greek mythology and essential phrases in the Greek language are all found at this site.

- Star Trek: WWW
www.stwww.com
    This comprehensive site from an Italian fan, has newsgroups, mailing lists, numerous links, and a searchable database.

- Stephen Sondheim Stage
www.sondheim.com
    This site has show schedules, plot summaries, history, awards, original casts (from *Company* to *Sweeney Todd*), articles in The Forum section, reviews, and interviews with people working on Sondheim theater and film projects.

- International Sinatra Society
www.sinatraclub.com
    This site has photographs and trivia of the late Frank Sinatra, plus merchandise for sale including CDs, books, movie videos, posters and magazines.

Your Health Daily

www.nytsyn.com/med

Health and fitness articles from major newspapers and medical journals distributed by the New York Times Syndicate, plus message boards, are found at this site.

Home Decoration

Ask A Designer

www.askadesigner.com

Ask home design questions by e-mail, browse design tips and past questions, or locate an interior designer by zip code.

Home Ideas

www.homeideas.com

Extensive articles on decorating are searchable by room, plus there are free product catalogs and brochures and message boards.

HouseNet

www.housenet.com

Offering extensive resources for home and garden improvement and decorating, this site has articles, estimators for how much paint or wallpaper you'll need, and contractors by zip code.

Martha Stewart Living

www.marthastewart.com

Highlights of Martha Stewart's magazine, television program, radio show, and books provide decorating, entertaining, gardening, and home improvement tips plus recipes.

Insurance

Insuremarket

www.insuremarket.com

This site from Quicken, the maker of the personal finance software Intuit, offers competitive prices from different companies on health, life, and auto insurance, plus advice on choosing a policy and figuring out how much coverage you need.

InsWeb

www.insweb.com

Receive competitive quotes from different companies on health, car, and life insurance on-line or by e-mail, plus articles and quizzes to help determine what kind and how much insurance you need.

Jobs/Careers

About Work

www.aboutwork.com

A community site on job hunting and career advancement, this site offers advice, weekly hot jobs profiles, bulletin boards, and sections for working at home, small business, and students.

Career Mosaic

www.careermosaic.com

Thousands of job listings, resume postings, and company profiles are included at this site. The extensive resource list includes professional organizations, salary and market trends data, career articles library, and news links.

CareerCity

www.careercity.com

Access to 4 million job openings, hot links to 27,000 employers, free resume posting, salary surveys, directories, and hundreds of articles on careers. From the publishers of *JobBank* and *Knock 'em Dead* books.

Cool Jobs

www.cooljobs.com

Learn how to apply for various glamour and fun jobs including Club Med, Ben & Jerry's, television, movies, circus, F.B.I., and space jobs.

Internet Career Plaza

www.careerplaza.com

Job listings and placement agencies at this site are searchable by industry and region. Tools to write and post resumes are included.

Monster Board

www.monsterboard.com

Thousands of job listings, resume postings, company profiles and career tips can be found at this site. Build a desired job profile, and a personal job search agent will e-mail likely job listings to you.

Legal

FindLaw

www.findlaw.com

An extensive directory of legal resources, this site has U.S. Supreme Court rulings, law firm listings nationwide, news, topics from labor to intellectual property, federal, state, and international laws, jobs, and message boards.

Maps

Mapquest

www.mapquest.com

Find a local map or get driving directions between two addresses by typing in any address in the United States, then zoom in for a closer look.

Music/Sound

Broadcast.com

www.broadcast.com

Sound clips available at this site range from concerts and CDs, live television and radio news, author interviews, business, sports and public affairs. This is biggest source of multimedia on the Web, due to partnerships with many television and radio interview networks and other companies.

CDnow

www.cdnow.com

Music CDs for sale—searchable by artist, album title, song title or record label—are available at this online store. Articles and reviews cover all music genres from rock and jazz to classical.

CD Universe

www.cduniverse.com

Music CDs for sale—searchable by artist, album title, song title, and genre—with many sound clips, are available at this online store.

Classical Insites

www.classicalinsites.com

Biographies of famous performers and classical, romantic, and opera composers, from Beethoven and Chopin to Verdi, plus lists of recommended recordings. Also included is a music history section, sound clips of concerts, a music CD store, and message boards as well.

Country Spotlight

www.countryspotlight.com

Country music news, reviews, celebrity interviews from Loretta Lynn to LeAnn Rimes, and chat can be found at this site.

E Music

www.emusic.com

This site has music CDs for sale, including many hard-to-find items.

JAM TV

www.jamtv.com

Featured at this site are sound clips of concerts and interviews with rock musicians, plus biographies, list of recordings, news, chat, and CDs for sale.

Jazz Central Station

www.jazzcentralstation.com

Jazz news, articles about musicians, sound clips of recordings, music CDs for sale, and message boards are all included at this site.

MTV Online

www.mtv.com

Rock music news, video and sound clips, interviews with musicians, and celebrity chats can be found at this site from the MTV cable channel.

Music Boulevard

www.musicblvd.com

At this site you will find music CDs and cassettes for sale—searchable by artist, album title, or song title—plus special content for rock, jazz, and classical fans. Music news from MTV and VH1 is also available.

Opera America

www.operaam.org

Find out when and where specific operas are being performed, and by which opera company, from this nonprofit group's database of schedules.

Tower Records

www.towerrecords.com

The Tower site has music CDs for sale—searchable by artist, album title, song title and genre, plus sound clips.

News

CNN Interactive

www.cnn.com

This site has late-breaking stories, with audio clips, from world, show business, and science/technology news.

C-SPAN

www.c-span.org

Video and sound clips of Congressional hearings, Washington press conferences, speeches and court sessions, and book programs are available at this site from the C-SPAN cable channel.

Electronic Newsstand

www.enews.com

A magazine lovers' site, featured are capsule summaries of stories from dozens of magazines, news about magazines, and "hype hell/hype heaven" features on who's getting bad and good press. Searchable by magazine name or category.

Los Angeles Times

www.latimes.com

The online version of this daily newspaper.

New York Times on the Web

www.nytimes.com

This online version of the paper has Book Review articles dating from 1980, and author interviews and readings, real estate and job classified ads, plus online features such as CyberTimes—articles concerning online issues—and many message boards on a wide range of topics. Easily searchable.

NPR

www.npr.org

National Public Radio online has sound clips of complete *All Things Considered* and *Morning Edition* shows (with RealAudio) plus news story summaries.

Pathfinder

www.pathfinder.com

A huge site for Time-Warner publications, included are *People*, *Money*, *Time*, *Fortune*, and *Entertainment Weekly* magazines. The database is searchable by topic or publication.

Total News

www.totalnews.com

This site has links to dozens of news sites, including newspapers, television, radio, and magazines. It is searchable by category (national news, business, opinion) and topic.

Wall Street Journal Interactive

www.wsj.com

Featuring highlights from the print version, this site also includes original articles on small business and technology and a library with articles from over 3,000 publications (per-article fees). Membership fee is required.

USA Today

www.usatoday.com

An online version of the daily newspaper, this site also has articles on noteworthy Web sites and Internet issues.

Washington Post

www.washingtonpost.com

An online version of the daily newspaper.

Package Tracking

Federal Express

www.fedex.com

Track packages sent worldwide by Federal Express, arrange for pickups, fill out and print air bills, and find out addresses and hours of the nearest drop-off locations.

United Parcel Service

www.ups.com/tracking/tracking.html

Track packages sent worldwide by UPS, arrange for pickups, and find out addresses, hours, and maps of the nearest dropoff locations.

Parents

Babies Online

www.babiesonline.com

This site has birth announcements with photographs and descriptions (searchable by baby's name and birthdate) plus free product samples and links to parenting sites.

BabyCenter

www.babycenter.com

This comprehensive reference site for new and expectant parents has pregnancy, baby care, health and nutrition information. Medical experts answer e-mail questions, and there is a store selling discount baby care products.

Family.com

www.family.com

At this site you'll find articles and message boards for parents on child rearing issues (from adoption, divorce, single parents, and discipline to family moves), planning activities, education—including helping with homework and gifted children—and games for children.

Parent Soup

www.parentsoup.com

A community site for parents with children of all ages, from teen-agers to babies. Features bulletin boards on topics from discipline problems, education to sibling rivalry, and news archives of interest ranging from product recalls to health and legislation issues. Experts offer advice to e-mail questions.

People Finders

Directories that list telephone numbers, addresses, and e-mail addresses of people nationwide include:

Bigfoot
www.bigfoot.com

555-1212.com
www.555-1212.com

Four11
www.Four11.com

Infospace
www.infospace.com

Internet Address Finder
www.iaf.net

Switchboard
www.switchboard.com

Pets

Animal Network

www.petchannel.com

At this site are breed descriptions and photographs of pets—from dogs, cats, horses to fish—plus message boards on care, health, and behavior.

Cat Fancier's Home Page

www.fanciers.com

A comprehensive cat lovers' site, you'll find breed descriptions and photographs, health care information, advice on raising a kitten and buying a purebred, resources on breeders and cat shows, and a bibliography.

Real Estate

Bank Rate Monitor

www.bankrate.com

Compare mortgage rates at specific banks in over 100 cities nationwide, and consult step-by-step tips in choosing and applying for a mortgage. A chart comparing credit card rates and tips on home equity loans and bank ATM rates is also offered.

Homebuyer's Fair

www.homefair.com/home

Compare schools, crime, demographics, and insurance rates in cities nationwide. Handy calculators figure out how big a mortgage you can afford, cost-of-living comparisons between domestic and foreign cities, monthly mortgage payments, renting versus buying a home, and the value of your home. Recent home sales in your city are also provided.

Reference

All-In-One Search Page

www.albany.net/allinone

A one-stop shopping for many reference sources, here you will find Bartlett's *Familiar Quotations*, Shakespeare's complete works, current U.S. legislation, people finders, and search engines.

Ask An Expert

www.askanexpert.com/askanexpert

Experts in many fields in a dozen broad categories—from career/industry, science/technology to health—answer questions by e-mail or offer helpful Web sites.

Encarta

http://encarta.msn.com/Encarta/Home.asp

A smaller version of Microsoft's Encarta CD-ROM encyclopedia.

Encyclopedia Brittanica Online

www.eb.com

This site has thousands of articles from the print encyclopedia plus many on-line articles, including pictures, maps, a dictionary, and Web links. Fee for membership, but there is a free trial period.

Encyclopedia Mythica

www.pantheon.org/mythica

Here you can learn about thousands of myths and legends—from Greek and Roman to Celtic, Norse, Aztec, and Native American—with pictures.

Grolier Multimedia Encyclopedia

www.gme.grolier.com

This site has thousands of articles from the CD-ROM encyclopedia, with pictures, maps, Web links, and a children's section. Fee but free trial.

Learn2.com

www.learn2.com

An excellent reference for practical and fun tips, here you'll find useful information on home repair (fix a leaky faucet or toilet, defrost a freezer, clean a bathroom), personal care (get a close shave, repair pantyhose, tie a necktie), and parenting (childproof a home, burp a baby).

National Association of Investigative Specialists

www.pimall.com/nais

A comprehensive resource for Web sites, books and articles on investigating people or businesses, this site is from a trade association for private detectives.

Reminder Service

E-Organizer

www.eorganizer.com

You'll never forget birthdays, anniversaries, parties and other important days again: this service will e-mail you a reminder. Post your lists of chores and notes as well on this free online electronic organizer.

Science

Discovery Channel Online

www.discovery.com

This site from the Discovery cable channel features articles on nature, exploration, science, and technology, with a searchable database.

Seniors

Senior.com

www.senior.com

A money club site, here you'll find FAQs on personal finance and business finance, chats, information on classes and events, and news from national and local publications for seniors.

SeniorNet

www.seniornet.org

This site from a nonprofit group that educates older people about computers features over 200 message boards for people age fifty-five and older, on topics from current events, health, religion, cooking, gardening, and computers to politics, plus e-mail pen pals.

Sports

CBS Sportsline

www.sportsline.com

From CBS Sports, this site has articles on men's and women's sports, scores, sound and video clips, and chat.

ESPNET Sportszone

www.sportszone.com

This comprehensive resource for daily sports news from the ESPN cable channel covers sports worldwide.

GolfWeb

www.golfweb.com

Articles, golf courses worldwide searchable by country or name, message boards, even a partner locator can be found at this site.

Mountain Zone Skiing

www.mountainzone.com/ski/index.html

News from championship skiing worldwide, articles, product reviews and tips, interview sound clips, and message boards are found at this site.

SkiNet

www.skinet.com

This travel-oriented site has a resort finder that helps you pick a resort in the United States based on criteria such as lodging, value, snow quality, or apres-ski nightlife, and vacation packages. A snow report for different areas, plus message boards about ski resorts worldwide, are also included.

Toys

Beanie Babies

www.ty.com

This site from the toy maker Ty has photographs and an official list of the tiny stuffed animals, from Mel the Koala and Fleece the Lamb to Bernie the St. Bernard. Many other stuffed toys, such as cat and dog collections, are included.

Dr. Toy

www.drtoy.com

Over 500 toys and children's products have been selected by a nonprofit organization for children's resources, based upon educational value and durability, and are described by age group, toy type, cost, and company name and telephone number.

Vermont Teddy Bear Company

www.vtbear.com

An on-line store for the hand-crafted stuffed animals, you can order bears for special occasions, bears wearing outfits, or bears in the buff. Same-day shipping is possible with gift boxes and cards.

Special Occasions

American Greetings

www.americangreetings.com

Many electronic greeting cards are available at this site from the well-known card company. Searchable by special occasion, plus a reminder service. A fee is charged for animated cards only.

The Cyber Greeting Collection

http://home.stlnet.com/~binnie/cybrcard.htm

Many electronic greeting cards, with instructions on how to personalize, are available in a variety of different categories.

Hallmark

www.hallmark.com

Over 1,000 electronic greeting cards, plus a reminder service, are available at this site from the well-known card company. A fee is charged for animated cards only.

How Are You.com

www.howareyou.com/cards.shtml

Electronic greeting cards in many different categories are searchable by occasion or specialty.

Internet Card Central

www.cardcentral.net

Many different categories of electronic greeting cards are available at this site.

Travel

American Airlines Net SAAver Fares

www.americanair.com

Reduced airfares on last-minute domestic and international American Airlines flights, plus lower hotel and car rental rates, are available to subscribers of its weekly e-mail list.

Arthur Frommer's Outspoken Encyclopedia of Travel

www.frommers.com

This site from Frommer, the author of the original *Europe on $5 A Day* guidebooks, offers sightseeing guides, customs and hotels for 200 top cities and islands worldwide, helpful articles on budget travel and travel tips, plus travel reservations.

CyberRentals

http://cyberrentals.com/homepage.html

Search for or post a short-term vacation rental for homes, chalets, and condominiums worldwide, with photographs, costs, and descriptions.

Expedia

www.expedia.com

Comprehensive travel resources, from making airline and hotel reservations to a huge travel guide organized by country, are available at this site. Helpful features include airfare comparisons, currency converters, and a low airfare finder by e-mail.

Fodor's Travel Service

www.fodors.com

The personal trip planner can customize trips to over eighty cities worldwide, allowing you to select hotels and restaurants based on price and location. A bed-and-breakfast finder lets you pick from over 2,000 in the United States, searchable by state, amenities (lakeside, romantic, etc.) and activities. Essential information and activities from Fodor's guidebooks, articles, plus a low airfare finder are included as well.

Preview Travel

www.previewtravel.com/index.html

Choose hotel rooms and make reservations worldwide; searchable by cost, amenities, and specific hotel chain.

The idea of community where people with shared interests can share information and feel they belong to a bigger group is behind many Web sites. Racial and ethnic communities are no exception, and sites have been built to draw members of a specific minority as well as others interested in their culture.

Channel A

www.channela.com

For lovers of things Asian, this site offers a rich mix of recipes from India, Thailand, Vietnam, and China, martial arts movies and other Asian entertainment, business and political news, plus products, such as cookware and Japanese animation videos for sale.

The Black World Today

www.tbwt.com/index2.htm

This site is a daily newspaper with articles of interest from the United States, Caribbean, Africa, and Europe, from the arts to politics. There are sound clips of interviews and message boards debating racial issues drawing a multiracial crowd.

African American Web Connection

www.aawc.com/aawc.html

This site offers a comprehensive mix of biographies of prominent blacks, from authors Toni Morrison and Maya Angelou, opera singer Marian Anderson, singer and toast of Paris Josephine Baker, to leaders from Martin Luther King Jr. to elected officials, history—from Library of Congress and Encyclopedia Brittanica to black achievements in sports and the armed forces, enter-

tainment and arts—ranging from gospel, jazz, and hip hop to Haitian and African art and crafts, and business. A list of a variety of black organizations and chats are included as well.

QRadio

www.qradio.net

This site offers sound clips of music from South Africa, from choral music to jazz, plus 24-hour news and talk rad h African radio stations.

Black Voices

www.blackvoices.com

This site offers news and business articles of interest to blacks, plus practical advice on topics like buying a home or car, and career information.

LatinoWeb

www.catalog.com/favision/latinoweb.htm

This site offers a searchable directory covering many Web sites from news, arts, business, education, and media, based in the United States, Latin America, and Spain.

Hispanic Online

(www.hisp.com) offers articles, live celebrity chats, a schedule of events, and links and is the online version of *Hispanic*, a monthly magazine.

Priceline

www.priceline.com

Pick the price you want, and PriceLine will try to match unsold seats and reduced airfares on major airlines for domestic and international flights.

Rough Guides

www.hotwired.com/rough

With information from the print guidebooks, this site emphasizes offbeat destinations in Europe, the United States, and India.

Spa-Finders

www.spafinders.com

A worldwide spa locator, this site is searchable by category—such as luxury, New Age, adventure, weight management, various sports, location, and cost. Online bookings and special offers are also available.

The Trip.com

www.thetrip.com

This site offers airline reservations, airport maps, hotel reviews, tips, and a low airfare finder by e-mail.

Travelocity

www.travelocity.com

A huge travel guide organized by country, this site features airline reservations, hotel bookings, and low airfare finder by e-mail, from SABRE, the airline reservation system.

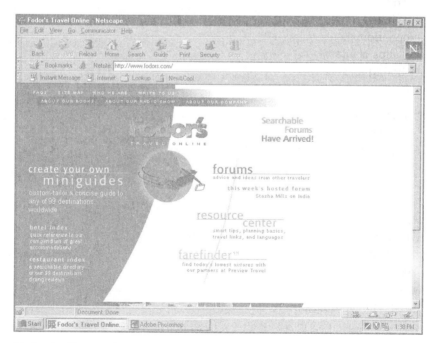

Fodor's Travel Service www.fodors.com

Worldview Systems

www.wvs.com

Organized by country, this site provides a detailed guide to hotels, restaurants, arts, and going out in over 200 destinations worldwide.

Women

Cybergrrl

www.cybergrrl.com

Features include Femina—a search engine for women's resources on the Web—Bookgrrl—reviews and interviews for books by women—forums, plus articles on careers, love and friends, family and travel.

Femina

www.femina.com

A clearinghouse of information for women, this site includes topics such as arts, business, health, family/motherhood, education, activities, and clubs for girls.

HomeArts Network

http://homearts.com

This site provides articles on family, food, home design and money, including many from *Good Housekeeping*, *Redbook*, and *Town & Country*.

Women's Wire

www.women.com/guide

A lifestyle magazine, this site has articles on careers, health, money, style, business owner profiles, forums, and daily "good news" for women. Specific information for certain cities is also available.

Zip Codes

U.S. Postal Service ZIP Code Lookup

www.usps.gov/ncsc

Find zip codes by typing in the address and city.

Travel
Education
News
Shopping
Music
Books

Wrap-up: Twenty-five Important Points to Remember

A great deal of ground was covered in this book, and much—or maybe all—may be unfamiliar. The Internet can be confusing because of the wide variation in many areas and the technical concepts.

Let's summarize twenty-five important points that will make your Internet experience easier, more positive, and productive:

1. Choose an Internet service provider or a commercial on-line service based upon your needs and desires. Consider:
   :-) the special content and members-only bulletin boards and chats of a commercial online service (such as America Online or Prodigy), which may guide you and make you feel part of something, versus the undiluted access of a straight Internet service provider
   :-) an easy-to-install automated sign-up program
   :-) cost (unlimited monthly use versus an limited number of hours)
   :-) local access telephone number
   :-) easy access, with no constant busy signals, and good technical support
   :-) no setup fee
   :-) e-mail and newsgroups included
   :-) compare national and local services in your area for the best overall deal
   :-) take advantage of trial offers before you buy

2. Use a 28.8 Kbps or higher modem for a speedier surf. You will regret using a slower speed.

3. Use a second telephone line for your Internet connection, unless you don't mind an answering machine or voice-mail system taking all messages for your household.

4. Type Internet addresses (URLs) EXACTLY as they appear. Carefully include the proper spelling, punctuation, any capital letters, and no spaces between letters.

5. Use search engines properly. Narrow your topic before you begin to search. Read search engines' instructions carefully, and use "AND," "OR," "NOT," plus or minus symbols, or quotation marks as the specific search engine recommends. Make a search engine your friend by learning its quirks and strong points.

6. Bookmark favorite sites so you can revisit them quickly without having to retype their Internet addresses. Bookmark at least one search engine. Organize your bookmarks and delete those sites you no longer visit.

7. Use commands such as "back" and "history" to revisit recently seen sites without having to retype their Internet addresses.

8. Use the "stop" command to halt a search or page from loading that is taking too long.

9. Respond to e-mail messages using "reply" so you don't have to type the sender's e-mail address.

10. Always fill in the subject of an e-mail message so the recipient has a general idea of what the message is about. Many people get a great deal of e-mail.

10. Locate sites, mailing lists, and/or newsgroups that share your interests or hobbies, and get involved. Read their content regularly, and post your comments or questions.

11. Observe proper netiquette. Read a newsgroup's postings and FAQ before posting your own message. Don't use all capital letters or send insulting messages.

12. Subscribe or unsubscribe to the mailing list owner directly without sending your message to the entire list.

13. If you want to create your own home page and don't know HTML, use your Internet service provider's or a community site's, such as GeoCities or Tripod, free home page building services.

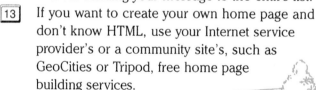

14. If you create your own home page, register its Internet address with various search engines. If it promotes a business, you possibly may want to use an announcement service as well.

15. Take advantage of the Web's many wonderful free

services, including reference, comparison shopping, travel bookings, newspapers, magazines and newsletters, reminder services, and product samples.

16 List yourself in people finder directories if you want to be found. Delete yourself from these directories if you want to protect your privacy.

17 If you have small or teenage children, monitor their online activity, urge them to tell you about favorite sites and online pals, and teach them not to disclose personal information. You can also childproof your computer by using filtering software to block objectionable material.

19 Protect your computer from viruses by using antivirus software.

20 Shop safely with a credit card on secure sites only (those using SSL or SET), which scramble information so it can't be read.

21 Use a current, or fairly recent, browser. Many Web sites note which browsers, and versions, are best, and some can only be viewed properly by fairly recent browsers.

22 Learn which plug-ins your browser may have built-in. Find out which may be required at sites you visit often to play sound, video, or animation.

23 Keep an on-line e-mail address book. This is a very handy feature for speed dialing. Instead of looking for a person's e-mail address, click on their name, type your message, and send.

24 Turn off images to increase your speed. Remember, you can always see a specific image if you wish. But turning off all images means you bypass many ads and images you don't need to see.

25 Know all the things you can do to protect your privacy. You can reject cookies, which allow Web sites to identify you on future visits, limit personal information you enter on online registration forms, and reduce the amount of spam—junk e-mail—you get.

Appendices:

Newsgroups Directory
Internet Organizations
Glossary
Bibliography

Newsgroups Directory

There are tens of thousands of newsgroups, discussing every imaginable (and some unimaginable) topic. Here is a sample of offerings in certain official categories (see more in chapter 6). Each is a separate newsgroup. Some have their own subcategories as well.

Recreation

rec.antiques
rec.arts.animation
rec.arts.books
rec.arts.books.childrens
rec.arts.books.hist-fiction
rec.arts.comics
rec.arts.dance
rec.arts.movies.current-films
rec.arts.movies.past-films.
rec.arts.movies.people
rec.arts.movies.reviews
rec.arts.mystery
rec.arts.poems
rec.arts.theatre
rec.arts.tv
rec.autos.driving
rec.autos.marketplace
rec.backcountry
rec.bicycles.misc
rec.boats
rec.climbing
rec.collecting
rec.collecting.dolls
rec.collecting.stamps
rec.crafts.glass
rec.crafts.jewelry
rec.crafts.pottery
rec.crafts.winemaking
rec.folk-dancing
rec.food.baking

rec.food.chocolate
rec.food.cooking
rec.food.recipes
rec.food.restaurants
rec.food.veg
rec.games.board
rec.games.computer
rec.gardens
rec.gardens.orchids
rec.gardens.roses
rec.humor
rec.humor.funny
rec.music.beatles
rec.music.classical
rec.music.country
rec.music.dylan
rec.music.folk
rec.music.opera
rec.music.rock-pop-r+b
rec.outdoors.camping
rec.outdoors.national-parks
rec.pets
rec.puzzles
rec.scuba
rec.skiing.backcountry
rec.skiing.resorts
rec.toys.action-figures
rec.toys.vintage
rec.travel.asia
rec.travel.bed+breakfast
rec.travel.budget.backpack

rec.travel.caribbean
rec.travel.cruises
rec.travel.europe
rec.travel.usa-canada
rec.woodworking

Society (Social and Cultural Issues)

soc.adoption.adoptees
soc.adoption.parenting
soc.college
soc.college.admissions
soc.college.financial-aid
soc.couples
soc.couples.wedding
soc.culture.austria
soc.culture.french
soc.culture.german
soc.culture.greek
soc.culture.japan
soc.feminism
soc.genealogy.britain
soc.genealogy.methods
soc.history
soc.history.ancient
soc.history.living
soc.politics
soc.rights.human
soc.singles
soc.support.depression
soc.support.pregnancy.loss
soc.veterans
soc.women

Talk (Debates About Politics, Ethics and Philosophy)

talk.abortion
talk.atheism
talk.environment
talk.origins (evolution vs. creationism)
talk.philosophy.misc
talk.politics.european-union
talk.religion.newage
talk.rumors

Miscellaneous

misc.activism.progressive
misc.business.consulting

misc.consumers
misc.consumers.frugal-house
misc.creativity
misc.education
misc.education.home-school
misc.entrepreneurs
misc.fitness.aerobic
misc.fitness.walking
misc.forsale.computers
misc.forsale.noncomputer
misc.health.alternative
misc.health.infertility
misc.immigration.usa
misc.int-property (intellectual property)
misc.jobs.offered
misc.jobs.resumes
misc.kids.breastfeeding
misc.kids.health
misc.kids.vacation
misc.legal
misc.rural
misc.taxes
misc.writing

News (Newsgroup news)

news.announce
news.answers
news.newusers.questions

Alternative

alt.abuse
alt.abuse-recovery
alt.activism
alt.adoption
alt.adoption.searching
alt.archaeology
alt.architecture

alt.aromatherapy
alt.art.marketplace
alt.astrology
alt.books
alt.books.anne.rice
alt.books.mysteries
alt.books.reviews
alt.business
alt.business.home
alt.clothing.designer
alt.coffee
alt.collecting
alt.collecting.teddy-bears
alt.college
alt.cooking-chat
alt.creative-cook
alt.discuss (wide variety, from announcing new newsgroups and Web sites to arts, hobbies, home pages, pets, etc.)
alt.food
alt.food.asian
alt.food.coffee
alt.food.sushi
alt.food.wine
alt.gossip.celebrities
alt.gossip.royalty
alt.journalism
alt.music
alt.psychology
alt.recipes
alt.restaurants
alt.travel
alt.true-crime

Biz (Internet business)

biz.jobs
biz.marketplace

Internet Organizations

These are some major organizations involved in Internet issues. Each has a Web site and publishes magazines and/or newsletters.

Electronic Frontier Foundation (EFF)
www.eff.org
San Francisco, CA
415-436-9333

This nonprofit group works to protect freedom of speech, privacy, and democratic access to the Internet. It has testified on these issues before Congress, expressed its views to states, and filed lawsuits on behalf of people whose constitutional freedoms have been tampered with online. News and activities are posted on its Web site, which has a searchable archive.

The foundation has published a book, *Protecting Yourself Online: The Definitive Resource on Safety, Freedom & Privacy in Cyberspace*, (Harper Edge, 1998) by Robert Gelman with Stanton McCandlish, EFF program director.

The group is currently working on a book, *Cyberlife*, and invites people to contribute first-person accounts of their online experiences. Any 1,000-word account earns a one-year membership in EFF.

Electronic Privacy Information Center (EPIC)
www.epic.org
Washington, D.C.
202-544-9240

This research center works to protect freedom of speech and privacy online, formed in 1994 as a project of the Fund for Constitutional Government. The fund is a nonprofit organization formed in 1974 to expose and correct corruption in the Federal government and other national institutions through public education and research.

Its resources include online guides to Congressional legislation on online issues, privacy protection tools such as PGP (Pretty Good Privacy), anonymous e-mail and Web surfing, plus Web sites, conferences, newsletters, and groups dealing with privacy issues—both online and in the real world. Detailed descriptions of computer security, scrambling (encryption) policy, and an A to Z listing of privacy issues (and its lack) in our society—from caller ID and wiretapping telephones to Social Security numbers.

EPIC has a newsletter, an online bookstore that sells books on freedom of expression and privacy online, and searchable archives.

The Internet Society

www.isoc.org
Reston, VA
703-648-9888

This is an international organization that works for global coordination and cooperation involving the Internet and its technologies. Members include companies, government agencies, nonprofit and trade associations, and foundations in the United States and abroad that helped create the Internet or invent its technologies.

Formed in 1992, the Internet Society holds an annual conference, many workshops and seminars, and aims to promote advances and common standards on the Internet. It publishes a bimonthly magazine and a monthly e-mail newsletter on Internet issues.

World Wide Web Consortium (W3C)

www.w3.org
Cambridge, MA
617-253-2613

This international industry group works to develop common standards to promote the growth and full potential of the World Wide Web. It was formed in late 1994, originally in collaboration with CERN, the Swiss physics laboratory where the Web was created, with support from the U.S. Department of Defense's Advanced Research Projects Agency (which created ARPANET, the Internet's ancestor) and the European Commission.

Its director is Tim Berners-Lee, the creator of the Web at CERN. Its United States headquarters is at the Massachusetts Institute of Technology, but other headquarters are in France and Japan. Members include big software companies, such as Microsoft, and many others involved with the present and future of the Web.

Its resources include a great deal of information on the Web for Web site designers and users, as well as sample code developed to show and experiment with new specifications for the Web.

W3C publishes a quarterly journal, a monthly newsletter and weekly update on its activities, plus technical reports.

Glossary

ActiveX control. A small add-on program that enhances the ability of Internet Explorer browsers to do specific tasks; similar to a plug-in.

ADSL (Asymmetric Digital Subscriber Line). A speedy way of using the nonvoice part of regular telephone lines to send data, also known as DSL.

AOL (America Online). The biggest commercial online service, it offers special content for members only, plus Internet access.

ARPANET (Advanced Research Projects Agency Network). The computer network developed by the U.S. Department of Defense to survive a nuclear attack; an ancestor of the Internet.

attached file (or attachment). A file sent with an e-mail message, which may be text, images, sound, or video.

bit. The tiniest amount of computerized data. Bits per second (bps) is a common way to measure the speed at which data is transmitted.

byte. Eight bits of computerized data.

bookmark. A way to save favorite Web pages so you don't have to type in an Internet addresses again.

browser. A software program that locates and displays Web pages and other Internet resources.

cache. A place on your computer's hard drive that stores recently viewed documents so they can be accessed quickly.

chat. Communicate by typing and receiving messages to other people in real time, without the delays of bulletin boards or e-mail.

client. A software program that communicates with another computer, called a server, to use its files or programs.

commercial on-line service. A company that offers special content, plus Internet access, through its computer network to members.

Compuserve. A commercial online service, now owned by America Online, its former rival.

configure. Adjust settings to tailor a device to work with something else. For example, your TCP/IP software needs to be configured to work properly with your Internet service provider, and your modem needs to be configured to work with your computer.

cookie. Information stored on your computer's hard drive by a Web page after you view it, which helps it "recognize" you on your next visit.

domain name. The name registered for an Internet site. The end is the top-level domain—.com, .org, .edu—which shows what type of entity is behind the site. The part before that is the second-level domain, which is more specific, is usually the name or shortened name of the company, organization, or person.

download. Copy a file or program from another computer onto your computer's hard drive.

DSL (Digital Subscriber Line). See ADSL.

e-mail. Electronic mail, which you can send or receive over a computer network.

emoticons. Punctuation symbols for emotions, used in e-mail and newsgroup postings.

encryption. Scrambling messages so they cannot be read without a decoding device.

FAQs (Frequently Asked Questions). Questions and answers on a topic, common in newsgroups and on Web sites.

filtering software. Software that blocks objectionable material—such as sexually explicit, violent, or hate-filled content—on the Internet, often used by parents to protect children.

flame. A hostile e-mail message or newsgroup posting.

frame. A separate and independent part of a Web page, which not all browsers can display.

FTP (File Transfer Protocol). A way of obtaining or sending files over the Internet from certain sites, which can be public or private.

GIF (Graphics Interchange Format). A common format used to display images on the Web.

gigabyte. A hundred times a megabyte, or 1 million bytes of computer data.

graphical browser. A software program that locates and displays Web pages and other Internet resources by letting users point and click a mouse. Mosaic was the first graphical browser.

home page. The front page of a Web site. Often used to designate a whole Web site.

hypertext. The system of linked pages of related material, created with HTML, which makes up the World Wide Web.

HTML (Hypertext Markup Language). The programming language used to create Web pages, which browsers can read.

HTTP (Hypertext Transfer Protocol). The command that moves hypertext pages over the Internet. It is the first part of an address located on the Web ("http://"), and is followed by the domain name.

icons. Pictures that are symbols for functions. For example, a mailbox, envelope, or paper and pen can stand for mail.

intelligent agent. A software program designed to locate information and understand context.

Internet. A network of computer networks that contains countless computers worldwide, each of which can communicate with any other.

Internet Explorer. A Web browser made by Microsoft.

Internet relay chat (IRC). A system that lets people type and receive messages in real time, without the delays of e-mail or newsgroups.

Internet service provider (ISP). A company that sells dial-up access to the Internet.

InterNIC. The registry of Internet domain names, which has been operated by Network Solutions, an American company.

ISDN (Integrated Services Digital Network). A speedy way to move data over regular telephone lines which is digital, instead of analog, at both ends.

JPEG (Joint Photographic Experts Group). A common format used to display images on the Web.

kilobytes. A thousand bits of data. Modem speeds are in kilobytes per second; for example, a 28.8 Kbps modem moves 28,800 data bits per second.

link. A word, phrase, or picture you can click on to connect to another Web page instantly.

Lynx. A text-only browser, often used on the UNIX operating system.

MacTCP. A Macintosh computer needs this connection software to be on the Internet (similar to TCP/IP for a IBM-type PC).

mailing list. A system that sends incoming e-mail to a group of subscribers who want mail on a specific topic.

megabyte (MB). A million bytes. For example, a computer's memory may be 32 MB, or 32,000,000 bytes.

modem. An electronic device that connects to your computer and telephone line and lets your computer talk to other computers.

Mosaic. The first graphical browser, which let users point and click a mouse to get around the World Wide Web.

MPEG (Motion Picture Experts Group). A common file format used for short video clips on the Internet.

Netscape Communicator. A software package, which includes the Netscape Navigator browser, an e-mail and newsreader program, home page building tools, and other features, developed by Netscape Communications Corporation.

Netscape Navigator. A browser developed by Netscape Communications Corporation.

newbie. A beginner on the Internet.

newsreader. A software program that lets you read and post messages in newsgroups.

newsgroup. A public discussion group on the Internet where you can read and post messages on a specific topic.

page. A document written in HTML on the World Wide Web, which can include text, picture, sound, or video files.

password. A secret word that allows entry; for example, a commercial on-line service or a Web page may require a password for access.

PGP (Pretty Good Privacy). A software program that scrambles e-mail to protect the user's privacy.

plug-in. An add-on that enhances the abilities of your browser to play sounds, display images or virtual reality, or take part in chat.

POP (Points of Presence or Post Office Protocol). A city or location where an Internet service provider can offer inexpensive dial-up access, often with a local telephone number. Or, a way in which a mail server on the Internet lets a user pick up mail.

PPP (Point-to-Point Protocol). An account with an Internet service provider, which means your computer is connected to the Internet.

push technology. A system that sends customized information directly to a computer without the user's immediate request or search based upon previously submitted preferences.

QuickTime. A common file format for short video clips on the Internet, invented by Apple Computer.

search engine. A software program that finds topics, words or phrases on the Web or in newsgroups and displays them as links.

server. A computer that offers services, ranging from e-mail to Web pages, to other computers, called clients, on a network.

SET (Secure Electronic Transaction). A standard used by some credit card companies to scramble information, such as credit card numbers, so a Web site can offer safe shopping.

shareware. Software that is free for a trial period, then requires a nominal fee paid to its developer.

SLIP (Single Line Internet Protocol). An account with an Internet service provider, which means your computer is connected to the Internet; an older version of PPP.

spam. Unrequested junk e-mail.

SSL (Secure Socket Layer). A system that scrambles information to protect privacy, often used by Web sites to offer safe shopping.

status indicator. The icon on a computer screen that shows a browser is active.

tags. Codes in HTML that are commands for certain functions, such as boldface, italicize, and create links.

TCP/IP (Transmission Control Protocol/Internet Protocol). The system of rules computers connected on the Internet follow to communicate. Your computer needs TCP/IP software to be on the Internet.

telephony. Technology that allows voice communication over the Internet, which may involve using microphones and computers, not telephones.

thread. A cluster of messages on the same topic in a newsgroup or on a bulletin board.

toolbar. A horizontal row of icons, which stand for browser commands, such as "back" and "bookmark."

UNIX. An operating system for computers before Windows was invented, which can still be used today.

upload. Copy a file or program from your computer's hard drive to another computer.

URL (Uniform Resource Locator). The Internet address of a page that includes the protocol needed. For example, "http://www." for a page on the World Wide Web, followed by the domain name.

Usenet. The thousands of newsgroups on many different topics on the Internet. It is an abbreviation of Users' Network.

virtual. "Almost" something. For example, virtual reality is a 3-D environment that offers the feeling of being within a real world.

World Wide Web. The graphical part of the Internet, rich in images, sound, and video clips.

Web site. A group of pages written in HTML on the World Wide Web belonging to one company, organization, or person.

WYSIWYG (what you see is what you get). A Web authoring tool that shows what the Web page will look like before you are finished creating it (pronounced "wizzy-wig").

Index

We Have

EVERYTHING

More Bestselling Everything Titles Available From Your Local Bookseller:

Everything **After College Book**
$12.95, 1-55850-847-3

Everything **Astrology Book**
$12.95, 1-58062-062-0

Everything **Baby Names Book**
$12.95, 1-55850-655-1

Everything **Baby Shower Book**
$12.95, 1-58062-305-0

Everything **Barbeque Cookbook**
$12.95, 1-58062-316-6

Everything® **Bartender's Book**
$9.95, 1-55850-536-9

Everything **Bedtime Story Book**
$12.95, 1-58062-147-3

Everything **Beer Book**
$12.95, 1-55850-843-0

Everything **Bicycle Book**
$12.95, 1-55850-706-X

Everything **Build Your Own Home Page**
$12.95, 1-58062-339-5

Everything **Casino Gambling Book**
$12.95, 1-55850-762-0

Everything **Cat Book**
$12.95, 1-55850-710-8

Everything® **Christmas Book**
$15.00, 1-55850-697-7

Everything **College Survival Book**
$12.95, 1-55850-720-5

Everything **Cover Letter Book**
$12.95, 1-58062-312-3

Everything **Crossword and Puzzle Book**
$12.95, 1-55850-764-7

Everything **Dating Book**
$12.95, 1-58062-185-6

Everything **Dessert Book**
$12.95, 1-55850-717-5

Everything **Dog Book**
$12.95, 1-58062-144-9

Everything **Dreams Book**
$12.95, 1-55850-806-6

Everything **Etiquette Book**
$12.95, 1-55850-807-4

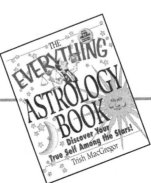

From the publishers of this book

CareerCity.com

Search *4 million* job openings at all the leading career sites with just one click!

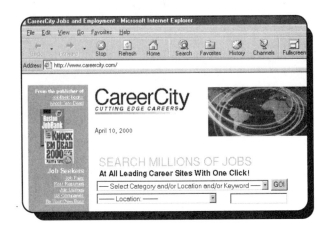

Find all the great job openings without having to spend hours surfing from one career site to the next.

Now, with just one click you can simultaneously search all of the leading career sites . . . at CareerCity.com!

You can also have jobs come to you! Enter your job search criteria once and we automatically notify you of any new relevant job listings.

Plus! The most complete career center on the Web including . . .

- Descriptions and hot links to 27,000 U.S. companies
- Comprehensive salary surveys in all fields
- Expert advice on starting a job search, interviews, resumes and much more

You'll find more jobs at CareerCity.com!

Post your resume at CareerCity and have the job offers come to you!

It's fast, free, and easy to post your resume at CareerCity—and you'll get noticed by hundreds of leading employers in all fields.